THE L WORD

Also by David P. Barash

Sociobiology and Behavior
The Whisperings Within
Aging: An Exploration
Stop Nuclear War! A Handbook (with Judith Eve Lipton)
The Caveman and the Bomb (with Judith Eve Lipton)
The Hare and the Tortoise
The Arms Race and Nuclear War
Marmots: Social Behavior and Ecology
The Great Outdoors
Introduction to Peace Studies

THE L WORD

An Unapologetic, Thoroughly
Biased, Long-Overdue
Explication and Celebration
of Liberalism

DAVID P. BARASH

WILLIAM MORROW AND COMPANY, INC.
New York

Grateful acknowledgment is made to the following individuals and publishers for the use of previously published material:

W. H. Auden, *Collected Poems*, ed. Edward Mendelson. Copyright 1940 by W. H. Auden. Reprinted by permission of Random House, Inc.

Bertrand Russell, "Unpopular Essays." Copyright 1950 by Bertrand Russell. Reprinted by permission of Simon & Schuster, Inc.

Arthur M. Schlesinger, Jr., "Origin of the Cold War," *Foreign Affairs*, Spring 1967. Reprinted by permission of *Foreign Affairs* (Spring 1967). Copyright © 1967 by the Council on Foreign Relations, Inc.

Arthur M. Schlesinger, Jr., *The Vital Center* (New York: Houghton Mifflin, 1949).

Franklin D. Roosevelt and the Future of Liberalism, ed. John F. Sears (Westport, Conn.: Meckler, 1991), pp. 80–81. Quoted by permission of the Franklin and Eleanor Roosevelt Institute.

"Economics with Power Steering" by Calvin Trillin originally appeared in *The Nation*. Copyright © 1990 by Calvin Trillin.

It is the policy of William Morrow and Company, Inc., and its imprints and affiliates, recognizing the importance of preserving what has been written, to print the books we publish on acid-free paper, and we exert our best efforts to that end.

Library of Congress Cataloging-in-Publication Data

Barash, David P.
   The L word : an unapologetic, thoroughly biased, long-overdue
explication and celebration of liberalism / David P. Barash.
     p. cm.
   ISBN 0-688-10882-2
   1. Liberalism. 2. Conservatism. 3. Right and left (Political
science) I. Title.
JA83.B2482 1992
320.5'13—dc20   91-7342
                                            CIP

Printed in the United States of America

First Edition

1 2 3 4 5 6 7 8 9 10

BOOK DESIGN BY PAUL CHEVANNES

To Anne and Nat Barash:
good liberals, great parents

Contents

Foreword
by George McGovern

This is the most important book on American politics and society that I have read in a long time. It is important because it deals honestly and intelligently with the most important, successful, and practical American political tradition—liberalism. It describes practical problem-solving as the chief function of government with authentic liberals justifiably proud of their achievements in the past and confident of their capacity and obligation to get on with the liberal agenda of the future.

Mr. Barash is a tolerant, open-minded, moderate man, as liberals should be. But he is disgusted with the phony conservatism of the Reagan-Bush era, which has displayed an excess of greed, irresponsibility, and militarism. He is equally disgusted with feeble, apologetic, and wavering liberals who have forgotten the great liberal victories of the past and fear the challenges of the present.

Mr. Barash believes, as I do, that liberalism has saved American capitalism from the excesses of the right and left since the 1930s. It did so by establishing an underpinning of minimum wages and collective bargaining, Social Security, farm price supports and rural electrification, guaranteed bank deposits, regulation of the securities markets, and government initiatives to strengthen the public services and infrastructure of the nation, plus timely government fiscal and monetary stimulus or restraint. These commonsense liberal safeguards have ended or greatly relieved the earlier pattern of crushing depressions that used to occur about every twenty years.

Liberalism is the "middle way" between the right-wing glorification of an unregulated "free market" and the left-wing advocacy of full-scale government ownership and direction. One hopes that the author is right in believing that the authoritarian regimes of Eastern Europe will, after their current salute to the "free market," eventually find their way toward the mixed economy that now serves Western Europe, the Pacific rim, and North America. This is the path of liberalism.

Paradoxically, American conservatives applaud the liberalism of such leaders as Poland's Lech Walesa, Czechoslovakia's Václav Havel, and, at times, the Soviet Union's Mikhail Gorbachev while deriding liberalism in the United States. Many American liberals seem to swallow the current failures of conservatism including the selfishness, ignorance, and jingoism that have been passed off as leadership vision in recent years.

I hope this highly informed, candid book will help to expose some of the contemporary political charades while giving a little more pride and spine to American liberals.

America has always needed both an authentic conservative tradition and an authentic liberal tradition. The creative tension between conservatism and liberalism is the genius of our constitutional democracy. There is ample room—and indeed an important necessity—for the conservatism of an Alexander Hamilton and a Dwight Eisenhower and the liberalism of a Thomas Jefferson and a Franklin Roosevelt.

I am old-fashioned enough to believe that our political system works best when Republicans are honest-to-goodness conservatives and Democrats are honest-to-goodness liberals. Perhaps this is why my longtime Senate colleague Barry Goldwater and I have long enjoyed an amicable relationship and a measure of mutual admiration.

While recognizing the contributions of an authentic conservatism in restraining excessive public expenditure and government interference—a caution not practiced during the

Reagan-Bush era, when the national debt was tripled—it is all the more important to recognize the need for positive government action in resolving public problems that cannot be resolved by individual actions. It is a historical fact that all or nearly all of the public programs now embraced by conservatives and liberals alike began as liberal initiatives over conservative opposition. This is true of achievements as diverse as Social Security, Medicare, rural electrification, pure food and drug protection, the environmental movement, civil rights, guaranteed bank and savings deposits, the women's movement, and the struggle to end the war in Vietnam.

I have always been proud to be a practicing liberal. This book makes me even more proud of the liberal spirit. But just as Judge Learned Hand warned long ago that the "spirit of liberty" is not too certain that it is right, author Barash warns that liberals must not be so convinced of their virtue that they become blind to the claims of other voices, perspectives, and experience. But with that word of caution in mind, I endorse the author's conclusion that "liberalism is precisely what we need for the 1990s and beyond." I believe that historian Arthur Schlesinger is also right in asserting that the political cycle is about to carry us into another era of liberal ascendancy—unless liberals themselves insist on surrendering the field.

THE L WORD

Chapter 1 Introduction: Bedrooms, Boardrooms, and Bombast

"THE MASQUERADE is over. It's time to . . . use the dreaded L word, to say the policies of our opposition . . . are liberal, liberal, liberal."

Thus spoke Ronald Reagan, at the Republican National Convention in New Orleans, in August 1988. And as the presidential campaign of 1988 unfolded, the "L word" did indeed appear time and again, as George Bush sneered and Michael Dukakis shrank away, like Dracula confronted by a cross. You would think the word *liberal* was political poison, a criminal accusation. Unfair, said the Massachusetts governor. Slander, he implied. The election was about competence, he protested, not ideology. In any event, the Democratic presidential candidate—who was, in fact, a liberal—squirmed and wriggled, refusing to accept the liberal label.

By denying his political heritage, Dukakis caused many voters to question theirs. The result was that millions of Americans—unclear about ideological labels even when they are honestly used and acknowledged—became convinced that there must be something shameful about that L word, trailing hints of witchcraft or black mass, of nasty rites to be practiced only in secret, on the darkest nights. Finally, during the last week or so of the campaign, Mr. Dukakis 'fessed up to being a liberal, "in the tradition of Franklin Roosevelt, Harry Truman, and John Kennedy." At that point, significantly, he began gaining ground, but too much had already been conceded. And even then, he never told us what liberalism was.

The people—many of them—were perplexed. What was this liberalism, this seeming abomination that dared not speak its own name? Others were infuriated. For liberalism is not only one of the fundamental political principles of the United States, it is in many ways *the* American political principle. In misrepresenting liberalism as somehow antagonistic to American values, Ronald Reagan, George Bush, and other conservatives have in fact misrepresented American values themselves. By sleight of hand more remarkable even than voodoo economics, and about on a par with calling the MX missile the "Peacekeeper" or labeling the Nicaraguan contras the "moral equivalent of our Founding Fathers," liberalism has somehow been painted as the enemy of the people. But if we swallow this, if we turn our back on liberalism, we turn our back on the best of our own past, and on our greatest hopes for the future.

THE 1988 presidential election is history. Although it highlighted the difficulties of being liberal in the United States, this one election did not begin those difficulties. For some time now, liberals have been feeling like the well-meaning, well-liked Nicholas Rostov, who found himself on the battlefield in Tolstoy's *War and Peace:* "Why are they shooting at me," he asked, perplexed, "of whom everyone is so fond?" Liberals and liberalism have become targets, and in their enthusiasm for the sport, the onlookers (if not those doing the shooting) have lost sight of just who and what is in the cross hairs.

Conservatives have been simplistic in thought, but very skillful in packaging, and Ronald Reagan represented the epitome of this combination. Liberals, by contrast, have been the opposite: subtle in thought, but relatively clumsy in popular exposition, either overly demagogic or excessively urbane and professorial.

During the 1980s in particular, liberalism was a political stance that politicians sought to deny and escape rather than to strengthen and renew. Or even to explain. This book was originally intended to be an explanation, with the thought that if it also helped to strengthen or renew, so much the better. To begin with, then, my goal was modest: to elucidate liberalism, its origins, its basic concepts, how it differs from conservatism, what it has done for us in the past, what it has done for us recently, and what it promises to do in the future.

Consider this dilemma: A neighborhood dog regularly chases passing cars, until one glorious day he catches one. What does he do with it? Not since the 1960s have American liberals elected a president. (The only intervening Democrat, Jimmy Carter, was the most conservative Democratic president since Grover Cleveland.) They chase after the White House every four years, yapping away, but to no avail. What if someday they actually win? (Ambrose Bierce once wrote that a conservative is "a statesman who is enamored of existing evils, as distinguished from the liberal, who wishes to replace them with others."[1])

But I soon realized that a stance of moderate, scholarly objectivity would be a misrepresentation of my own position, as well as a disservice to what is, in actuality, a very good "cause," that of liberalism itself. The result, *The L Word*, is part didactics, part diatribe, a polemic as well as a primer. In short, a manifesto.

By the time we are done examining liberalism, you should have a pretty good idea what a liberal agenda would involve, although my purpose in this book is not to advise liberals on how to package themselves or their ideas; rather, it is to enumerate and celebrate those ideas. Like an overenthusiastic golden retriever puppy, who sniffs eagerly at your outstretched finger instead of following the direction of that finger to see what you are pointing at, American liberals have slobbered all over the American public's disillusionment with them, trying to fathom its basis, while ignoring the direction in which it points: the need to explain what liberalism is all about and to acknowledge its wisdom.

This book is not intended for the pundits, politicians, or

---

[1] Ambrose Bierce, *The Devil's Dictionary* (Mount Vernon, N.Y.: The Peter Pauper Press, 1958).

professors of political philosophy, but for the people, those who were misled, angered, or just plain confused by the 1988 presidential election, and by what has been passing for political dialogue ever since. It is also directed to those millions of liberals—both acknowledged and those hiding nervously in their closets—who could use a reaffirmation of their "faith."

I also write this partly out of anger and frustration, outraged that a good, decent, well-meaning, and highly serviceable old friend and benefactor has been so disparaged, that—as comedian Rodney Dangerfield likes to say—it doesn't get any respect. Because it deserves a whole lot.

THE STORY of the United States is in fact the story of the greatest triumph of liberalism in the history of the world. Its framework is the Constitution and the Bill of Rights, and its clearest embodiment is the Declaration of Independence:

> We hold these truths to be self-evident, that all men are created equal, that they are endowed by their Creator with certain unalienable rights, that among these are Life, Liberty, and the pursuit of Happiness.—That to secure these rights, Governments are instituted among Men, deriving their just powers from the consent of the governed.

The above two sentences are liberalism in a nutshell.

What is the United States of America? Its identity does not lie in buildings or dried-up documents, or even in the land itself with its purple mountains' majesty from sea to shining sea. Nor does America reside in a shared ethnic consciousness (we are a diverse people, as Jesse Jackson likes to say, a rainbow of many patterns and many colors), or even a common history (America is a nation of immigrants, who have brought their own history with them). Rather, the U.S.A. locates its soul in a shared system of values. And these values are overwhelmingly liberal: democracy, national self-determination, the rule of law, freedom of speech and of worship, taking care of ourselves and of one another.

Liberalism may have become an unpopular word, but it represents an honored tradition. Indeed, noted historian Louis

Hartz[2] has suggested that liberalism *is* the American political tradition. Why, then, was liberal-baiting so successful in 1988? How has the L word become the virtual equivalent of the A word in Nathaniel Hawthorne's *Scarlet Letter*? Or the C word to 1950s McCarthyites? One reason is that in the 1980s, the L word assumed some of the connotations of the S words, socialism and statism. This is deeply ironic, and would be especially so to our Founding Fathers, since historically liberalism has meant opposition to a strong, monarchical state. And furthermore, as we shall see, liberals are at their best when defending personal rights and freedoms. The ACLU, so derided by candidate Bush during the 1988 presidential campaign, is in fact the American *Civil Liberties* Union, and this preeminently liberal organization remains true to its name, fiercely committed to civil liberties, as set down in the Bill of Rights. Those opposed to the work of the ACLU might honestly be asked which of our civil liberties they would care to abandon: freedom of speech, of religion, of assembly, the right to a jury trial?

Conservatives, for their part, supposedly favor personal freedom and inconspicuous government. Yet they have a decided fondness for telling us what we can or cannot do with our bodies, whether making love or obtaining an abortion. The difference between conservatives and liberals is, in part, whether the country should stick its nose into corporate boardrooms or into our private bedrooms. And if their obsession with running our sex lives wasn't hypocrisy enough for people who claim to speak for small, nonintrusive government, conservatives are positively entranced with precisely those federal agencies—the Defense Department, the FBI, the CIA—that comprise some of the most excessive and wasteful government expenditures, and that are most threatening to civil liberties.[3]

Conservative ideologues and George Bush's handlers would

---

[2] Louis Hartz, *The Liberal Tradition in America* (New York: Harcourt Brace, 1955).
[3] How many people noticed that George Bush's proposed 1991 federal budget called for a 2 percent increase in education funding, which was ballyhooed as a "major increase," and another 2 percent increase in military spending, which was packaged as a "major decrease"?

have us believe that liberals are soft on crime, short on patriotism, rotten with permissiveness, seeking only to "tax and
tax, spend and spend." Liberals are made out to be amoral
relativists who threaten American values such as home, family, and God. The truth, as we shall see, is quite different. The
upper echelons of liberalism, according to George Bush, are
made up of "remnants of the 1960s, the New Left, campus
radicals grown old, the peace marchers and the nuclear-freeze
activists." This is closer to the truth. Many of us, remnants of
the 1960s and the New Left, campus radicals grown old that
we are, peace marchers and nuclear-freeze activists indeed,
are rather proud of our past and our present. We were not
alone then, nor are we now.[4]

NOT THAT liberalism is perfect, of course. In their assaults
on liberalism, George Bush and Ronald Reagan tapped a reservoir of legitimate public distrust; liberals often tend to be
powerful, hypocritical "limousine liberals," both snobby and
condescending. "We who are liberal and progressive," wrote
Lionel Trilling, "know that the poor are our equals in every
sense except that of being equal to us."[5] Such skewerings have,
at least on occasion, been earned. As their stock-in-trade, liberals offer "programs"—that is, things to be done, organized
ways of trying to make things better, and this necessarily involves a definite role for government. So liberalism's largeness
of spirit (something of which conservatism has never been accused) is often housed within the timid narrowness of bureau-
cratic officialdom, paper-shufflers, bunglers, infuriating *petty*
civil servants in every sense of the word.[6]

And liberals don't often agree with each other; they tend to
be a scrappy, contentious lot. "I don't belong to any organized political party," noted Will Rogers. "I'm a Democrat."

---

[4] In countless polls, more than 80 percent of the American public during the
early 1980s declared themselves in favor of a bilateral nuclear freeze, for
example.

[5] Lionel Trilling, *The Liberal Imagination* (New York: Doubleday, 1950).

[6] Bureaucracy itself, however, is not an illness confined to the liberal tradition. For example, consider the Chinese public service agencies, which have
endured for more than one thousand years. And Russia under the czars—
hardly a liberal environment—spawned one of the most sluggish and stul-
tifying bureaucracies of all times.

On the other hand, liberalism has been known to degenerate into a kind of ineffectual, wishy-washy, neither-fish-nor-fowl, flabby in-between moderateness, not likely to inspire passionate devotion. Maybe this is why we have "rock-ribbed" Republicans and "staunch" conservatives, but no comparably stalwart and sturdy, John Wayne–like adjectives for the liberals among us. And of course, liberals tend to be intellectuals (although not necessarily pointy-headed, as Governor George Wallace used to claim[7]), ivy-tower types with grand schemes for the nation and the world, but who can't even park their bicycles straight. The rallying cries of liberalism—when sounded at all these days—have tended toward an accent that seems almost foreign, calling to Americans in a tone that is more and more alien, and that seems to emanate from an outmoded political tradition. And on occasion, liberal programs don't even work (although, as we shall see, they have worked a whole lot better than we have been led to believe). Worst of all, liberals have been almost as guilty as conservatives when it comes to a narrow-minded and dangerous chauvinism; I am thinking here of the notorious "Cold War liberals," who follow a progressive agenda on domestic issues but have a history of competing with the far right to flourish the most red-necked anticommunist credentials when it comes to foreign policy.

Actually, liberals have difficulty with evil, notably the evil of monsters of either political extreme, whether of the far right like Hitler or the far left like Stalin. Similarly, they are surprised, troubled, and honestly hurt by welfare cheats, greed,[8] or street thugs. This is not really surprising in view of the basically optimistic, forward-looking, and (some would say) naïve mind-set from which liberalism springs. For their part, the more pessimistic perspective of conservatives puts them closely in tune with human nastiness, perhaps because they tend to be imbued with no small degree of it themselves. And just as liberals have difficulty dealing with evil, conservatives are ill-prepared for goodness and virtue. It is only a slight ex-

---

[7]". . . the overeducated ivory-tower folks with pointy heads looking down their noses at us."

[8]We assume that the conservatives will be greedy: It seems to come with the territory.

aggeration to say that to the liberal, no one is truly and irre-
deemably bad, and to the conservative, no one is good.

Paraphrasing Winston Churchill on democracy, we can conclude from all this that liberalism is probably the worst possible political ideology . . . except when we compare it to any
of the others! Because in fact, liberalism, for all its faults, is
head and shoulders above the alternatives, conservatism and
neofascism on the right, radicalism on the left. On balance—
in its mix of ideals and practicality, heart and head—liberalism
is almost certainly the best political philosophy ever developed. "Radicals, who would take us back to the roots of things,
often fail," according to Louis D. Brandeis, "because they disregard the fruit Time has produced and preserved. Conservatives fail because they would preserve even what Time has
decomposed."[9] And liberals, when they succeed, do so by
preserving that which is useful from the past, while adapting
it to the present and future. When they fail, it is generally
because they stray too far in the direction of either radicals or
conservatives, overlooking perfectly good fruit or preserving
the rotten stuff.

LIBERALISM HAS been the dominant United States political
movement of the twentieth century, and it has given Americans most of those things that they most prize. Liberals have
helped this country grow and thrive by embracing the principle that it isn't government's job to enrich the rich, but rather,
to help those who need help . . . which, to some degree, is
all of us. Imagine the United States without the benefits that
liberalism has bestowed: Social Security, unemployment compensation, the right to form labor unions, farm price supports,
student loans, civil rights legislation, child labor laws, a minimum wage, Medicare and Medicaid, workplace safety regulations, and environmental protection. This is only a partial list.

In foreign policy, it was during the liberal presidency of
Woodrow Wilson that the United States defeated Germany and
its allies in World War I, and then, with one of the century's
great liberals, Franklin D. Roosevelt, at the helm, did it again
in World War II. It is worth noting that while Roosevelt sought

[9]Solomon Goldman, ed., *The Words of Justice Brandeis* (New York: H. Schu-
man, 1953.

to aid Britain and western democracy in their hour of need, the conservative America Firsters clung to isolationism, along with an ill-concealed fondness for Adolf Hitler as a possibly useful antidote to communism. Then it was another liberal, Harry S. Truman, who gave us the most generous—and hard-headedly effective—program of international aid in human history, the Marshall Plan for the rebuilding of Europe. Truman also presided over the repulsing of North Korean and Chinese aggression in the early 1950s. And both the Roosevelt and Truman administrations gave us the United Nations, once more over the strenuous objections of the political right. In all fairness, however, we should also note that two other liberal presidents, John Kennedy and Lyndon Johnson, gave us the quagmire of Vietnam. Overall, liberal internationalism has been a mixed bag, perhaps, but a rich one, and on balance, a remarkable and worthy legacy.

In the twentieth century, liberalism and conservatism in America have played leapfrog, cycling between (liberal) periods of public activism and (conservative) times of private retrenchment. The following paragraph does a fine job of describing the conservative resurgence that occurred in the 1980s:

> No intellectual phenomenon has been more surprising in recent years than the revival in the United States of conservatism as a respectable social philosophy. For decades liberalism seemed to have everything its way. The bright young men were always liberals; the thoughtful professors were generally liberals. . . . But in the last year or two, it has all seemed to change. Fashionable intellectual circles now dismiss liberalism as naïve, ritualistic, sentimental, shallow. With a whoop and a roar, a number of conservative prophets have materialized out of the wilderness, exhuming conservatism, revisiting it, revitalizing it, preaching it. . . . Today, we are told, the bright young men are conservatives; the thoughtful professors are conservatives; even a few liberals, in their own cycle of despair, are beginning to avow themselves conservatives.[10]

But this was written more than thirty years ago! The so-called neoconservatism in the 1980s was in many ways a re-

---

[10] Arthur M. Schlesinger, Jr. "The Politics of Nostalgia," *Reporter*, June 16, 1955.

play of the New Conservatism of the 1950s (the Eisenhower years), which in many ways repeated another conservatism—the so-called New Era philosophy—of the 1920s (the heyday of Harding, Coolidge, and Hoover). As we shall examine later, there is some reason to think that people get tired of good deeds, worn out in the service of great causes, whereupon they return to their narrower, more private, selfish lives. Liberalism has been the philosophy of the "doers" (or, if you will, the "do-gooders") while conservatives prefer to do good unto themselves.

If you think liberals have gotten out of touch with mainstream American concerns, that they have lost their street smarts, think again. On abortion, on "trickle-down" economics,[11] on the repressive social dictates of the Moral Majority, on dragging their heels in acknowledging the new political landscape vis-à-vis the Soviet Union, it is the conservatives who are lumbering, outmoded dinosaurs.

It was liberalism that broke the back of the Depression, and of the Axis, while conservatism gave us . . . what? At best, a respite. Take, for example, Ronald Reagan's education program, which, as historian Robert McElvaine puts it, had three parts: "cut federal funding for education, launch a teacher into space, and pray."[12] Following a decade of conservative neglect, educational levels have sunk so low that schoolchildren are barely able even to read George Bush's lips.

And when it comes to the overall economic impact of Reaganism, it is significant that even a conservative such as Kevin Phillips has shown himself to be deeply troubled by the blatant favoritism toward the rich that has characterized conservativism's recent heydays. As Phillips sees it, the 1980s largely recapitulated the pattern of the Gilded Age (1880s and 1890s) and the roaring twenties, when government policies saw to it that wealth flowed toward the already rich, and the middle class lost out—not to the poor but to the wealthy. This should occasion no real surprise: Phillips recognizes, for example, that

[11] Crusty old George Meany, licensed plumber and long-time head of the AFL-CIO, once said that in his career he had seen many things trickle down, but money wasn't among them.

[12] Robert McElvaine, *The End of the Conservative Era* (New York: Arbor House, 1987).

the historical role of conservative Republicanism has been "not simply to revitalize U.S. capitalism but to tilt power, policy, wealth and income toward the richest portions of the population."[13] At the same time, public "goods" have been devalued and allowed to deteriorate, giving us private splendor amid public squalor. The two most striking legacies of such illiberalism are the newest demographic groups in the United States, both of which (significantly) experienced skyrocketting growth during the past decade: the billionaires and the homeless. As to the billionaires, "no parallel upsurge of riches had been seen," according to Phillips, "since the late nineteenth century, the era of the Vanderbilts, Morgans and Rockefellers." And as to the homeless, no such upsurge had been seen since the Great Depression.

Liberalism's zenith was in the early 1960s, when LBJ trounced Barry Goldwater and initiated the Great Society, the War on Poverty, and the Voting Rights Act, while the horrors and divisiveness of Vietnam were not yet upon us. But even today, with liberalism supposedly in ignominious decline, the reality is that most people support liberal positions on issues, even as they reject the liberal label. They want to see government more active in opposing drugs, reducing the East-West confrontation, defending the environment, caring for the needy, improving educational opportunities and medical benefits, and, to achieve these ends, taxing those who can afford it. During the ruckus over the 1990 federal budget, conservatives came out foursquare in favor of retaining tax breaks for the wealthy, while liberals sought to return to a basic principle: People earning more money should pay a higher percentage of their income in taxes. In short, fairness. Liberals were even so disrespectful as to suggest that millionaires, who profited mightily by Reagan-era preferences for the wealthy during the 1980s, should pay a special surtax; conservatives, by contrast, made it clear that by "no new taxes," they meant, "no new taxes *for the rich*." Watch this, the so-called fairness issue. It will surface again for the 1992 elections, as well it should.

To liberals, government has a role—a crucial one—in mak-

---

[13] Kevin Phillips, *The Politics of Rich and Poor* (New York: Random House, 1990).

ing things better. FDR put it this way: "As new conditions and problems arise beyond the power of men and women to meet as individuals, it becomes the duty of the government itself to find new remedies with which to meet them."[14] One difficulty confronting modern-day liberalism is that Roosevelt's liberal programs were presented as just that: programs that were needed, and that worked, rather than as coherent exercises in social democracy. We never actually became liberal in theory, only in practice! These liberal practices were not accompanied by a firm philosophical or ideological rationale. So most people don't realize that their most beloved United States government programs were and still are unremittingly liberal. Like Dickens's Mr. Micawber, who was astonished to learn that he spoke prose, Americans would probably be astonished to learn that most of the time, they think liberal.

LIBERALS AND liberalism gave birth to the basic notion of affirmative government, the idea that people are not meant to be isolated and alone, dog-eat-dog and devil take the hindmost. The alternative to affirmative government is indifferent government, or—worse yet—antagonistic government. In its positive, affirmative form, government is our shield against the profound selfishness and callous disregard for others that is represented by modern conservatism. Two hundred years ago, liberalism gave us the Bill of Rights, and now it seeks to preserve these rights. Perhaps the next liberal step will be what we might call a Bill of Responsibilities: to one another, to the future, and to the environment. When Ronald Reagan announced that "Government is not the solution, government is the problem," he was proclaiming a radically regressive concept of interpersonal responsibilities, essentially one of beggar—or bugger—thy neighbor, "go for it," and to hell with anyone else. Not surprisingly, it is a viewpoint that has always found favor with those who are comfortable and well-to-do. Fairness is an unlikely rallying cry for those who are

---

[14] Franklin D. Roosevelt, *The Public Papers and Addresses of Franklin D. Roosevelt*, Introduction, Vol. 7, compiler Samuel I. Rosenman (New York: Random House, 1938–1950).

already getting more than their share. These are the people who, like conservative economic guru George Gilder, can unblushingly suggest in one breath that the poor need the "lash of their poverty" to keep them working, and then proclaim in the next that the rich, by contrast, need *reduced* income taxes and a special break on their capital gains transactions to keep them productive. (Former Texas Agriculture Commissioner Jim Hightower identified one of these types when he described George Bush as someone who "was born on third base, so he figured he must have hit a triple.")

Liberals feel that the poor, the disenfranchised, must be protected. Conservatives feel that the rich must be protected, from the potential political power of an envious and good-for-nothing majority. Liberals have been accused of fomenting class warfare, whereas in fact they challenge us to acknowledge the existence of such conflicts, a necessary precondition if we are to remedy them. Meanwhile, such accusations typically come from conservatives, who blithely are engaged in the most blatant forms of class cruelty. As we shall see, conservatives have been surprisingly successful in hoodwinking many people into thinking that liberalism is in the interest of "them" as opposed to "us," often with racist inuendo. Having become experts at manipulating imagery, conservatives managed to fool too many of the people, too much of the time. (Politics, it has been said, is the art of getting votes from the poor and money from the rich by promising to protect each from the other.)

To the self-satisfied middle-class suburban home owner, or even the urban-dwelling blue-collar laborer, liberal programs were painted as "handouts" or efforts to extend aid to others who were too lazy to earn it. Columnist Mike Royko had the courage to point out that as part of that manipulation, liberal came to mean "nigger lover" to many people. Liberals, in other words, were said to be out to help *them*: uppity women, the poor, black, gay, immigrant, handicapped, and so forth. The conservative agenda has been to set up divisions within society, in part by studiously ignoring that any divisions exist and therefore refusing to do anything about them (except to promote policies that exacerbate these divisions). Liberals, by contrast, try to bring us together, through caring, sharing, and hard work.

As a result, liberals can be annoying. They are a goad to our complacency. Ronald Reagan told us that it was morning in America; he had eyes only for the successful and the up-and-coming, and even a disbelief that anyone could really be poor, unemployed, sick, or homeless. And Americans listened, because it was what they wanted to hear. It gave them permission to "take care of number one." Liberals, on the other hand, point to our problems, not because they are constitutionally morose or pessimistic, but because they feel a sense of involvement and responsibility, and because they are committed to making things better. The first step in doing this is taking a clear-eyed look at the way things are—even if people would rather listen to a cheerleader who reassures them that everything is fine, that they should just go ahead and have a happy day, because after all, those people sleeping on the heating grates are actually there because they like it.

Liberalism is driven by social conscience. Hence, it takes a very different view of our responsibility to one another. In his book *All I Need to Know I Learned in Kindergarten*, Robert Fulghum wrote that "When you go out into the world, watch out for traffic, hold hands, and stick together." What Fulghum was really saying was that he received a liberal education.

Liberalism takes a favorable view of democracy in particular. Hence, it sees government (exactly as the Declaration of Independence defined it) as nothing more nor less than *ourselves*, our representative in a profound sense, ministering to us, correcting us if need be, standing for us, our goals, our hopes, and our way of reaching out to one another. It is our instrument of public purpose. Imperfect, to be sure. Sometimes wasteful, sometimes frustrating, sometimes even counterproductive, but a whole lot better than what the conservatives prefer to dish up: greed mixed with social indifference, spiced with pieties about the virtues of self-reliance.

Liberalism embraces people and hence, democracy. When, in 1988, the Neanderthal-conservative Republican Party of Arizona proclaimed that the United States was a "Christian nation," it also announced that it was "not a democracy." This may be shocking to some, but not to anyone familiar with the essential difference between liberalism and conservatism when it comes to democracy. Edmund Burke, one of the leading conservative thinkers of his day, was especially incensed by the French Revolution, with its upstart assertion that "the people" had a right to decide their own form of government. According to William Gladstone, prime minister of Great Britain eighty years later, "Liberalism is trust of the people tempered by prudence; conservatism is distrust of the people tempered by fear."

We've come a long way, as a country and as individuals, thanks to liberalism. Few people, at the turn of the last century, would have predicted that in the century to come, the United States would have become a racially integrated society, that the federal government would actually concern itself with the health and well-being of its people, or that the country would have undertaken a vast network of international commitments. This is the liberal program, and it has largely been achieved. Fewer yet would have predicted that having been so successful, liberalism would then be rejected . . . and that while renouncing it, even its detractors would cling enthusiastically to most of its accomplishments. Liberalism was not assassinated by right-wing death squads; instead, it has been victimized by its own success. Those born in the 1940s and later take their social "safety net" for granted, they have benefited so much from liberal programs that many have come to think they can afford to vote conservative! What they cannot afford, however, are the results of that vote.

IT IS easy to criticize liberals and liberalism: the bleeding-heart do-gooders who wallow in guilt and try to make you do the same, brimming over with plans for the nation and the world, and who are especially liberal with other people's money. But in fact, liberalism represents more than anything a way of thinking and feeling, a commitment of citizens to the future and to one another, an optimistic attitude that has the courage to put its money and its reputation where its mouth is. Said President John F. Kennedy:

> Liberalism is not so much a party creed or a set of fixed platform promises as it is an attitude of mind and heart, a faith in man's ability through the experiences of his reason and judgment to increase for himself and his fellow men the amount of

justice and freedom and brotherhood which human life deserves.[15]

To conservative disciplinarians, the way to insure domestic tranquility is to carry a bigger stick, to imprison wrongdoers who are often society's victims no less than victimizers (just last century, conservatives fought tooth and nail against abolishing debtors' prisons, for example), to demand responsible behavior and if it isn't forthcoming, to come down hard on those who are caught, especially if they are poor, minorities, or otherwise helpless. In fact, the United States currently imprisons a higher percentage of its population than any industrialized state in the world, including—are you ready for this?—the Republic of South Africa and the U.S.S.R., which come in second and third. And still we have crime. In fact, we have the highest crime rate in the industrialized world.

Yet American society—and Western society generally—has on balance been doing rather well for itself, well enough for it to be the envy of the planet, and a model for the newly democratizing countries of Eastern Europe. One of Karl Marx's great miscalculations was his failure to appreciate that capitalist societies could ever develop a heart, that they could care for the needy or display a sense of responsibility toward the future . . . in short, that they could become *liberal*. Liberalism gave us capitalism with a human face, thereby saving capitalism from itself, from its worst excesses of selfishness and greed. But the job is not finished, and probably never will be. In the words of an old Talmudic injunction, "The day is short, the work is urgent. It is not your duty to complete the work, but neither are you free to desist from it."

Thus, if the Reagan years have taught us anything, it is that avarice and irresponsibility are always with us, waiting only for society to let down its guard. The liberal impulse stands astride these tendencies, challenging them, rechanneling them, thwarting them when it can. Liberalism is the humanizing impulse, the softening of our nastier, fiercer, more unpleasant inclinations. George Bush may not like hearing this, but when

---

[15] Quoted by David Peterson, in a speech at JFK School of Government, Harvard University, March 15, 1989.

he called for a "kinder, gentler nation," he was calling for a more liberal one.

To CONSERVATIVES, freedom is the absence of constraint. It is getting the government, and liberal scheming, "off our backs." Take, for example, the childproof aspirin bottle. This simple and often infuriating device might serve as a metaphor for triumphant liberalism: It is well-intentioned, and probably a good idea. But in pursuit of social responsibility, childproof medicine containers (that often cannot be opened by adults) may well represent social do-goodism carried just a bit too far. As with these frustrating aspirin bottles, liberals would rather constrain our actions, if need be, in the interests of a greater good. Conservatives would rather have the buyer beware, even if some kids get poisoned—especially if, by deregulation, they can sell more aspirin.

And yet, liberals—as we shall see in the next chapter—take a back seat to nobody when it comes to devotion to freedom; indeed, liberalism originated out of the deepest commitment to freedom, and a willingness to stand up to despotic monarchies (the same monarchies and aristocratic privileges that conservatives *supported*). But here and now, in the late twentieth century, long after overcoming King George III and Louis XVI, liberals recognize that freedom means more than freedom *from*. It must also include freedom *to*: freedom to develop one's potential, in a world that often is less than free, or fair.

In Gilbert and Sullivan's *Iolanthe*, we learn that every child "born into this world alive, is either a little liberal or else a little conservative." Maybe so, but liberals know that a poor child—whatever its inclination at birth—assuredly isn't born free to compete on an equal footing with, say, the offspring of Leona Helmsley ("We don't pay taxes; the little people pay taxes"). They know that the children of Donald Trump, or Michael Milken, or William Buckley, or for that matter, George Bush, hardly start out on a "level playing field" with the rest of us. They know that people aren't free when they are discriminated against because of their skin color, when they can't get adequate medical care, a decent education, an opportunity to live without the threat of drugs, environmental destruction, or nuclear war. Liberals know that in such a world, government isn't some evil, outside force. It is *us*, the agent of our collective will, and we need it desperately. They know that government isn't perfect, anymore than people are, but they also know that we establish government not only for negative reasons—to protect ourselves from one another and from shared enemies—but also for positive ones, to take care of one another, to make ourselves better.

To be sure, there is a natural tension at work here, produced by the liberal striving to achieve freedoms *to* without losing freedoms *from*. No one—liberals included—likes the idea of creating excessive state authority, and thereby perhaps endangering individual freedoms. But in fact, the restrictions that liberals imposed upon private enterprise have, on balance, greatly enhanced the domain of personal liberty. Writes Arthur M. Schlesinger, Jr., scholar of American political history, enthusiast of liberal causes, and one of John F. Kennedy's most articulate White House aides:

> The individual freedoms destroyed by the increase in national authority have been in the main the freedom to deny black Americans their elementary rights as citizens, the freedom to work little children in mills and immigrants in sweatshops, the freedom to pay starvation wages and enforce barbarous working hours and permit squalid working conditions, the freedom to deceive in the sale of goods and securities, the freedom to loot national resources and pollute the environment—all freedoms that, one supposes, a civilized country can readily do without.[16]

The goals of liberalism are to make life better. It is that simple. And just as war is too important to be left to the generals, and politics too important to be left to the politicians, the goals of liberalism are too precious to be entrusted to conservatives.

LIBERALS KNOW that you don't have to believe in a smothering welfare state to believe in decency, compassion, helping, and caring. They know that you don't have to believe in a rigidly planned economy or a bloated bureaucracy to believe

---

[16] Arthur M. Schlesinger, Jr., "Is Liberalism Dead?" *The New York Times Magazine*, March 30, 1980.

that personal and corporate greed are not always the best guideposts to a decent future. And yet, the accusations of the 1980s are not new. In 1960, speaking to New York State's Liberal Party, Senator John F. Kennedy asked:

> What do our opponents mean when they apply to us the label "liberal"? If by liberal they mean, as they want people to believe, someone who is soft in his policies abroad, who is against local government, and who is unconcerned with the taxpayers' dollar, then the record of this party and its members demonstrate that we are not that kind of "liberal."
>
> But, if by "liberal" they mean someone who looks ahead and not behind, someone who welcomes new ideas without rigid reactions, someone who cares about the welfare of the people—their health, their housing, their schools, their jobs, their civil rights, and their civil liberties—someone who believes that we can break through the stalemate and suspicions that grip us in our policies abroad, if that is what they mean by a "liberal," then I'm proud to say that I'm a "liberal."

And what of the future? What will people mean when they speak of liberalism in the next century? Is it, as critics insist, devoid of new ideas? What sort are required? In fact, one defining characteristic of liberalism has been its openness to ideas, its willingness to experiment, to integrate government direction with private implementation. It may not sound terribly exciting, but the truth may well be that liberalism has already found its crucial idea: a humanization of capitalism, a softening of private greed by public purpose. This may not be the best of all imaginable worlds but rather, the best of all practicable ones.

The years to come seem likely to demand a renewed compact among government, industry, and labor—with science, technology, and the arts thrown in. Just as the New Deal of the 1930s was urged upon the United States by the exigencies of the Great Depression, and the liberalism of JFK and LBJ in the 1960s by a realization of the unfinished work of a socially responsible polity, the driving force of the next great phase of liberalism—that of the 1990s—may well come from a realization of the limits to growth and the need for environmentally and ecologically sound practices in a world of too many people and too few resources.

Probably the enduring myth of American history has been that of the rugged individualist, the solitary frontiersman, the hard-driving captain of industry, carving out a livelihood and a nation by force of character and indomitable entrepreneurial spirit, without the benefit of society, or government. To the contrary, the United States government, as the most prominent and best-endowed agent of the American people, has a lengthy tradition of affirmatively entering into the lives of its citizens, and to the overwhelming benefit of those citizens. As historian Schlesinger points out, there is ample precedent for government resuming such a role, navigating between the tyranny of state overcontrol and the unfairness of the unregulated market. Well-considered, humane coordination between government and the private sector, according to Schlesinger,

> calls for the restoration of the spirit in which the republic was founded, the spirit of commonwealth, of the public good, of the general welfare. The tradition of affirmative government is quite as authentically American, quite as deeply ingrained in our national history, quite as strongly identified with our greatest statesmen, quite as expressive of American ideas and character, as the competing tradition of self-interest and scrambling private enterprise.[17]

The most important new idea of liberalism is modest enough, but in its own way crucial: a return to the principles of liberalism itself. But first, let's take a look at those principles, starting with how they came to be.

---

[17] Arthur M. Schlesinger, Jr., loc. cit.

Chapter 2 A Bit of History: Jeffersonian Ends and Hamiltonian Means

FRANCIS FUKUYAMA is assuredly no liberal. He is a State Department official in the Bush administration, and one of the darlings of American conservatives. Why then do we encounter his name in a chapter on the history of American liberalism? Because in his essay, "The End of History,"[1] which celebrated the crumbling of communism in Eastern Europe, Fukuyama concluded that we have won. But note how he put it: "The ultimate triumph of Western *liberal* democracy is at hand" (italics added). The outcome is not, he assured us, "a convergence between capitalism and socialism . . . but an unabashed victory of economic and political *liberalism*" (italics added). People may be forgiven for being confused at this point, for presumably this conservative is not claiming victory for the ideals of Ted Kennedy, Mario Cuomo, George McGovern, and Michael Dukakis. Rather, he means that democracy and particularly the free market have triumphed (whether this is really true, incidentally, remains to be seen, since it is likely that the

---

[1] Francis Fukuyama, "The End of History," *The National Interest*, Summer, 1989.

31

states of Eastern Europe will ultimately adopt a kind of social democratic model, along the lines of Sweden).

Our purpose here is not to debate the supposed "end of history," but to note its author's use of the terms *liberal* and *liberalism*. In doing so, he points up the fact that these words have undergone a major metamorphosis, especially in the United States. Two hundred years ago, today's conservative would have been called a "liberal," whereas today's liberal scarcely existed at all before the early twentieth century. Fukuyama's usage is thus a bit archaic, but it helps emphasize some of the changes that have taken place.

LIBERALISM FIRST came into being in its "classical" form. In particular, the classical liberals—men such as John Locke, David Hume, Jeremy Bentham, John Stuart Mill, and Immanuel Kant—believed passionately in the freedom, independence, and rights of the individual. While this may not seem so extraordinary today, several hundred years ago it was nearly revolutionary, since European society was rigidly organized by hierarchy, with monarchy at the top, the landless peasants at the bottom, and shopkeepers and merchants in between. There was relatively little industry, in the modern sense. Privilege and wealth were hereditary, and aristocracy was the order of the day. Individuals didn't count, except for a few in the nobility.

Joining the upstart political thinkers of the European and American Enlightenment with their newfangled ideas of personal autonomy and freedom were some notable economists, especially Adam Smith and David Ricardo. That's right, the founding fathers of capitalism, virtual deities in the pantheon of modern-day conservatives, were the renowned *liberals* of their day! And this should not really be surprising, since free enterprise is a system in which mere individuals—some of them, to the consternation of the aristocracy, lowly born—actually proceed to go into business and create wealth for themselves, regardless of their ancestry and pedigree. Capitalism was, in its time, a revolutionary doctrine, a way of turning the world upside down.

Not surprisingly, conservatives of the day resented it. Of all biblical statements about politics, none had been more quoted and discussed during the Middle Ages than the following, from St. Paul (Romans 13: 1–5):

> Let every soul be in subjection to the higher powers: For there is no power but of God, and the powers that be are ordained of God. Therefore he that resisteth the power withstandeth the ordinance of God: And they that withstand shall receive to themselves judgment. . . . And wouldst thou have no fear of the power? Do that which is good, and thou shalt have praise from the same: For he is a minister of God to thee for good. But if thou do that which is evil, be afraid; for he beareth not the sword in vain: for he is a minister of God, an avenger for wrath to him that doeth evil.

It is precisely this conception of authority—hierarchical, divinely empowered, beyond question—that the classical liberals were to overthrow, and which conservatives such as Edmund Burke of England were to protect. Liberalism was a critique of the old system (the *ancien régime*) and an effort to establish a new political order. Conservatism sprang into being in response, as a defense of the way things were.

The stage was set for a clash of ideologies. We should note here that the term *ideology* was originally a product of the French Enlightenment; it referred to a body of revolutionary thought aimed at overcoming traditional beliefs and social structures, and replacing them with something better. We would do well to linger awhile on the concept of ideology, since liberalism is one, along with conservatism, Marxism, fascism, and so forth. Ideologies are complete schemes for the good life, which purport to tell us how to run human society. They also provide a framework for understanding why things are as they are, and for consoling ourselves when they go awry. In fact, one of the most attractive things about ideologies—for their followers— as well as one of the most frustrating things, for their opponents, is that most ideologies are so complete that they cannot be refuted. That's partly why they are so successful. If things go well, it is because the ideology has been followed; if badly, then it must have been thwarted, ignored, or incorrectly applied. Fukuyama's pronouncement of the end of history was, interestingly, preceded several decades ago by a sociologist, Daniel Bell, who bemoaned the end of ideology.[2]

---

[2]Daniel Bell, *The End of Ideology* (New York: Free Press, 1962).

But let's return to the classical liberals. Their conservative opponents quickly developed a more negative variant of the term *ideology*, and it has stuck. Thus, it was while opposing the upstart European liberals and their seemingly radical ideas that the term *ideologue* was first coined. The French political philosopher Antoine Rivarol (1753–1801) complained that the ideologues have "aspired to nothing less than the reconstruction of everything, by means of a revolt against everything. And without remembering that they themselves are in the world, they have torn down the pillars that support the world."[3] To Rivarol, the liberal ideologues had "an appearance of boldness and loftiness that enchanted youth and conquered mature men, a readiness and a simplicity that obtained everyone's approval and eliminated all resistance. Indeed, instruments of destruction are so very simple."[4]

But of course, classical liberalism was not destructive, except insofar as it successfully overcame the structures of monarchy and aristocracy. Rather, the classical liberals were apostles of the Industrial Revolution, of building and growth, industry and commerce, liberated thinking and unlimited frontiers. To the classical liberals, government should do only whatever was minimally necessary to preserve order and private property at home, and to provide defense against aggression from abroad. (And of course, conduct a little aggression now and then, when it might be profitable.) The classical liberals, in short, favored a so-called night-watchman state, in which the powers of government were essentially those of the police and the military. Not that these powers were to be overbearing. Quite the contrary: Thomas Jefferson was a liberal in the classic sense, and he is best known as an advocate of strictly limited government power.

Thus, Ronald Reagan was a dyed-in-the-wool, *classical liberal* when he proclaimed, in his first inaugural address, that "Government is not the solution to our problem; government is the problem." Of course, conservatives soon also came to

---

[3] Quoted in William T. Bluhm, *Ideologies and Attitudes: Modern Political Culture* (Englewood Cliffs, N.J.: Prentice-Hall, 1974).
[4] Ibid.

recommend a minimal government role, all the better to un-
chain the free market and let it work its magic. Possessing a
much deeper sense of irony than Mr. Reagan, the English
conservative Benjamin Disraeli noted before the House of
Commons in 1845 that "A conservative government is an organized hypocrisy."

As public religion declined from its zenith during the late
Middle Ages, individual freedom was on the upsurge, and the
proper role of government was to protect those freedoms, especially to defend each citizen's claim to his or her property.
Governments were to enforce contracts and to protect life and
property. Government itself was to be a limited contract, established by a willing citizenry and as such, revocable. In England, the result was a parliament made supreme over the
monarch; in the United States, classical liberalism gave rise to
a system of constitutionally limited government, with ample
checks and balances to prevent any branch of government from
becoming too big for its eighteenth-century britches.

Furthermore, the early liberals argued that even before taking part in any social contract, people in a state of nature retain certain fundamental perquisites, their "human rights." This
inspired the French Declaration of the Rights of Man and of
the Citizen, and in the United States, the Bill of Rights. Behind it all, undergirding the whole flow of social events: the
Individual, reigning supreme.

Of course, the ideal society as envisioned by the classical
liberals was not one in which individuals had complete freedom of action. The night watchman, after all, was on duty.
But the slogan "Don't tread on me" was suitable not only for
the early United States flag; it also served as a motto of the
classic liberal conception of individuals in relation to society
and government.

I⊤ is a big step from the theoretical writings of any ideology to the actual reality of its practice. Compare, for example,
Karl Marx's theory—a classless society and a government that
will eventually "wither away"—with reality in the Soviet Union
or China, where everyone is equal, but some are more equal
than others, and the state most assuredly hasn't withered. A
similar gap separates the writings of John Locke and Thomas

Jefferson on the one hand from the reality (and even the theory) of modern-day liberalism. Liberals in fact are much less attuned to their predecessors than are Marxists. Whereas Marxists will diligently study and explicate the writings of Saint Karl, relatively few liberals have read Locke. Similarly, most conservatives haven't attempted Edmund Burke, Disraeli, Plato, or even Goldwater. Nonetheless, there is much to be said for understanding one's intellectual antecedents, if only to discover how far away they are.

Liberalism developed gradually, almost shapelessly, over time. It began as an outgrowth of the rising capitalist class, the merchants and industrialists. It reflected part of the transition from an agrarian and rural life-style to industrial and urban society. It was fundamentally a mechanistic creed: secular, rational, and oriented toward progress. And it expressed primarily the aspirations of the growing middle class.

For classical liberals, the primary source is John Locke. The Enlightenment was essentially the dawn of the age of the individual, and it was liberal philosophy that illuminated this dawn. At a time when the modern nation-state was being formed, when the hierarchical, unquestioned authority of the Church had been fragmented by the Reformation, John Locke expressed a new kind of faith: in the individual. In his *Letters on Toleration*, Locke wrote that social life was a "Commonwealth," a "society among men constituted only for the processing, preserving, and advancing of their own civil interests . . . life, liberty, health . . . and the possession of outward things, such as money, lands, house, furniture, and the like." Again, this seems tame enough to American sensibilities in the final decade of the twentieth century, but in 1689, it was virtual heresy, suggesting that governments existed as a result of the voluntary coming together of people for their individual benefit. Notably missing from Locke's formulation was the role of national leader, or as European writers of that era used to put it, the Prince, ordained by God to rule over land and people. Government authority, in short, derived from the consent of the governed.

Locke's ideas were eventually taken up by Europeans and Americans eager to create their own futures. As one scholar puts it, "About two hundred years ago, the idea that truth was made rather than found began to take hold of the imagination . . ."[5] Platonic Ideas and the mind of God began to give way to new conceptions of reality: science, capitalism, the French Revolution. The result was a kind of relativism which liberals found intoxicating at the time, and which still illuminates the mind-set of liberals today.

It is sometimes claimed that Thomas Hobbes (1588–1679) was one of the founders of liberalism, since, like John Locke, he maintained that governments are established because individuals organize themselves voluntarily, to avoid the chaos that would otherwise result in a "warre of each against each." But in fact, Hobbes's views are far more congenial to modern-day conservatives, because his primarily pessimistic view of the human condition sees people's lives in nature as "solitary, poor, nasty, brutish, and short," and their behavior as motivated largely by fear and by desire for power. Moreover, Hobbes's most famous political argument, *Leviathan*, showed the colors of a true-blue conservative in its eagerness to subordinate individual rights to the straitjacket of authority.

To the liberal, even the classical liberal of three hundred years ago, authority was inappropriate unless it derived from the consent of those underneath. Moreover, John Locke was equally bold with regard to religious authority, which, like political authority, was to be the tool of its members rather than a supreme power and goal unto itself. "A Church," he explained, "I take to be a voluntary society of men, joining themselves together of their own accord [for] . . . the public worshipping of God . . . a free and voluntary society." It is also noteworthy that Locke wrote "*a* Church," not "*the* Church." Thus, he not only prefigured the separation of Church and State, but also the very liberal notion that there might actually be more than one church and more than one way to worship, each of them equally legitimate.[6]

---

[5]Richard Rorty, *Contingency, Irony, and Solidarity* (New York: Cambridge University Press, 1989).

[6]Or even, by extension, that it might be legitimate to refrain from worshipping altogether. Not that liberals are necessarily atheists or opposed to religion, despite what Christian fundamentalists would have you believe. They simply advocate tolerance, something most fundamentalists, whether Christian or Islamic, find even more incomprehensible than atheism. However, I suspect that atheism and agnosticism are far more widespread among liberals than among conservatives. "There is no God," James Mill confided to his son, the brilliant John Stuart Mill, "but this is a family secret."

In the economic sphere, the medieval world had sought to suppress the importance of worldly possessions. In his *Essay on Kingship*, Thomas Aquinas had called on rulers to limit the appeal and spread of commercial pursuits, which distracted people from their only true pursuit: salvation. Lending money at interest had been prohibited. Prices were extensively regulated by civil government and monopolistic guilds in favor of the "just price," which typically was not determined by a free market. At the same time, however, a middle class of merchants and entrepreneurs was arising in the towns, and usury (criminal) gradually was transformed into banking (respectable at last).[7] In addition, classical liberals weighed in on the battle to produce, to overcome scarcity. Locke noted that "He who appropriates land to himself by his labour, does not lessen but increases the common stock of mankind."[8] Locke was not simply a devotee of what in modern times has become environmentally destructive land "development." It must be remembered that three hundred years ago, great tracts of land were officially owned by the state, kept essentially as vast private hunting preserves for distant monarchs, while most people were desperately poor and landless.

Classical liberalism basically derived from two primary heritages, both of them espousing liberty: from the English philosophers such as Locke, liberty of individual rights, especially the right to personal property, and from the American and French revolutionary tradition, democratic liberty and popular rule. As to the preferred structure of a new democratic government, the early Americans turned to the work of another renowned liberal, this time a Frenchman, Charles Secondat, Baron de Montesquieu (1689–1755). A member of the French aristocracy who traveled widely throughout Europe and lived for a time as an exile in England, Montesquieu greatly admired English democracy and roundly criticized the French aristocracy. (Interestingly, John Locke also spent many years as an exile, in Holland.) Political freedom became Montes-

---

[7] At least to most people; in Bertolt Brecht's *The Threepenny Opera*, Mac the Knife asks, "What is the robbing of a bank compared to the founding of a bank?"
[8] *Second Treatise of Civil Government.*

quieu's overriding passion; he is credited with the liberal doctrine of "separation of powers," which puts limits on excessive government authority through an ingenious series of checks and balances among the executive, legislative, and judicial branches.

But classical liberals had a dilemma. With government primarily occupied keeping tabs on itself, so as to prevent undue power in any one branch, and with people free to do as they pleased, what would now motivate them to work, given that as part of their newly unfolding doctrine, neither the Church nor State could rightfully compel the individual? Their answer: self-interest. People would be industrious and hard-working (as the burgeoning middle class already was prepared to be) if they were guaranteed the products of their labor. And conversely, they wouldn't slouch so long as they knew that if they did, their lot would be poverty, misery, sickness, and an early death. The classical liberals most assuredly did not envision a welfare state.

Albert Dicey, an Englishman, wrote of the Poor Law of 1834 that its function was "to save the property of hard-working men from destruction by putting an end to the monstrous system under which laggards who would not toil for their own support lived at the expense of their industrious neighbors."[9]

The work ethic, or Protestant ethic, as Max Weber later called it, was integral to classical liberalism. Under the watchful eye of medieval theologians, this "ethic" in its early forms had been intended primarily as honor to God. But the bustling middle class and their classical liberal thinker-colleagues rapidly transformed the very concept of work itself, enshrining rational thought and purposive, industrious action directed toward accumulating wealth rather than benedictions, profits rather than salvation. Indeed, salvation soon became equated with material well-being itself. Without self-interest providing the engine of personal motivation, and classical liberalism providing its intellectual justifications, capitalism would not have been very dynamic. It might even have been a dud. As we

---

[9] Quoted in Harry Girvetz, *The Evolution of Liberalism* (New York: Collier, 1963).

shall see, this was not the last time that liberalism was to save capitalism.

ALTHOUGH THE "classical liberals" are now widely known by that phrase, they were not identified as such at the time. The word *liberal* first seems to have appeared as the name of a Spanish political party, the "Liberales," advocates of constitutional government in Spain during the nineteenth century. It was later taken up to indicate a preference for freedom over totalitarianism, especially by those in Europe and North America who sympathized with the various nationalistic struggles then under way within the Austro-Hungarian and Ottoman empires: Serbs, Croats, Czechs, Moravians, Bulgars, Greeks, Albanians, Montenegrins, Italians—all sought national self-determination, and "liberals" sympathized with their plight and identified with their aspirations.

As we have seen, classical liberalism's first battles were with the aristocracy and the Church. The fact that classical liberals were no more sympathetic to the downtrodden than was monarchy didn't necessarily do the new doctrine any harm; after all, virtually no one was sympathetic to the downtrodden, and they had no power anyhow. For their part, the classical liberals at least had a firm alliance with the burgeoning middle class. Liberalism's first crisis took place after it triumphed: The liberal order was based largely on a self-reliant middle class, with ambition, skills, and, increasingly, property and wealth. But the workers and peasants began to reason that if each individual mattered, as the liberals claimed, then the impoverished and uneducated also had certain entitlements, notably, the right to a say in their leadership and their lives.

This impulse toward democracy has taken many directions. It has included the English Leveler Movement (which was largely rational and nonviolent) and the Jacobin phase of the French Revolution (which was neither). In our own day, it has motivated the prodemocracy strivings in China that met such bloody repression in Tiananmen Square, as well as the 1989 "velvet revolutions" in East Germany, Hungary, Poland, and Czechoslovakia . . . so named because they were conducted nonviolently, even gently. And about two hundred years ago, it helped separate classical liberalism from its descendants—conservatism and modern liberalism.

It was liberal, prodemocracy doctrine that freed the English Parliament from control by the monarchy. It was the liberals among the American Founding Fathers who favored freedom to vote, to elect representatives directly and not by proxy, to design federal budgets and to tax—with these decisions to be made by the representatives of those being governed.

Conservatives objected to democracy, to participation of the hoi polloi (the "great unwashed") in the serious business of governing. Liberals—less and less of the classic variety—showed themselves increasingly in sympathy with democratic reforms, and eventually succeeded in doing away with property requirements for voting, over the ferocious objections of the conservatives. The transition was quite striking: Capitalism and democracy were at one time allies against monarchism and the abuses of feudal aristocracy. And supporters of capitalism and democracy were "liberals." Then, the traditions diverged: Those whose primary devotion was to capitalism wanted the new entrepreneurs to be left to do as they wished (laissez-faire), with government following a strictly hands-off policy . . . except, of course, for certain tax breaks and other benefits that could be wheedled. They came to be known as conservatives. On the other hand, those whose primary identification was with the democratic impulse—that is, with widespread freedoms regardless of wealth or social status—gave rise to the modern-day liberal.

It is no calumny to say that conservatives are uncomfortable with democracy, with one-person, one-vote. It is the simple truth, historically accurate and valid even today, although most right-wingers make ritualistic obeisance to democratic ideals. The conservative Patrick Buchanan, who wrote speeches for Richard Nixon and served for a time as Ronald Reagan's communications chief, at least has the virtue of saying out loud what most conservatives mutter only in private. Thus, in a column written just after the South African government announced that the African National Congress was being unbanned, Buchanan was unabashedly grumpy about the prospect of democracy in South Africa. He asked rhetorically why we should celebrate movement toward democracy in the land of apartheid.

Comes the answer: Because we stand for democracy! Because white rule of a black majority is inherently wrong! But, where did we get that idea? The Founding Fathers did not believe this. They did not give the Indians, who were still living a tribal existence, the right to vote us out of North America. When they created the Republic, they restricted the franchise to property-owning males, believing that not every man was qualified to rule, nor every people prepared for self-government. If the past 30 years taught us nothing else, it has surely taught us that.[10]

Let us remember, by contrast, the greatest liberal manifesto of all time, which announced: "We hold these truths to be self-evident . . ." But in 1776, the "self-evident" truths of equality were not widely recognized; indeed, their very pronouncement was breathtakingly new. And some people even today—notably, conservatives of whom Mr. Buchanan is, unfortunately, typical—evidently need to have these truths repeated and updated. Who better than liberals to do it?

LIBERALS TODAY are less self-assured than they were in the heyday of classical liberalism, or in the salad days of American liberalism, between 1933 and 1968, when its modern form became the ascendant ideology in the United States. An elusive, fluid doctrine, even today liberalism lacks towering figures like Locke or Adam Smith, largely because it has achieved most of its goals. Today's liberals are distrusted by the right wing and held in contempt by the far left. They want to retain private enterprise and the benefits of the marketplace, but unlike conservatives, they recognize a need for government intervention on behalf of social justice, education, workplace safety, medical care, housing, public welfare, defending the environment, as well as government regulation to prevent monopolistic practices and other excesses of capitalism run wild.

Still, today's liberalism continues to see society as existing for the sake of the individual; in that sense it is a natural extension of the seventeenth-to-nineteenth century, classical variety. How did it get here from there?

---

[10] *Seattle Post-Intelligencer*, February 7, 1990.

As we have seen, Jefferson was a classical liberal, and so, in a sense, was Alexander Hamilton. Yet there were noteworthy differences between these two giants of American history. Jefferson spoke for democracy, Hamilton for wealth and privilege. Jefferson's ideal America was a land of small towns and rural communities, peopled by farmers and other "freeholders." Hamilton's ideal America was a bustling, commercial metropolis, in which bankers and industrialists held sway.

In the early United States, Thomas Jefferson—widely recognized and revered for his contributions to democratic ideals and the freedom of the individual—opposed substantial government expenditures and involvement in civic life. It was Jefferson who espoused minimal government, who wrote, "That government is best which governs least." In his first inaugural address, Jefferson called for a frugal government that "shall refrain men from injuring one another, shall leave them otherwise free to regulate their own pursuits in industry and improvement, and shall not take from the mouth of labor the bread it has earned." In other words (read his lips), low taxes. By contrast, Alexander Hamilton—champion of the merchant, banking, and industrial class—favored government expenditures on their behalf. Thus, it was Hamilton, by modern standards the "conservative," who advocated an affirmative activist government, and Jefferson, the "liberal," who opposed it. It was also Jefferson who criticized the Federalist party of John Adams, Alexander Hamilton, and George Washington for being too close to the wealthy and the privileged; after leaving office, Jefferson (founder of the Democratic Party) noted, "I hope we shall crush in its birth the aristocracy of our monied corporations."[11]

In the early nineteenth century, there was a shortage of capital in the fledgling United States, and "government programs" were essentially directed toward improving the economic sinews of the new and growing country. These were not Head Start, Aid to Families with Dependent Children, or food stamp programs for the poor, but rather, the building of roads, canals, and ports, to develop the national economy.

---

[11] Quoted in Eric Foner, *Politics and Ideology in the Age of the Civil War* (New York: Oxford University Press, 1978).

The major beneficiaries, initially at least, were the corporations and the wealthy. In his first message to Congress, President John Quincy Adams pointed out the potential for abuse,
if, in its enthusiasm for growth and development, the needs
of the people are forgotten:

> The great object of the institution of civil government is the
> improvement of the condition of those who are parties to the
> social compact, and no government, in whatever form consti-
> tuted, can accomplish the lawful end of its institution but in
> proportion as it improves the condition of those over whom it
> is established.

Later, Andrew Jackson, perhaps our only president who was
truly a populist, vetoed schemes that would have induced the
federal government to make additional investments that—according to Jackson—should have been made by private enterprise. Jackson saw business seeking to milk funds from the
federal treasury; as a populist democrat (both small and large
D), he preferred laissez-faire to the Hamiltonian dream in which
private enterprise would be guided and abetted by a generous
national government.

Early in our history, no one seemed to consider seriously
the prospect that the federal government, or for that matter
the states, might ever bestir themselves on behalf of those who
were not well-to-do. It should be remembered that what we
call the "Revolutionary War" had actually been a war for political independence and national self-determination, not a true
revolution in domestic social relations as the French Revolution would soon become. Some have claimed that to understand American liberalism it is necessary to recall that at its
inception, the United States had no resistant feudal class to
overthrow. Looking at it differently, on the other hand, we
might say that the American feudal class was never really
defeated; the wealthy merchants and landowners—the Wash-
ingtons, Adamses, Jeffersons, Hamiltons, and Madisons—
engineered a separation from England, so that power was
essentially transferred from Europe to North America, but
within the United States itself, social and economic relations
continued more or less unchanged.

In any event, Jefferson and Hamilton had very different ideals, and the tension between them illuminates much of the distinction between liberals and conservatives. The project of modern-day liberals has been described as seeking to achieve Jeffersonian ends by Hamiltonian means: equality and liberty, through the actions of government. Or as Swedish Nobelist Gunnar Myrdal once observed, "America is conservative . . . but the principles conserved are liberal and some, indeed, are radical."[12] By contrast, even as liberals try to employ government power to achieve fairness, conservatives have an opposite goal: to use Jeffersonian means to gain Hamiltonian ends—using governmental *in*action for the benefit of the few, the select, the privileged, the wealthy, and the powerful. (This is why conservatives have been so much enamored of Social Darwinism, with its bogus version of "survival of the fittest.")

Today's liberal goals are unquestionably those of Thomas Jefferson: the "common good," equality of opportunity, widespread democracy, a nation of competent citizen participants. But as times have changed, so have the means to achieve these worthy ends. We are no longer an agrarian nation of small landowners (if indeed, we ever were). Jeffersonian "hands-off" government was—and certainly is today—a vestigial dogma of a long-gone past. The Jeffersonian tradition of antigovernmental "liberalism" ceased long ago to protect the individual. Instead, it began endangering the nonrich, by crimes of omission rather than commission.

Local, minimal government had been the Jeffersonian ideal. But as powerful local interests developed, the poor and dispossessed had to appeal over the heads of local interests and local government, to a more encompassing authority; namely, the federal government. Local bigotry, local tyranny of the neighborhood financial bully or the regional industrial plant—all these required the civilizing influence of those who did not have a direct, selfish interest in a specific conflict. Power abhors a vacuum: If society won't exercise power on its own behalf, wealthy industrialists and corporations will be only too happy to do so. Under these conditions, government's rightful role is to help overcome various obstacles to freedom, whether im-

---

[12] Gunnar Myrdal, *An American Dilemma* (New York: Harper, 1944).

posed by foreign powers, by bad luck and accident of birth, or by the excesses of corporate greed.

The 1892 Populist platform stated this newfound liberal reliance on government: "We believe that the powers of government—in other words, of the people—should be expanded . . . to the end that oppression, injustice and poverty shall eventually cease in the land." Alexander Hamilton, never a populist himself, would have been surprised to have been appropriated by such egalitarianism. And whereas the Populists no longer exist as a political party, today's liberals have continued to embrace Hamilton's conception of an active, affirmative federal government, to serve as the agent of national will and to accomplish worthy aims that cannot be achieved by individuals acting alone. (It may be ironic that—in the liberal conception—government is supposed to be the organ of public caring and sharing, and yet government agencies only rarely display a human face to their constitutents. This is a serious problem for implementing liberal goals, but it should not be confused with these goals themselves, which actually have changed remarkably little in hundreds of years.)

There is, in fact, a crucial strand of consistency linking classical liberalism with its modern descendants. Liberals of the seventeenth, eighteenth, and early nineteenth centuries must be seen in the context of their times. They opposed government activism when the greatest danger to humanistic values came from those governments themselves. Classical liberals sided with the individual versus the state at a time when the government was monarchical, tyrannical, and inimical to freedom. In the last hundred years or so, with the triumph of democracy and capitalism in the West, the greatest threats to the individual have shifted. Now, they emanate not from society or government, but from the excesses of capitalism itself, and with the collusion of *too little* government.

Liberals turned to government intervention after industrialization created great concentrations of wealth and a poor working class, far from Jefferson's idyllic vision. In his world of independent farmers, protection was needed (and feasible) against a rapacious government. But faced with child labor, sweatshops, union busting, and monopolistic practices, those interested in the widest possible well-being of the citizenry (that is, liberals) increasingly saw government not as an enemy, but as a necessary ally. The basic difference between today's liberals and conservatives lies not in their attitude toward government—which, as we have seen, has switched places—but in their commitment to people and to a socially oriented generosity of spirit. In this respect, modern-day liberals have kept faith with the prodemocracy, even the early procapitalist, traditions of the classical liberals, while conservatives have remained true to the antidemocracy, proprivilege orientation of the monarchists and the entrenched.

"I feel confident," said Woodrow Wilson, "that if Jefferson were living in our day, he would see what we see. . . . Without the watchful interference, the resolute interference of the government, there can be no fair play." And we can be equally confident that if Locke or John Stuart Mill were alive today, they too would almost certainly side with modern liberals and not with the conservatives. They would recognize that defending the individual, which required opposition to government in the age of monarchy, requires active involvement by democratic government in the age of capitalism. In the past, capitalism (along with democracy) was the ideology of the people, of those who believed that rights and rewards should be independent of hereditary advantages. With capitalism triumphant, the need has shifted: to ameliorate the excesses of free enterprise itself.

In some countries—China, for example, and Myanmar (formerly Burma), as well as notably several Islamic and African states—authoritarianism prevails and society more closely resembles the eighteenth-century tyrannies. In such cases, governments are still the prime enemy and threat to individual freedom. Locke or Mill would doubtless be dissidents in these countries, or in the Soviet Union as well, for all its rapid democratization. Significantly, people like Boris Yeltsin, and even Mikhail Gorbachev himself, are called liberals, as opposed to the conservatives who prefer to retain the old nondemocratic system of entrenched minority privileges. (Notably, when Gorbachev began cracking down on the various democratically oriented independence movements, he was said to be moving toward the hard-liners and the conservatives.) Soviet and Chinese liberals aren't politically to the left of their opponents;

economically, in fact, they are to the right. Rather, they favor "liberalization," and greater freedoms. This, as we have seen, is the founding idea of liberalism, and the founding idea of the United States as well. By contrast, it is perfectly accurate to describe the old guard, those who prefer an authoritarian "ancien régime," as communist conservatives.

It has been said that the United States was born a liberal society, never going through a clearly "feudal" stage; the U.S.S.R., by contrast, went from feudal to communist, without ever being a liberal society. The Soviets have suffered because of this lack of a liberal political tradition, and as they struggle to liberalize today, the signs of strain are evident. Less appreciated is the fact that the United States also suffers— although much less—from the fact that it was "born free." Thus, with no clear legacy of feudal institutions, we also lacked a forthright conservative tradition that tried to defend these institutions.[13] We also never spawned a tradition of revolutionary socialism, fired with fervor to overthrow the last vestiges of medieval aristocracy. (Significantly, a large proportion of the American left-wing revolutionaries turned out to be European immigrants.) Had we experienced more of the far right, in short, we would also have doubtless known more of a homegrown far left. As it is, the American political experience ranges from conservative to liberal, a depressingly narrow swing of the pendulum, compared, say, with most European countries.

For better or worse, therefore, Governor Mario Cuomo was quite correct when he pointed out that "Liberalism properly understood is not just consistent with the American idea; liberalism properly understood *is* the American idea."[14]

THE PROBLEM of American liberalism has essentially been the problem of consolidating victory. Thus, as we have seen, liberalism's first phase was especially concerned with marketplace freedom, with buying and selling, getting and spending. This achieved, the second phase seriously began by the turn of the century, with the populist recognition that the market

---

[13]Southern defense of slavery came closest.
[14]Speech to the Liberal Party of New York, October 31, 1988.

alone cannot secure justice. The need was clear: to add political controls, to start tinkering with a system which, if anything, was working all too well. First-phase, or classical liberals, felt themselves relieved of the obligation of coming to grips with inequity. In part this was because wealth first had to be created—and in great abundance—before its maldistribution could become a problem. And even then, the market would surely take care of everything. Today's conservatives continue to believe this. Second-phase liberals, however, agree that intervention is needed, even on such hallowed ground as private property, especially the private property and practices of megacorporations.

In its most modern form, second-phase liberalism found its voice around the turn of the century, under the leadership of the Progressives, who picked up the mantle of the Populists. Many of them were in fact members of the Republican Party: men such as Senators Hiram Johnson of California, William Borah of Idaho, George Norris of Nebraska, and most notably, Theodore Roosevelt, governor of New York, and later president. Teddy Roosevelt fought the "robber barons," particularly John D. Rockefeller's Standard Oil, and Morgan's United States Steel Corporation. In a speech in 1910, Roosevelt clearly laid out his challenge to the plutocrats: "We are face to face with new conceptions of the relations of property to human welfare, that property is subject to the general right of the community to regulate its use to whatever degree the public welfare may require." TR's prescription is one that many of the classical liberals would have had a hard time swallowing, and that today's conservatives find anathema, since it elevates the "general right of the community" over the rights of individuals to dispose of their property as they please. But it fits right in with modern liberalism.

In a sense, it is another version of the fundamental Enlightenment idea that concentrations of power must be limited and constrained by checks and balances. This applies not only to the various branches of the federal government, à la Montesquieu, but also to the role of business versus government, business versus the people, and the people versus themselves. Those stymied in their attempts to ride roughshod over their neighbors often responded by appealing to Jeffersonian ideals and/or States' Rights or, better yet, local governmental control or no control at all, because the smaller the public unit, the more likely it is to be under the thumb of powerful interests. Accordingly, such appeals were often a cloak for unlimited corporate or private power.

Not that the issue has been clearly resolved, even among modern-day liberals themselves. In particular, the concept of "distributive justice" remains elusive, not only as a practical matter (what, precisely, is to be distributed—money, education, health?—and how: grants, workfare, minimum wages?) but also as an ideal (what exactly is being sought: equality, or just an end to gross *in*equality?) Even more troublesome is the question of *re*distribution, implying not only giving *to* but also taking *from*.

The Progressive tradition gave us not only the trust-busting of Teddy Roosevelt, but also the progressive income tax, the eight-hour workday, and child labor laws. Its goal was a kind of equality to be achieved not by leveling downward, as European ideology has long favored, but by leveling *upward*. American liberalism came to be inspired by an ideology that, as Tocqueville wrote, "incites men to wish all to be powerful and honored."[15]

IN THE United States, the term *liberal* as opposed to *conservative* only emerged in the 1930s, ironically just when American liberalism was going most explicitly beyond the antistatist attitudes of classical liberalism. For a time, opponents and critics of Franklin Roosevelt's New Deal called themselves "the true liberals." Only later did they accept the label *conservative*.

The New Deal was the defining episode of modern American liberalism. At the time, however, it was neither intended nor publicly justified as a means of achieving cooperative social good or of fundamentally changing the social system of the United States. Rather, liberalism was simply a way of overcoming the Depression and safeguarding traditional American values: individualism and freedom. To some extent,

---

[15] Alexis de Tocqueville, *Democracy in America* (New York: Random House, 1990).

the New Deal, with its watered-down version of European Social Democracy, was therefore actually "conservative." Thus, it was designed to stave off deeper reforms, in that by improving the lot of the American people, other, more radical changes—notably socialism—were preempted. As a result, liberalism acquired the enmity of True Believers from the far left no less than from the far right.

Many New Deal programs survived FDR and the end of the Depression, including broad-based efforts in education, health care, highway construction, veterans' benefits, and notably, Social Security. Even the relatively conservative 1950s were more a time of retrenchment than of retreat from basic liberal principles and practices.

Then, the 1960s witnessed yet another flowering of liberal energies, with real progress in civil rights, environmental protection, and benefits for the elderly. During the 1960s, however, liberalism got tripped up by several factors. It has not yet recovered its balance: For one thing, the disaster and tragedy of Vietnam was initially undertaken and promoted by liberals. (We shall examine the checkered relationship of liberalism and war in Chapter 9.) The divisiveness and bitterness of the Vietnam War has outlasted one generation; like the Civil War, it may prove to have permanent and painful repercussions within American society. The convulsions of the 1960s turned liberals against each other, and stripped liberalism of the moral certitude it had possessed. Hubert Humphrey, for example, was Lyndon Johnson's vice president and one of the great figures of American mid-century liberalism. But he couldn't quite separate himself from LBJ's Vietnam tar baby, which not only gave Richard Nixon the presidency in 1968, but also led many American liberals to become disillusioned with liberalism itself, since the "best and the brightest" had brought such dishonor to their country and themselves. LBJ himself, although a moderate/conservative while a senator, became increasingly liberal, at least on domestic issues, while president. (Indeed, he was the most successful president since FDR in furthering liberal social legislation.) But this only exacerbated the disillusionment and self-doubt among many liberals, who, although pleased at Johnson's progressivism at home, found liberal ideology tarnished by the fact that the Vietnam War—with all its

divisiveness and brutality—was being prosecuted by an acknowledged liberal.

There were other problems for liberals in the 1960s. The
civil rights movement, by its very success, created splits within
the Democratic Party, especially between northern liberals and
southern conservatives. Liberalism found itself under attack
from the New Left as "corporate" or "Cold War" liberalism,
and from the middle class, because of its association with busing and other threats to ethnic white enclaves in the North,
as well as the breakup of the white-centered social order in
the South. Life-style issues also became problematic: America's youth—increasingly alienated by the Vietnam War—turned
to practices that were distasteful to many of their elders, and
which, fairly or not, were attributed to such "liberal values"
as excessive permissiveness. In 1972, the Democrats and their
liberal standard-bearer, George McGovern, were branded the
party of "acid, amnesty, and abortion."

LBJ's Great Society programs moved, as political philosopher Michael Walzer put it, from "majoritarian welfarism to
minority welfarism," and in doing so, "it lost its grip on national feelings." Liberal programs, as we have seen, became
associated with spending for "them." At the same time, a
conservative backlash was stirred by a progression of liberal
legal victories, including *Roe* v. *Wade* on abortion, court-or-
dered busing, and affirmative action, which gave the impression that judges were legislating liberalism against the interests
of the middle class. And finally, the economy: Economic growth
through the 1960s and early 1970s had allowed liberal programs to go forward without overtly redistributing wealth. As
John F. Kennedy had put it, "A rising tide lifts all ships." But
by the late 1970s, economic stagnation combined with inflation and the Arab oil boycott caused a massive financial crunch.
The tide began to recede, and with it, the reputation of liberalism.

Liberalism had enjoyed a relatively easy time so long as the
economy was expanding. For example, during World War II,
some income redistribution was achieved, but almost entirely
by "leveling up": Between 1941 and 1945, the income of the
richest 20 percent of Americans increased by 20 percent; at the
same time, that of the poorest 20 percent also increased, by

68 percent. This was a painless redistribution, in which the poor became richer somewhat faster than the rich grew richer. (Absolute increases were still greater for the rich, but hardly anyone complained.) The point is that when times are good, redistribution needn't *lower* anyone's income. But when they turn bad, as happened in the late 1970s, the result is trouble.

The stage was therefore set for Ronald Reagan, who fed voter resentment while offering a cheery hope of selfish aggrandizement. Reagan provided show without substance, circuses without the bread, while at the same time promising to help America "stand tall" and recover from our embarrassments in Vietnam and over the Iranian hostages.

Liberalism, meanwhile, was pushed to the sidelines. But as we shall now see, that has happened before . . . and it probably will happen again, just as, predictably, the glory days of 1980s conservatism are already beginning to fade.

Chapter 3 The Bi-Cycles: From Private Greed to Public Purpose

Lᴇꜰᴛ ᴡɪɴɢ and right wing are a kind of mirror image for each other—almost like up and down, in and out or tall and short—spanning the range of options. They seem to divide up the imaginable universe. Moreover, they tend to alternate in power and influence. A century and a half ago, Ralph Waldo Emerson identified two political traditions that "divide the state." One of these he called "the party of Conservatism" and the other, "that of Innovation." He went on to point out that they "are very old, and have disputed the possession of the world ever since it was made. . . . Now one, now the other gets the day, and still the fight renews itself as if for the first time, under new names and hot personalities."[1]

Look around your house or your neighborhood on a warm summer day. Walk outside, comfortable in shirtsleeves, and try to remind yourself that the same streets and trees and grounds that are so accessible today were remote, forbidding, cold, wet, or possibly frozen hard and covered with snow,

---

[1] Ralph Waldo Emerson, 1841 lecture "The Conservative," in *Nature* (Boston: Houghton Mifflin, 1903).

just a few months before. Moreover, they will be that way again, just a few months from now. Immersed in things-as-they-are, it takes a powerful effort of the imagination to picture them being quite different, even when deep inside we know that once—not so very long ago—they were, and that they will be, again.

What applies to the seasonal patterns of warmth and cold also applies to political cycles. Immersed in politics-as-it-is, we require real imagination to remember that things were different in the past, and to realize that they may well be that way yet again in the future. But there is good reason to believe that political events—just as seasonal events—do in fact move in cycles.

According to historian Arthur M. Schlesinger, Jr.,[2] there is a thirty-year cycle of liberalism (which he calls "periods of public purpose"), alternating with eras of conservative restoration (when "private interest" is ascendant). During periods of public purpose, the emphasis is on *responsibilities*, what we owe to each other and to society at large; on the other hand, the ascendancy of private interest is characterized by a stress on *rights*, what each of us, as a private citizen, is entitled to do— generally for ourselves. Public purpose held sway with the election of Teddy Roosevelt in 1904, FDR in 1932, and JFK in 1960, while private interest was reasserted during periods of conservative reaction, which characterized the 1920s, the Eisenhower years of the 1950s, and the 1980s of Ronald Reagan.

THE CYCLIC nature of American liberalism and conservatism was first pointed out by the senior Arthur M. Schlesinger, also an historian, and then picked up and elaborated by his son. As the Schlesingers see it, the process is almost physiological, like the alternating contractions and relaxations, systole and diastole, of the human heart. Social activism is exhausting, demanding stuff. It takes its toll in the personal life of the activist, as well as on the national psyche. "Burnout" happens as people simply grow tired of commitment and weary of effort, impatient with the clamor and clash that char-

---

[2] Arthur M. Schlesinger, Jr., *The Cycles of American History* (Boston: Houghton Mifflin, 1986).

acterize struggles for social betterment and exhausted by the stress and strain of building a better world. Social activism is emotionally and often physically draining. It offers long hours, low pay, and all too often little in the way of positive reinforcement. (After all, the nation is big, the world is bigger, and each of us, small; after a while, we tire of the mismatch. And besides, social activism almost by definition promises more than it can deliver.) Small wonder that burned-out 1960s activists have gone on to earn MBAs and do leveraged buy-outs, Jerry Rubin sells respectability, and Abbie Hoffman dies of a drug overdose.

After a high level of citizen participation, most people are eager to hear a message of "at ease," from their leaders. Do your own thing, they say, make money, be a little greedy, it's OK, it's the American Way. Even the less prominent—but often, no less committed—long for peace and quiet, an opportunity to lick their wounds, feather their own nests, raise children in tranquillity and an immediate, if illusory, security; in short, to enter a conservative cocoon. "Worn out by the constant summons to battle," writes Schlesinger, "weary of ceaseless national activity, disillusioned by the results, they seek a new dispensation, an interlude of rest and recuperation."[3] Passion, idealism, reform, and public action decline. Or, as long-time liberal strategist Joseph Rauh, Jr., put it, "There is a national fatigue with progress. People think *we've* done enough for *them*."[4]

But any biologist can tell you that although it seems inactive, there's a lot going on inside a cocoon; a butterfly (or if you prefer, a moth) is getting ready to emerge once again, and to resume its hectic dance among the blossoms of social commitment. Thus, even during times of conservative dominance, things aren't altogether quiet. Periods of conservatism, of private focus and personal enrichment such as we have just been through in the 1980s, are also times when an undercurrent of criticism, dissatisfaction, frustration, and anger grows silently beneath the surface. Neglected injustices fester and social unfairness builds like an abscess, fulminant and needing to be

---

[3] Ibid.
[4] *The Wall Street Journal*, April 15, 1986.

drained.[5] In some cases, they actually erupt, as with the anti-nuclear activism of 1981–1986. Clever palliatives, such as the INF Treaty and Reagan's endorsement of a Star Wars scheme to make nuclear weapons "impotent and obsolete" served to confuse and confound the most vocal components of the 1980s peace movement. At the same time, social problems remained largely intractable, and accordingly, as in all periods of conservative retrenchment, there developed a growing, growling undertone of disappointment and disaffection. As Schlesinger describes it, during periods of social inaction:

> People grow bored with selfish motives and vistas, weary of materialism as the ultimate goal. The vacation from public responsibility replenishes the national energies and recharges the national batteries. People begin to seek meaning in life beyond themselves. They ask not what their country can do for them but what they can do for their country. They are ready for a trumpet to sound. A detonating issue—some problem growing in magnitude and menace and beyond the capacity of the market's invisible hand to solve—at last leads to a breakthrough into a new political epoch.[6]

However, these new epochs also tend to be time-limited as well. After a period of heady activism, such as this nation experienced during the 1930s and 40s and again during the 1960s and early 1970s, people once again grew weary of causes and of political enthusiasm itself. "Americans tire, after twenty years," wrote H. L. Mencken from another viewpoint, "of a steady diet of . . . highfalutin and meaningless words; they sicken of an idealism that is oblique, confusing, dishonest and ferocious. . . . Tired to death of intellectual charlatanry, [the citizen] turns to honest imbecility."[7]

"Honest imbecility" would be a good description of the Reagan Administration . . . especially if we delete the first word.

---

[5]Unfortunately, this particular period of conservatism left us with a right-wing judiciary (including the Supreme Court) that will serve to stifle progress and delay the correction of injustice for some time after the political pendulum has swung back once again.
[6]Arthur M. Schlesinger, Jr., op. cit.
[7]H. L. Mencken, *The American Scene* (New York: Knopf, 1965).

Although Ronald Reagan's special brand of imbecility is doubtless unique, it is more the uniqueness of personal idiosyncrasy than a response to some altogether novel historical and political demand. Thus, looking for surcease from caring, we have turned to similar forms of imbecility at other times in this century. Such a turning occurred after the first two decades of the twentieth century, after a national exhaustion with Teddy Roosevelt's eager trust-busting and a degree of internationalism that this country had never known before, culminating in Woodrow Wilson's hyperidealistic "war to end all wars" and to "make the world safe for democracy." The country's response was to turn its back on Wilson's League of Nations, and to embrace the reassuring (if incompetent) Warren G. Harding and his much longed-for "return to normalcy," which continued through the somnambulistic administrations of Coolidge and Hoover. As Schlesinger reminds us, Harding summed up the country's mood in his own words, when he observed that the United States wants "not heroics but healing, not nostrums but normalcy, not revolution but restoration, not agitation but adjustment, not surgery but serenity."[8] (And we also got the Teapot Dome scandal—which had its reflections in the Reagan Administration's Iran-Contra, Savings and Loan, and HUD scandals. Under Reagan, we may well have sought not intensity but indifference, not thoughtfulness but theatrics, and we got not competence but corruption. But even then, it turns out, we didn't really mind, since our hearts were set on respite and retrenchment.)

During the self-indulgent, conservative decade of the 1920s we involuted, amusing ourselves with flappers and bathtub gin, the Charleston and high-flying stock speculation. After all, the business of America, we reminded ourselves, was business, especially minding our own business, and even the scandal-ridden and inept Harding administration didn't dampen our enthusiasm for "keeping cool with Coolidge," and for that red-hot radical who was next in line: Herbert Hoover.

Finally, after Hoover came the deluge.

The 1930s and 1940s, not surprisingly, were marked by a

---

[8] Samuel H. Adams, *Incredible Era: The Life and Times of Warren Gamaliel Harding* (Boston: Houghton Mifflin, 1939).

return to activism: two decades of it, under Franklin Roosevelt and Harry Truman. The Great Depression was upon us—at least in part a result of the devil-may-care, self-indulgent conservatism that had preceded it—and Americans responded with the New Deal and a remarkable array of social programs. We rose to the challenge of "one third of a Nation ill-fed, ill-housed, ill-clothed," as well as the challenge of fascism. World War II demanded a nationwide commitment and immense effort, following which we collapsed once more into the arms of another feel-good decade, this one symbolized by a smiling, fatherly, reassuring war hero who somehow never seemed especially bloody or demanding: Dwight Eisenhower.

The social energy of the 1950s was matched by the intellectual depth expressed in the most popular political slogan of the day, "I like Ike." What we really liked was another return to normalcy after the tumult of the 1930s and 1940s. Again, national exhaustion led to another predictable era of public stagnation and retrenchment, the Eisenhower years of the 1950s.

Then, by 1960, Americans were ready once again to heed a more activist trumpet, to bestir ourselves so as to "get this country moving again." So we elected a president—John F. Kennedy—who told us: "Ask not what your country can do for you; ask what you can do for your country." And the 1960s were indeed a tumultuous time, with the assassinations of John and Robert Kennedy and Martin Luther King, Jr. ,the Great Society programs of Lyndon Johnson, the Vietnam War, hallucinogenic drugs, and social upheavals. The tide began turning once more as early as 1968, with the election of Richard Nixon. Nixon's 1968 speeches were actually far more conservative than Goldwater's in 1964, who was clobbered for being too conservative. But by 1968, times had changed. Nonetheless, liberalism continued to hold sway, at least as measured by the programs actually implemented: the Comprehensive Employment and Training Act (CETA), the Occupational Safety and Health Act (OSHA), the Environmental Protection Act (EPA), etc. Even conservative appointees, such as Walter Hickel as secretary of the interior, wound up marching under a liberal banner.

But eventually, the activist mood soured, worn out by the Vietnam War and the Watergate scandal, and the country turned, right on schedule, to conservatism as a balm to soothe its jangled nerves. The presidency of Jimmy Carter was in many ways a gradual transition to the full-fledged national (or rather, private) self-indulgence of the Reagan years. Although Carter himself was singularly unavaricious and not especially self-indulgent, he came to the White House with a distrust of government generally and social programs in particular, and he initiated—although on a smaller scale—many of the deregulation schemes that Ronald Reagan and his minions ultimately brought to fruition. As the second decade of 1960s–1970s public activism sputtered to a close under Jimmy Carter's administration, we turned—right—on cue, to yet another decade of conservative retrenchment, with Ronald Reagan as the leading man, starring in the 1980s version of 1950s Eisenhower, or Harding-Coolidge-Hoover of the 1920s. And similarly, the Bush presidency—whether it lasts one four-year term or two—seems likely to be another such transition. The American national mood, beginning either in 1992 or 1996, will almost certainly be activist, socially responsible, and internationalist—in a word, liberal.

E VEN AS the political pendulum has swung from left to right and back again, some things have remained more or less the same. One of them, not surprisingly, has been a tendency on the part of our wealthiest and most influential people and corporations to blame government for what it gives to others, while never ceasing to get all that they can for themselves. Of late, many politicians themselves have joined in the chorus. For more than a decade now, it has been popular to hoot about the abuses and inefficiencies of the "welfare state," populated by two kinds of folks: the undeserving poor and the hard-working taxpayer, with the former greedily soaking the latter for every possible penny. In addition to these two—which do exist, to be sure—there are others, many of whom do not fit into the all-too-simple conservative bestiary. Most notably, there are the hypocrites, especially those free-market conservatives—supposed opponents of government subsidies—who are the first to line up at the public trough when it comes to government handouts to the large corporations with which they are associated.

Consider this observation by William Simon, arch-conservative secretary of the treasury during the Nixon administration:

> During my tenure at Treasury I watched with incredulity as businessmen ran to the government in every crisis, whining for handouts or protection from the very competition that has made this system so productive. I saw Texas ranchers, hit by drought, demanding government-guaranteed loans; giant milk cooperatives lobbying for higher price supports; major airlines fighting deregulation to preserve their monopoly status; giant companies like Lockheed seeking federal assistance to rescue them from sheer inefficiency; bankers, like David Rockefeller, demanding government bailouts to protect then from their ill-conceived investments. . . . And always, such gentlemen proclaimed their devotion to free enterprise and their opposition to the arbitrary intervention into our economic life by the state. Except, of course, for their own case. . . .[9]

Mr. Simon's "incredulity" is a bit surprising. After all, in itself, there is nothing new or disreputable about big business trying to get the best deal that it can from Uncle Sam. In many cases, the public interest may actually be served by keeping some of these organizations solvent, especially when—like Lockheed or Chrysler—they employ tens of thousands of people. The problem (ethical, if not political) arises when those same folks who eagerly crowd around for a government handout for their corporations loudly proclaim their opposition to government assistance to individual people, especially poor people.

It is also ironic, and deeply inconsistent, that so many Americans begrudge meager government aid to human beings, whereas in fact the government has long been extraordinarily generous to big business. Much of this generosity has long been found in military contracting:

> More than 50 percent of all defense procurement is negotiated with an exclusive single contractor; less than 12 percent goes through a formal advertised competition. According to one lit-

---

[9] William Simon, *A Time for Truth* (New York: McGraw-Hill, 1978).

tle-known but often-used law passed during the Cold War in the 1950s, the Department of Defense is empowered to declare firms on the edge of bankruptcy "essential to the national defense," and provide them with overgenerous contracts and outright case grants. From 1958 to 1980, this law was invoked 5,644 times. But this is only the icing on the cake. Almost every category of military spending not directly paid out to servicepeople subsidizes a commercial interest. When the revolutionary government of Iran canceled its purchases of undelivered arms in 1979, the military budget was used to compensate private arms suppliers with hundreds of millions of dollars in termination payment. Many large contractors have been spared the necessity of capital investment. For example, LTV Aerospace, one of America's largest military manufacturers, at one point owned only 1 percent of the 6.7 million square feet of offices, plants, and laboratories it used; the rest was leased from the Department of Defense.[10]

Such largesse is nothing new. After World War II, the United States government sold—at bargain-basement prices—fifty aluminum mills it had constructed, thereby creating the Kaiser and Reynolds empires. Similarly, fifty-one synthetic rubber plants were sold off at less than one half the original investment. The beneficiaries? Goodyear, B. F. Goodrich, etc. Similar windfalls were bequeathed to many other industries, notably steel and electronics.

Nor is government generosity to large corporations limited to start-up investment and help in time of need. Quietly, with very little fanfare and in response to intense lobbying from highly paid and skillful industry representatives, United States tax policy has been very good indeed to America's moneyed interests. Whereas direct payments—as in the form of welfare—are directly visible, indirect payments to large corporations—in the form of tax credits, accelerated depreciation schedules, etc.—are largely hidden, and thus, unlikely to arouse taxpayer ire. Moreover, since they are presented (when they are presented at all) as a tax *decrease*, they generally do not produce resentment, although the reality is that massive corporate tax breaks of this sort wind up costing the rest of us exactly the same amount as if the money were given

---

[10]Gar Alperovitz and Jeff Faux, *Rebuilding America* (New York: Pantheon, 1984).

directly as a welfare subsidy . . . and to the least needy of Americans.

Some examples: In 1980, AT&T paid an 8 percent income tax rate on earnings of $7.7 billion; Bank of America paid 3.1 percent on earnings of $1 billion; Exxon paid 3.1 percent on $2.5 billion; Chase Manhattan Bank, Squibb Pharmaceuticals, and Monsanto paid no federal income taxes whatever, despite the fact that they earned nearly $500 million. Talk about welfare handouts! And not only large corporations, but also wealthy individuals have traditionally benefited during periods of conservative retrenchment. One reason why the Roaring Twenties roared—at least for the richest Americans—is that the top personal income tax rate was reduced from 73 percent to 25 percent. By the 1980s, America's wealthy people were once more paying a substantial share of their income in taxes (70 percent), whereupon this rate was again lowered, to 28 percent . . . with the middle class being stuck with the remarkable "bubble" of 33 percent.

Then comes the Savings and Loan crisis with its attendant bailout, threatening to exceed $500 *billion*. Certainly, there is plenty of blame to go around, enough for Republicans and Democrats, conservatives and liberals; that is, greed and shortsightedness have been characteristic of individual politicians, across the American ideological divide.[11] But when we switch from the failings of individual people (Neil Bush, the Keating Five, etc.) and examine the role of ideology, the picture becomes much more clear: The Savings and Loan fiasco is a textbook case of what happens when we combine greed and corruption with the conservative penchant for eliminating government regulation.

One of the most beloved ambitions of Reagan administration conservatives was to get government "off our backs," which generally meant getting the regulators off the backs of

---

[11] It is noteworthy that money-driven scandals have been significantly less frequent during periods of liberal social activism than when conservatism has been ascendant. This may be because liberalism tends, by definition, to be based upon social conscience and concern for others, whereas conservative politicians, once in power, are more likely to act on their own heartfelt conviction that self-interest is not only the best public policy but also an appropriate guide in one's private affairs.

the industries—such as the so-called "thrifts"—they were supposed to regulate. Unregulated, these institutions and their unscrupulous managers were free to invest in high-flying real-estate and construction schemes, using depositors' money without risk to themselves because their questionable investments were guaranteed by the federal government (that is, you and me). If they made a profit, they got to keep it; if they did not, we picked up the tab. The result? Corporate capitalism at its most blatant, with Big Government underwriting the losses of some of this country's major financial players, while politicians proclaimed proudly—and incorrectly—that they were upholding the banner of the free market. Profits had in fact been privatized, while losses were socialized. In such cases, the free market is more like a free ride, not for the down-and-out, but for the up-and-coming and well connected. For the great majority of Americans, the outcome has been a horror movie come to life: The Revenge of the Living Debt.

THE COMING liberal resurgence will be none too soon. Problems, brewing and bubbling through the Reagan and Bush years, have been generating more and more pressure, too much to be relieved by quick fixes and electorally popular safety valves. Greenhouse warming, acid rain, rainforest destruction, the gap between haves and have-nots (both domestically and internationally), the dangers and grotesque absurdity of the nuclear arms race—these will not be solved by more study, by presidential commissions, by taking the short-term profits and running, by fervent entreaties to the miracle of private enterprise, or by studiously looking the other way.

It has been claimed that the Reagan years were marked by a unique convergence of ideological and social conservatism. But in fact, even the social conservatism of the 1980s (including Jerry Falwell and his Moral Majority, Jimmy Swaggart, and Jim Bakker) repeated earlier patterns: Billy Graham and Norman Vincent Peale of the 1950s, Billy Sunday and Aimee Semple McPherson of the 1920s. There is nothing new in an alliance of economic conservatives and right-wing evangelicals; however, the coalition has always been uneasy at best, and as the 1990s dawn, such issues as prayer in schools, birth control, and especially, abortion rights, seem poised to split it down the middle.

(Ironically, as with liberalism in the economic sphere, conservatives are finding themselves victims of their own success: It was easy, and electorally useful, to oppose abortion so long as abortion rights were not seriously in doubt. This is because antiabortion voters would rally round a "prolife"[12] stand, whereas prochoice advocates, not feeling threatened, felt they could ignore the issue. But with an antiabortion majority on the Supreme Court and abortion rights under attack, prochoice voters have begun feeling nervous and making themselves heard. And conservatives, finding themselves on the wrong side of a popular issue, have begun jettisoning their supposedly "moral" antiabortion stance.)

Liberals, at the same time, are getting more serious. Even during the 1950s, with a moderately conservative president, liberalism persisted as the dominant intellectual and political tradition. That curious creature (now nearly extinct), the liberal Republican, even roamed the political landscape, giving us such fossil memories today as "Rockefeller Republican," along with the likes of George Romney, William Scranton, John Lindsay, and Jacob Javits. But there was something of a thinning out of liberal thinking, as liberals rested on their New Deal laurels. Today's liberals, on the other hand, seem ready for a new burst of energy, as memories of the New Deal fade but the country's problems—poverty, racial disharmony, sinking international competitiveness, inadequate education and health systems, a crushing military budget, environmental degradation—remain as real as ever.

As always happens at the tail end of a conservative era, there is currently a growing sense of United States drift and decline, especially with regard to our economic uncertainty, our environmental failings, our educational dunce cap, our deteriorating roads, bridges, and industrial plants, our drug-riddled cities. George Bush may have overcome his wimp image by sending other people to kill and die in Panama and by making war on Iraq, but the overall wimpishness of conserva-

---

[12] There is a particular irony in describing a policy that forces women to continue unwanted pregnancies or to resort to the butchery of back-alley abortionists as "prolife." Moreover, the conservative stance in this respect has typically been combined with a notable indifference to the fate of mothers and infants; as Representative Barney Frank pointed out, conservatives seem to think that life begins at conception and ends at birth.

tism—namely, its inability to solve the nation's problems—is becoming clearer than ever. There is a well-founded concern that governmental laxity, especially in the executive branch, has allowed things to get out of hand. As a result, we are approaching another one of those times "to get this country moving once again." And liberals are in a position to do just that. It is they who can champion a far-reaching domestic revitalization. Moreover, with the Cold War rapidly winding down, it is the liberals—as opposed to the conservatives who are mesmerized by their love for military spending—who are ready and willing to help this country reap a genuine peace dividend . . . assuming, of course, that any such dividend will remain to be paid out in the aftermath of the Iraq War.

Even with Ronald Reagan's vice president elected president in 1988, the fact remains that the Reaganite tide in the United States is ebbing. It is, at long last, bedtime for Bonzo.

ALTERNATING SPASMS of energy and fatigue are not the only factors driving the liberal-conservative cycle in American politics. An important factor is related to human memory. Thus, liberals typically have suggestions and proposals for social activism of one sort or another. By their programs shall ye know them. Conservatives, by contrast, have antiprograms. Their most consistent "program" is opposition to those suggested or initiated by liberals. As Ralph Waldo Emerson saw it, conservatism "vindicates no right, it aspires to no real good, it brands no crime, it proposes no generous policy, it does not build, nor write, nor cherish the arts, nor foster religion, nor establish schools, nor encourage science, nor emancipate slaves, nor befriend the poor, or the Indian, or the immigrants."[13] In short, to redirect Gertrude Stein's observation about Oakland, California, "There is no there, there." Or, as George Bush has made abundantly clear, no "vision thing."

The party of reform (that is, liberalism), Emerson admitted, "runs to egotism and bloated self-conceit," but at least it is the self-conceit of good purposes rather than personal selfishness.

Liberals, in short, provide the motive force, the engine, for domestic innovation. When liberal programs succeed, they gain

---

[13] Ralph Waldo Emerson, op. cit.

credit for the success; when they fail—or when the public thinks they fail, even if the truth is otherwise—they get the blame.[14] But success, once incorporated into our common expectation, becomes part of the social landscape, and thenceforth taken for granted.

The Wagner Act of 1935, for example, made labor unions legal, and was a monumentally important piece of liberal legislation. It has been so successful that now we worry about the abuses of excessive union power, taking their very existence for granted, and blaming liberals for catering to labor as a "special interest." Nearly 50 percent of union households even voted for Ronald Reagan in 1984. So in part, liberal-conservative cycles are like a cross-country skier or a person on skates: a few good strokes and skier or skater moves along briskly, but after a while, the glide comes to an end . . . until the next push sets him or her moving once again.

When slowing down, however, or even coming to a halt, the skier/skater is unlikely to thank the earlier push for accomplishing so much; more likely, he or she resents that the glide didn't go on forever. The recession of 1982–83—at that time the worst since the 1930s—was brought on by the excesses of conservative economic hands-off dogma, and was only kept from becoming a full-fledged depression by the economic controls set in place by New Deal liberalism. But liberals didn't get the credit (although, at the time at least, conservatives got the blame).

The writer of Ecclesiastes was probably wrong: Every now and then there does seem to be something new under the sun (e.g., nuclear fission, microcomputers, microwaved popcorn). But only rarely is this something a political idea. Ronald Reagan's vision of the "common good," for example, was to lower taxes for the very rich, the idea being that if treated similarly, the poor and middle class would just spend their money foolishly: on food and rent, for example. But the rich would invest it, to everyone's benefit. There was nothing new in this idea, which was actually as old as Coolidge in the 1920s, or McKinley in the 1890s. These "new" ideas only seemed new because they were so old that no one remembered them.

The explanation for political cycling, however, doesn't lie

---

[14]The war on poverty, as we shall see, is a notable example.

only in fatigue, laziness, or forgetfulness. To some extent, we do get tired, but often in the sense of "sick and tired." The truth is that governing—whatever one's approach or ideology—is a difficult and often thankless task. Familiarity breeds contempt; old faces and old ideas wear thin and we long for new leaders and new approaches (or at least, new packaging). And so, after either side has been in power, perhaps four years, or eight, or twelve, or sixteen, the voters get restless. Successful candidates typically run *against* those in power. And the most effective of all political slogans, certainly the most enduring, appears over and over again, in one form or another: "Had enough?" Had enough sacrifice? Or, had enough selfishness, indifference, and mean-spiritedness? Once again it's house-cleaning time, time to "Throw the rascals out!"

Sometimes, of course, they really are rascals, or worse. We have already seen that the United States, unlike Europe, did not go through a traditional feudal and monarchical stage. It also never had any close and serious encounters with fascism or Nazism. The result is interesting, and somewhat to the disadvantage of liberals. Thus, most Americans know that liberalism is somewhere left of center on the political spectrum. They also know that farther yet to the left is socialism and communism. And so, liberals often wind up spending disproportionate time looking worriedly to their left, fending off the lurking image of socialism and communism, reassuring the electorate that they are different from their extreme cousins.

On the other hand, it seems that very few Americans are concerned that conservatism—situated as it is on the political right—bears the same relationship to fascism and Nazism that liberalism does to communism. Ever since World War II, communism has been the dominant bogeyman to the American public, the ever-present specter that must be held at bay, while fascism and Nazism have shrunk to distant memories and war movies. And so, conservatives (even ultrarightists), have only rarely had to disclaim any connection with fascism and Nazism. It is interesting to compare this situation with that in Europe, where memories of ultraright extremism are still painful and acute. The European experience may not have produced absolute immunity against some future swing to the far right, but at least it has given both liberals and conservatives a more level playing field.

But even though conservatives in the United States do not generally have to tote around the ideological baggage of fascism, they do have to worry about being discredited by some of their more rabid and kooky allies: the superreligious fundamentalists, the wind-bag hyperpatriots, and the moral imperialists. Americans have a strong sense of decency, fair play, and respect for individual rights. Appeals to their baser inclinations—and modern conservatism frequently does precisely that—have occasionally been successful in the short run, but the long-term prospects are for balance and a swing the other way, toward a more liberal point of view.

Finally, some of the liberal-conservative cycling can be attributed to the lag between generations. Although people sometimes change their political stripes, their position on the liberal–conservative spectrum is by and large strongly influenced by the prevailing ideological climate when they first reach political consciousness. Those who were teenagers and young adults during the Progressive era at the turn of the century got their chance to govern during the 1930s and 1940s, which, not surprisingly, were parallel in their activism. Similarly, the next political generation—most strongly influenced by the conservative 1920s—gave us the relatively conservative 1950s, while the activists of the 1960s had grown up admiring the equally activist New Dealers of Franklin Roosevelt. We can therefore expect that the 1990s will give us leadership that was imprinted and inspired by John F. Kennedy's generation, and that sometime after that—God help us—we'll start hearing from those who imbibed Reaganism along with their mother's milk.

Of course, people are not simply empty vessels, to be filled with the prevailing social-political-economic wisdom. Sometimes they even rebel. Elliot Abrams, arch-conservative armchair general of the contra war during the Reagan years, was a university student during the turbulent, socially conscious 1960s . . . and was aghast at the liberalism of it all. And consumer advocate Ralph Nader, a liberal activist if ever there was one, was a student during the somnolent 1950s.

In general, the nonrich are more likely to resonate with liberalism and left-wing politics, while the well-to-do are more conservative. To some degree, this is pure self-interest, although of course, there are exceptions, such as the Kennedy and Harriman families, extraordinarily wealthy and yet traditionally liberal in their politics. The most common pattern, however, is for people to grow more conservative as they grow richer. Whereas the Republican Party has long been dominated by WASPs, the Democrats became home to first-generation immigrants: Italians, Greeks, Scots, Germans, Eastern European Jews, and, most notably, Irish. They tended to be working class, often unionized, and left-liberal . . . that is, until they got "established" and adopted establishment politics, which is to say, conservatism. To some extent this is a natural transition, from liberal-minded have-not immigrants with an understandable penchant for social justice, to the more successful, self-satisfied second generation, which has "made it" and tends to be more conservative about keeping it.

Jews, however—as is so often the case—are an interesting exception: Typically left-liberal as immigrants, they have tended to remain so, even as they began to achieve their "American dream." Conservative spokesman Irving Kristol, on the other hand, went through the kind of transition more typical of non-Jews, in that he began as a liberal, then switched to conservatism. The persistent liberalism of his Jewish brethren has been a constant annoyance and frustration to Kristol. "Jews in this country," he complains, "have the economic status of white Anglo-Saxon Episcopalians but vote more like low-income Hispanics."[15]

There seems little question that this is so. Jewish support for liberals such as Governor Mario Cuomo and Senator Alan Cranston has typically run 25 to 30 percent higher than among the general population. And Jewish voters turn out in disproportionately high numbers; thus, although only 3 percent of the population, they comprise 5 percent of the vote and tend to be generous with political contributions. In 1988, Jews voted for Dukakis by nearly three to one. The fact of Jewish liberalism is undeniable. The reasons for it, however—and for Jews' refusal to "cycle" like most other ethnic groups—are complex and multifaceted.

Some claim that Jewish religious tradition is inherently liberal. Thus, the Hebrew prophets were passionate about social

[15]Irving Kristol, "Liberalism and American Jews," *Commentary*, October 19–23, 1988.

justice. Isaiah, for example, urged his listeners to "seek justice, oppose oppression, defend the orphan, and plead for the widow." Deuteronomy commands the Israelites to "execute justice for the fatherless and the widow and love the stranger." And yet, the Old Testament is not an especially liberal document; moreover, conservative Jews are less liberal than those in reformed congregations, and orthodox Jews (who, presumably, are closest to Old Testament tradition) are the most conservative of all.

Another possible explanation is that right-wing politics, both in Europe and in the United States, has often been strongly tinged with anti-Semitism. The Ku Klux Klan, for example, targeted Jews along with blacks and Catholics, and it was the extreme right, in Europe, that persecuted Jews while liberals in the United States fought to loosen restrictions on Jewish immigration. At present, fundamentalist Christians and the Moral Majority—both strongly identified with conservative politics, and both threatening to erode the separation between Church and State—make most Jews deeply uneasy. Jewish involvement with civil rights also has a long and noble history, as well as a somewhat self-serving one, insofar as the "politics of inclusion" have a powerful appeal for people who feel themselves always at the risk of being excluded. And civil rights has long been on the liberal agenda, opposed by conservatives, who historically obscured their racist motivations behind the banner of "states' rights."

Kristol writes that "In all existing capitalist societies, Jews have done and do extremely well for themselves. And in all existing societies Jews—especially younger Jews—are profoundly uneasy about the legitimacy of their own success."[16] And so, they support an ideology of equal social rights, in part because they feel themselves outside the mainstream and hope that what goes around will come around. To some extent, most Jews—even the assimilated and nonobservant—have a secret fear of discrimination and intolerance. They sit quietly fearing, and half expecting, the next pogrom. They also tend to assume that it will be less likely in a liberal political and social environment. And they are right.

---

[16] Ibid.

To some extent, cycles from conservativism to liberalism and back again may reflect developmental changes as well. Conventional wisdom has it that people grow more conservative as they age. "We expect old men to be conservative," wrote the Reverend Henry Ward Beecher, an influential clergyman of the late nineteenth century,[17] "but when a nation's young men are so, its funeral bell is already rung." There is a saying: Anyone under forty who is not a socialist has no heart, while anyone over forty who is still a socialist has no head. This is at least partly an exaggeration. There have been many middle-aged and elderly socialists who were positively brilliant: Bertrand Russell and J.B.S. Haldane in England, Norman Thomas and Dorothy Day in the United States. And certainly, there are any number of relatively youthful conservatives such as writer/commentators Richard Perle, George Will, or Kenneth Adelman. But I've never met one with a heart.

THERE MAY be truth in the maxim attributed to Santayana, that those who forget history are doomed to repeat it. But whether or not we know the history of liberalism and its alternating cycles with conservatism, it seems likely that this cycling periodicity will continue. We may derive satisfaction from this, or consternation, as we wish. And of course, the liberal-conservataive cyclicity is not absolutely guaranteed, certainly not in any way that can be precisely measured; it may be delayed, speeded up, or otherwise modified by the press of events and the peculiarities of personality. It's a long way from the days of Bull Connor's ugly police dogs, teeth bared and menacing, fire hoses rolling children over and over in the Birmingham streets, to today's America, in which a moderate-liberal African-American was elected to the governorship of Virginia, the former capital of the Confederacy. Yet it is also a long way from Roosevelt's New Deal to Reagan's Rotten Deal. And the 1990 reelection of reactionary, hate-mongering Senator Jesse Helms in North Carolina was achieved by an appeal to racism that would have been familiar to the supporters of Governor George Wallace, Orville Faubus, or Lester Maddox. It may also be that George Bush's extraordi-

---

[17] Also widely considered a possible presidential candidate.

nary popularity in the aftermath of the Gulf War will propel him to a second presidential term.

But one thing at least seems undeniable: The king's counselor was right. Thus, the story is told about the king who asked his wisest counselor for a statement that will always be true, whenever it is uttered, whether in morning or night, summer or winter, sickness or good health, joy or grief, youth or old age. And the counselor proved to be wise indeed, because he said: "This too will pass."

Chapter 4 Connectedness: Them Is Us

O<small>NE OF</small> the key differences between liberals and conservatives shows up in how they view the individual. As we have seen, classical liberalism was fully committed to each private, separate, solitary person as an entirely autonomous, independent being. Classical liberals, in fact, have actually been criticized for putting too much faith in the "atomized" individual, doing his or her own thing (mainly, making money and holding property), without regard for anyone else. By contrast, conservatives of the eighteenth and early nineteenth centuries saw people as enmeshed in society, community, tradition. They resented liberal efforts at change, especially if such efforts were directed toward democracy and away from monarchy and privilege.

As we have seen, by the late nineteenth century, and certainly by the twentieth, an interesting thing had happened: This distinction between liberals and conservatives reversed by 180 degrees. Conservatives began advocating individualism and liberals argued for social networks and shared responsibility, although conservatives generally continued to oppose change, and liberals kept espousing it. To conservatives, nothing was more precious than the independent, atomized individual. Celebrants of an unbridled free market, conservatives came to see private enterprise as the ultimate expression of triumphant individualism. To liberals, on the other hand, we were no longer atoms, but molecules. We were connected to each other.

This connectedness—an unabashed effort at achieving social solidarity—became one of the cornerstones of late nineteenth-century Populism, which served in many ways as a precursor of today's liberalism. But times have changed. As Lawrence Goodwyn, historian of the Populist movement, puts it:

> Older aspirations—dreams of achieving a civic culture grounded in generous social relations and in a celebration of a vitality of human cooperation and the diversity of human aspiration itself—have come to seem so out of place . . . that the mere recitation of such longings, however authentic they have always been, constitutes a social embarrassment.[1]

For the modern-day conservative, the ultimate touchstone is not the common good, but individual laissez-faire. Barry Goldwater, patron saint of conservatism, wrote in his manifesto:

> Everyman, for his individual good and for the good of his society is responsible for his own development. If the Conservative is less anxious than his Liberal brethren to increase Social Security benefits, it is because he is more anxious than his Liberal brethren that people be free throughout their lives to spend their earnings as they see fit.[2]

Other changes came along. For example, in its traditional guise, and even up until recent decades, conservatism had always spoken in a sour, dour tone. It was somber, pessimistic, and glowering. As Harvard University professor Robert B. Reich puts it, "People regarded traditional conservatism the way they

---

[1] Quoted in Kevin P. Phillips, *The Politics of Rich and Poor* (New York: Random House, 1990).
[2] Barry Goldwater, *Conscience of a Conservative* (New York: Hillman Books, 1960).

regard a bitter medicine or a strict diet—good for you, perhaps, especially after you have gone on a binge, but fundamentally unpleasant nonetheless."[3] The new-fangled conservatism of the late 1970s and 1980s, however, was quite different, in part because in Ronald Reagan it found a genial, reassuring spokesman who was both too lazy and too shallow to let conservative ideology challenge his own deep-seated optimism. But Reagan was not the sole reason—or even the most important one—why conservatism was able to shed its gloomy image and become so much more appealing. No, the trick to conservatism's newfound clothes was its redefinition of who had to take the bitter medicine, who had to go on a diet, who had to suffer: *they, them,* the other guys, the blacks, the mentally ill, the Latinos, the impoverished single mothers, the scheming welfare Cadillac queens, and of course, the evil Commie Russians and all their nasty ilk.

We, on the other hand—white, relatively comfortable—could do whatever we wished. There were no limits to how far we could go, how much money we could make, once government was "off our backs." Because after all, it was "morning in America."

Liberals, by contrast, seemed to have taken up the discarded conservative mantle of sour-faced prophets of doom. Carter (actually not very liberal) spoke of a national "malaise" and was hated for it. Liberal environmentalists warned that the world's resources were finite, while conservatives professed their faith in "growth, growth, and more growth," as Nevada Senator Paul Laxalt gushed at the Republican National Convention in 1984. Liberals pointed out that tens of thousands of people were homeless and millions out of work; conservatives, unfazed, said there weren't really so many, they're probably just lazy, and besides, they can always find a bed somewhere, maybe even a hot meal. Peace activists pointed with alarm at the risks of nuclear war, while President Reagan chuckled and made jokes and piled the bombs ever higher, claiming they would scare "them" while protecting "us."

On the domestic front, the same liberal attitudes that had

---

[3]Robert B. Reich, *Tales of a New America* (New York: Random House, 1987).

once offered a share of the American dream to everyone seemed more and more to reflect softhearted, lily-livered, do-gooder altruism. But it should be emphasized that liberalism had never been based on simple altruism, on giving to others. Rather, it depended on a term recently made famous by the Polish trade-union movement: solidarity. Pogo once said, "We have met the enemy and he is us." Liberalism says, "We must work together, and help one another, for the other is us."

The liberal creed is based on an important and typically un-stated assumption: that there are no fundamentally irreconcil-able interests among people, classes, or nations, no matter how deep-seated the disagreements may be. For radicals and con-servatives, the world is typically a "zero-sum game," a contest in which if you win, then I lose, and vice versa.[4] But for lib-erals, things are more complicated, and ultimately, more hopeful. You and I can lose together—as in a depression, or a nuclear war—but we can also win together. We can play "pos-itive sum games," in which everyone comes out ahead. As a result, the "bleeding heart liberal" is not just sympathetic and compassionate, although he or she is that, too. Rather, liberal action derives from a sense of what is possible, as well as de-sirable: The world can be made a better place for you without hurting me (at least, not in the long run). And in the process, it will eventually become better for us both.

The conservatives, let us be clear, have become the new "atomists," the proponents of dog-eat-dog competition, of separation, of disconnection. In their enthusiasm, they even got evolution wrong: Darwinism belongs in the biology class-room, not in public policy. Liberals know this. Conservatives, by contrast, would like to reverse things, banning Darwin from the schools, but enshrining their own version of "survival of the fittest" in our interactions with each other, aided by locat-ing *them* far away from *us* . . . in the inner cities, the gay bars, the Indian reservations, the Kremlin.

Following both World Wars I and II, it was the conser-vatives who wanted America to withdraw from the world, who were the isolationists. True to conservative inclinations, they

---

[4] Thus, the sum of your losses and my wins always equals zero.

wanted to keep the United States separate from the rest of the planet, and especially Europe, just as they have always wanted to keep themselves isolated from the plight of the unemployed, the sick, the weak, and the ethnic minorities. It was liberals such as Woodrow Wilson who tried (unsuccessfully) to involve the United States in the League of Nations, and then other liberals such as FDR and Harry Truman who (successfully) engineered the United Nations, NATO, the Marshall Plan, and the Truman Doctrine. Left to their own inclinations, conservatives would have opted out of postwar solidarity with the rest of the planet, just as they try to opt our of solidarity with the downtrodden within their own country. Conservatives eventually accepted the liberals' insistence that we include ourselves in the world, after liberals dragged them into reality. In fact, it didn't take very long before they found themselves quite taken with the idea, especially because they could organize their thinking around their favorite "us versus them" mentality, this time emphasizing the Free World versus communism. And furthermore, they could also steer vast profits in military spending to their pals in the big corporations.

Conservatives, it turns out, are actually delighted to see Uncle Sam spend money, so long as it goes to the military (preferably by way of General Dynamics, Martin Marietta, Lockheed, Northrop, or the like). But otherwise, conservatives can't abide federal outlays. Business investments are fine, but investments in people or in the land warrant a tight fisc.[5] Conservatives claim to have a vision of community, but one that turns out to be sadly outdated, an image of close-knit, rural, small-town America, whose citizens help one another to clear land, replace a burned-out barn, or cooperate to build the local school or church. It harkens back to the America of Thomas Jefferson, which, as we have seen, gave birth to the classical liberal political tradition.

But that was a long time ago; for most of us, things are very different today. Communities tend to be transient and thus,

---

[5]This delicious phrase appeared in Robert Kuttner, *The Life of the Party* (New York: Viking, 1987). I assume it was intentional, and not a typographical error.

superficial. Sure, there are neighborhoods, but most people work outside their homes, returning at night to their own apartments or houses, unlikely to form deep attachments with their neighbors. And sure, people still sometimes join together in the interest of community betterment, but only those dangerously out of touch with today's America would argue that the local block party or back-alley cleanup brigade is the level best suited to address our most serious domestic problems. And yet, this is precisely the conservative agenda: Do it on the local level, don't look to the federal government. According to the Republican platform for 1984: "By centralizing responsibility for social programs in Washington, liberal experimenters destroyed the sense of community that sustains local institutions." So they would have us decentralize, and destroy whatever is left.

One of liberalism's great accomplishments (begun by Franklin Roosevelt and continued to this day) was the recognition that America was one nation, that Maine fishermen had an obligation for the dust-bowl–bedeviled Okies, that the Oregon lumberjack was connected to the woman at the soup kitchen in New York's Bowery. Social benefits and services were presented as legal rights, not charity. Since the New Deal, in short, one of the defining phrases of liberalism has been "social conscience." It is worth meditating on these words, for they say a lot about the creed. *Social* means concern with others, an insistence that people be considered in their relationship to others, and *conscience* means a sense of deep and personal moral responsibility, with the proviso that we owe a special ethical obligation toward our fellows.

Compare the stunted myopia of conservatism—which seeks to enshrine callous disregard under the guise of "local institutions"—with the encompassing liberal vision, revealed, for example, by Mario Cuomo at the 1984 Democratic National Convention. Governor Cuomo spoke movingly of the "politics of inclusion," and when he referred to "family," he meant not just one's personal family, but the wider, more inclusive family that encompasses a society and a nation: "No family that favored its strong children—or that, in the name of evenhandedness, failed to help its vulnerable ones—would be worthy of the name. And no state, or nation, that chooses to ignore its troubled regions and people, while watching others thrive, can call itself justified."

SEPARATION OF us from them wasn't only the work of conservatives. In an important way, liberals—with the best of intentions—added to the "us versus them" distinction. The case of "the poor" is perhaps the most significant. There were always poor people in the United States, just as there were always rich ones, and those more or less in between. But before the 1960s, "the poor" did not have the identified existence that they have since achieved. Then Michael Harrington wrote an eye-opening book on poverty in the United States, titled (significantly) *The Other America*. Lyndon Johnson initiated his "war on poverty," and the United States mobilized resources to help "them" out. A "poverty line" was established, so as to identify who needed the most assistance; those below it were poor, those above it were not. "They," of course, were in the first group. "We" were in the second.

It must be reemphasized that this was all done with good intentions;[6] moreover, a whole lot of good did in fact come out of it, despite what conservatives would have us believe. But it is also true that by separating "the poor" from the rest of "us," many of the liberal antipoverty programs of the 1960s changed the terms of the social contract. As Robert B. Reich has analyzed it:

> When the poor could be any one of us, public assistance was assumed to entail reciprocal benefits and responsibilities. Now it was a matter of charity, assigning no response and presuming no responsibilities on the part of recipients. This emphasized the redistributive nature of the transaction—our magnanimity and their dependency. This perception tended to project itself on us and them alike, undermining whatever sense of reciprocity there might otherwise have been.[7]

Wealthier people enrolled their children in private schools, leaving inner-city schools predominantly black, Latino, and,

---

[6]Cynics may wish to point out that the road to hell is supposedly paved with such intentions.
[7]Richard B. Reich, op. cit.

increasingly, southeast Asian, so that public education came to seem more like a dole than an expression of social solidarity via our offspring. The affluent took themselves on vacations or joined private health clubs, so that government spending on public parks and recreation centers seemed more like a gift to the impoverished than a means of enhancing everyone's environment. Eventually, with the "Reagan Revolution," this transition—from shared responsibilities and obligations to an "us" versus "them" mentality—reached its extreme, and programs for social betterment were seen as further proof that government was "the enemy" . . . because it catered to "them."

It is one thing to favor equal opportunity, as by access to education, to jobs, to equal pay for equal work. But it is quite another when people begin to feel that they are being penalized so as to improve opportunities for others, having their children bused long distances so as to integrate someone else's schools, or having to buck affirmative action that excludes some whites so as to make up for past injustice to blacks. Not surprisingly, the backlash struck. The federal government began acting much less affirmatively. Angry white parents protested against busing. Eligibility requirements were tightened for child nutrition programs, housing assistance, Medicaid, food stamps. Others were severely cut back: Job Corps, vocational training, compensatory education, Head Start. Taxes were also cut back, but notably for the rich, while not only the poor, but also large segments of the middle class, were hard-put just to keep from backsliding.

The politics of compassion is limited in its appeal so long as it is limited to compassion for someone else. By contrast, conservative politics—of laissez-faire and unchecked self-interest—are more primitive and universally effective, since they are directed at private greed and resentment, things much closer to home. Moreover, there is an underlying misrepresentation in the very word *compassion*, because it implies a transaction motivated by generosity. Anything given out of the goodness of one's heart can be taken back when one's heart doesn't feel so good anymore, such as when the economy stagnates or takes a nosedive. By contrast, the special appeal of liberal programs such as Social Security, Medicare, the GI Bill, the Voting Rights Act, and so forth was that they were not presented as the fruits of compassion, but as entitlements—meaning not some privilege kindly granted to one group or another, but benefits to which Americans are fundamentally *entitled* because they live in this country and are part of it.

In the 1988 campaign, conservatives accused Michael Dukakis of making a divisive appeal to class consciousness when he expressed his most effective slogan (unfortunately too late to make much difference): "He's on their side. I'm on your side." An ironic accusation indeed, given the Willie Horton ads, which were as divisive (and racist) as anything American politics has seen. And if conservative enthusiasm for a reduction in the capital gains tax combined with staunch opposition to a surtax on millionaires isn't class consciousness, then what is? It is revealing to consider the public reaction to Bush administration proposals for reducing the tax on capital gains: Instead of seeing it as an outrageous pandering to the wealthy, many Americans—including those who wouldn't know a capital gain from the Capitol Dome—respond blandly, because they would like to hope that someday, they too would profit by benefits now being directed toward the rich.

It is hard to make political hay defending the downtrodden when no one wants to admit being downtrodden. Yet it is precisely these people who most need laws and the affirmative action of society on their behalf. One of the great scams of American conservatism has been to convince millions of people that their interests are best served by a government that refuses to help them. And thus have conservatives succeeded in bamboozling the middle class into acquiescing in its own mugging.

Conservatives who claim to be opposed to class consciousness or class conflicts bring to mind the corrupt police chief in the movie *Casablanca* who, after profiting from and even participating in the gambling inside, finally orders Rick's Café to be closed, announcing, with studied self-righteousness, that he is "shocked, shocked," to find that gambling is actually going on.

While they pursue policies that benefit the wealthy at the expense of the poor and the middle, conservatives proclaim the myth of a classless society so dear to almost every American's heart, especially the underclass who do not like to think of themselves as an underclass, and the wealthy who claim that by taking care of the rich, they are helping everyone. Without even a hint of embarrassment, conservatives have even argued that the poor need their poverty (or at least, the threat of it) to keep them industrious, while at the same time, the rich need their wealth, and the prospect of adding to it . . . for the same reason!

There is a legitimate debate: how to balance mutuality against individual obligation. Too much individualism threatens social reciprocity; too much mutual care-taking encourages a lack of personal responsibility. Deny unemployment benefits and whole families will suffer (American history confirms this); provide guaranteed jobs and people may well work less hard (Soviet history confirms this).

We simply cannot absolve the poor of all responsibility for their situation. But the basic instinct of liberals is also correct: Far too many people are *socially* disadvantaged, deprived of good educations, good jobs, health care, the respect of others and of themselves. When individuals fail, society often bears a heavy responsibility as well.

The hard-conservative view, a caricature of reality, has come to be that welfare *created* the problem. For example, welfare payments are tied to the number of one's children. So teen-aged mothers find it in their interest, we are told, to stay home and have additional children whom they can't support, while the fathers are encouraged to abandon them. The recommendation of the punitive right? Discipline: "Leave the working-aged person with no recourse whatsoever except the job market, family members, friends, and public or private locally funded services."[8]

And so, while liberals blame deprivation, conservatives blame dependency. Their claim—that welfare causes poverty—is like saying that the civil rights movement caused segregation, or that social security causes old age. The answer must be to en-courage productive work and self-control, "workfare" de-signed not to make welfare less available or to punish people for needing it, but to help them become independent, con-

[8]Charles Murray, *Losing Ground* (New York: Basic Books, 1984).

tributing citizens. In addition, government must be more than an updated Pontius Pilate, washing its hands of responsibility, all the while justifying its callous indifference by the self-serving claim that if it tried to help, all it would do is make things worse.

THE REAL crisis of liberalism began in the 1960s, just when—ironically—liberalism seemed most successful. (There is nothing unusual in this: Success often bears the seeds of its own destruction.) Thus, probably the greatest threat to liberalism came from the economic and social accomplishments of liberalism itself. Many people became, if not wealthy, then wealthier than they had ever been. They found they could afford cars, a house in the suburbs, kids in college; they had it made, at least enough so that a caring, giving society no longer felt obliged to care about them, or give to them. Rather, they were expected to care about, and give to, a new *them*—many of whom were black, Latino, welfare recipients, people with the effrontery to demand their civil rights, and so forth. In the words of Reich: "The stories Americans told one another had less to do with reciprocal obligation and mutual benefit than with the painful necessity of helping 'them.' "[9] And *them* no longer felt like us.

Barbara Ehrenreich, one of our most astute social commentators, points out that the American middle class began a "retreat from liberalism" when it went from "the naive mid-century idea that the middle class was America, and included everyone, to a growing awareness that the middle class was only one class among others, and an isolated, privileged one at that."[10] Those others were blacks, Jews, Hispanics, gays, the handicapped, the elderly, women, labor unions, welfare recipients, students . . . in short, the various "special interests" that actually make up a large proportion of America, but which seemed like distant and differentiated parts, whose sum appeared to be less than the whole. Those in the middle found themselves too rich to get publicly assisted housing, loans, food stamps, or medical care, but too poor to afford what they wanted on the open market. An additional problem was that

[9] Robert B. Reich, op. cit.
[10] Barbara Ehrenreich, *Fear of Falling* (New York: Pantheon, 1989).

those who benefited most immediately from these and other liberal-initiated social services typically did not vote (and still don't).

At the same time, conservatives continued to have their own "special interests," including oil companies, power utilities, insurance and banking firms, physicians and lawyers, agribusiness conglomerates, and arms manufacturers. But they also managed to persuade a gullible population—who have never liked to think of themselves as poor—that their interests coincided with those of the upper classes. Hence, the special charm of "trickle down." Take good care of the people at the top, we were told, and everyone would benefit. And besides, came the seductive, optimistic whisper in our ear, pretty soon you might also be at the top! We were to build a superstructure of prosperity on the shifting sands of an immense federal deficit and massive trade imbalance, saddling our children with the costs of our own profligacy—but they, too, were "them," not "us."[11] No wonder yuppies liked Reagan. And no wonder hard-nosed conservatism seemed more appealing than ever before: It promised to be hard-nosed, not with "us" but with "them," with everyone else. It told us that our problems have been caused by our being too naïve, too generous, too indulgent of others, too flabby in our definition of self-interest, too reluctant to be tough. It tells us that we don't really have to concern ourselves very much with anyone other than "number one."

Barbara Ehrenreich argues that the main reason that the middle class has become increasingly conservative is because of their "fear of falling." Thus, these people—lawyers, doctors, teachers, professors, accountants, store managers, insurance and real-estate agents—have neither the confidence of the born-wealthy that they will always be on top, nor the despair of the utterly poor that they will never get off the bottom. Instead, their lives are a continuing, anxious struggle to keep their position, and one result of this anxiety is that they have begun to distance themselves from those below.

Is it a caricature to say that conservatives like Senators Jesse

---

[11] I cannot help but wonder whether Ronald Reagan would have had a more caring attitude toward the future if he had had a better relationship with his own children and grandchildren.

Helms and Phil Gramm, or Ronald Reagan long to grind their heels in the faces of the weak? Maybe, but in fact, a mixture of indifference and outright brutality is very definitely a part of the conservative program, even part of its appeal. In the United States of America, thanks largely to conservative policies, we provide less support to families raising young children than any Western society. Among the eight leading Western industrialized nations, we have the highest rate of child poverty, and the highest rate of infant mortality. The trick is to make the majority of voters feel that they are among the strong, not the weak, and moreover, that they are somehow threatened by the weak.

Liberalism, on the other hand, calls us to a wider, more encompassing definition of ourselves, a healing of rifts, a uniting of people, not through simple altruism but by a more complex recognition of our shared interests. The truth is that corporations need a healthy, productive labor force, taxpayers need a population capable of paying its own share of taxes, city residents (including the well-to-do) need safe streets, and even the military needs recruits who are at least able to read and write. As Barbara Ehrenreich understands it, we can begin to appreciate our interconnectedness even on the mundane level of consumer goods, the "congealed labor of others." All we need do, she says, is listen:

> The computerized appliance speaks of Asian women straining their eyes on a distant assembly line; the gourmet take-out food speaks of immigrant workers chopping food in a sweltering kitchen; the towering condominium building speaks of lives risked at high altitude; and everything speaks of the tense solitude of the over-the-road truck driver.[12]

The American Catholic bishops' Pastoral Letter on the United States Economy, released in 1988, began with this: "Every perspective on economic life that is human, moral, and Christian must be shaped by two questions: What does the economy do *for* people? What does it do *to* people?"[13] The bishops went on to declare that "the poor have a special claim on our

---

[12] Barbara Ehrenreich, op.cit.
[13] Italics in original.

concern because they are vulnerable and needy. We believe that all—Christians, Jews, those of other faiths or no faith at all—must measure their actions and choice by what they do *for* and *to* the poor." Not surprisingly, this document was roundly criticized by conservatives, who would rather measure their actions and choices by what they do *for* and *to* the wealthy, or not at all.

But of course, our mutual interdependence goes beyond our commodities, or our degree of affluence and poverty, extending to peace and war, the structure and very preservation of our planet. And, let us emphasize once more, the difference between liberal and conservative is crucial in this respect, with conservatives denying our connectedness, urging us to tough it out, go for it, go it alone, do it by ourselves, and the liberals calling on us to recognize our mutual relatedness, our shared responsibility, and our shared fate.

There are two images of mutuality that are particularly instructive, that might help clarify this crucial difference between liberal and conservative. Both are well known to social scientists, although not, unfortunately, to the general public. To my knowledge, moreover, this is the first time that either of these images has been linked to the liberal/conservative distinction. The first is known as the Tragedy of the Commons; the second, the Prisoner's Dilemma.

Both the Tragedy of the Commons and the Prisoner's Dilemma are parables, simple situations with wide-ranging significance. The Tragedy of the Commons was first described by ecologist Garrett Hardin. It goes like this. In traditional England, shepherds each owned small patches of land, on which they would occasionally graze their sheep. But there was also additional pasture, known as "the Commons," because it was owned in common, by everyone. The shepherds, not surprisingly, became greedy. They preferred to graze their sheep on the commons rather than their own land, since it didn't cost them anything to use the publicly owned grass, and by doing so, they saved their own pasturage. The Commons became overgrazed and began to suffer. Yet, shepherds continued to use it, reasoning as follows: "I know the Commons is in bad shape and getting worse. I could behave responsibly, and keep my sheep off, but if I did, then my neighbor will just take advantage of me and keep grazing his sheep there. In the meanwhile, I'd be wearing out my own land, while the Commons will lose out just the same. So I may as well get in on the action."

Similar problems exist today, with international whaling, for example. Whales are a kind of Commons. Japan argues that if it refrained from slaughtering whales, then someone else (Iceland, Norway, Korea, the Soviet Union) would simply do them in . . . and also reap the profits. So it may as well be the Japanese (or the Icelanders, or the Norwegians, or the Koreans, or the Soviets). Conservatives have no good way of resolving the Tragedy of the Commons, except to let the tragedy work itself out. They are so in love with free enterprise and the unfettered market, and so averse to the notion of shared responsibility, that they resist committing themselves to interfere, even when the outcome is, in fact, a tragedy.

The answer, on the other hand, is fairly simple. It is a liberal's answer. It is to recognize that each separate actor—whether shepherd or whaling nation—is connected to the other and to the Commons. If they are unwilling or unable to regulate their actions, then someone else had better do it . . . for everyone's benefit (including the Commons'). In the case of grazing land, that someone should be the federal government, through agencies like the Bureau of Land Management.[14] In the case of whaling, it is the International Whaling Commission. The Earth's atmosphere is also a Commons. So are the rivers, the lakes, the oceans, the groundwater, the world's wildlife and wild places. Liberals know that in some cases, people simply cannot be trusted to act out of a sense of abiding common interest, even if that interest is real, because the sense may be lacking. And so, the factory owner will try to pollute the air or to use the nearby river as a sewer for his industrial effluent, deriving short-term benefit while shifting the costs onto everyone's shoulders. Liberals also know, accordingly, that because we are all connected, there is a contin-

---

[14] Whether such organizations do an adequate job—especially, whether they are too much under the thumb of those interests they are supposed to regulate—is another matter. Our point is why we have such agencies at all.

uing need to enforce respect for that connection and to make sure that tragedies are averted.

To liberals, economic activity must be in tune with the long-term interests of our people and our planet. Certainly, private initiative must be encouraged, not inhibited; enterprise must be liberated and not smothered by excessive regulation, paperwork, and restrictions. But at the same time, the shepherds, whalers, and industrialists must be harnessed, and not—as conservatives would have it—allowed to trample all over us.

Next, the Prisoner's Dilemma. This one is a bit more complicated, and yet on balance, simple enough that at some level we all understand it. Imagine two suspects in a bank robbery, and a district attorney who wants to get them to plead guilty. He jails them in separate cells, and offers each the same deal: Both plead guilty, and you spend five years in jail. On the other hand, says the DA, if you plead guilty and your buddy pleads not guilty, then with the evidence you provide we'll lock him up for twenty years and let you go free. And there's also one other possibility: If both you and your partner plead not guilty, you'll be convicted of a lesser crime—illegal possession of a gun—and get just a year in jail.

Do you see the dilemma? The best payoff for the two prisoners is if they would both plead not guilty, and serve their one-year sentences. But neither one can be blamed for reasoning as follows: "I have two choices, guilty or not guilty. So does my partner. Let's see—if he pleads guilty, then what is my best move? Well, if he pleads guilty, then I'd better plead guilty too, or else I'll rot in jail for twenty years while he goes free. And how about the other possibility? If he pleads not guilty, then my best bet once again is to plead guilty, because that way I get to go free (even if he winds up with twenty years)." The result is that either way, our prisoner is led to plead guilty. And so does the other one, who looks at the situation identically. The dilemma is that each of them therefore winds up spending five years in jail, whereas both prisoners could have gotten a much lighter sentence—one year—if only they could have figured out some way to stick with not guilty, that is, to cooperate.

Each prisoner was stymied by fear that if he cooperated, he

would be suckered by the other. And so, each winds up taking the uncooperative stance, and suffering as a result.[15] What does this have to do with liberalism and human connectedness? Just this: The Prisoner's Dilemma is a mistake. The apostrophe should be moved, revealing it as the Prisoners' Dilemma, a shared problem, not a private one. As with the Tragedy of the Commons, there are ways out of what we'll call the Prisoners' Dilemma. In real life (unlike our jail example) people can communicate with one another, express their concerns, provide reassurances. They can base a relationship on shared interests and build a reservoir of mutual trust. Sometimes, nonetheless, they may need a third party to get them to behave as they should.

Liberals know that people can get caught in many different versions of the Prisoners' Dilemma, forced into making bad decisions by greed and by fear that if they don't screw the next guy, they will wind up getting screwed. Let's say you are driving east to west during the rush hour; traffic is bumper-to-bumper and you are at a major intersection when the light changes. Traffic is equally heavy going the other way, north to south. Do you stop short of the intersection, letting the north–south traffic go by, which probably means that someone will almost certainly block you when the light changes again? Or do you block them? The resulting gridlock can be helped by outside authorities such as the police (conservatives like this solution, because of its law-and-order ring, but otherwise, they resent external controls on "personal freedom"). Liberals, on the other hand, recognize the need for some sort of positive, socializing influence, which makes everyone better off. The goal is to make the political community a kind of mutual-benefit club, by inducing people to cooperate, as a result of which they all come out ahead. We are back, once again, to the notion of humanizing, of liberalizing a worldview until it includes not just a narrow sense of self-interest, but a broader vision of ourselves in relation to others, even a kind of self that includes the other.[16]

---

[15] Uncooperative with each other, that is. Each winds up cooperating with the district attorney.

[16] The philosopher Martin Buber referred to this as an I–Thou relationship, instead of I–It.

These tragedies and dilemmas have a lot to do with everyday life, especially in a free enterprise society. For example, it is the responsibility of corporate managers to increase the wealth of their shareholders (including, not least, themselves). According to Adam Smith, if every enterprise proceeds this way, then somehow the wonders of the free market will—as by the working of a marvelous "unseen hand"—make everybody happy. Adam Smith and his ideological descendants such as Milton Friedman or George Gilder sometimes recognize the importance of Others, but at the same time they insist that big business be left free to ignore those Others: the environment, the health and safety of the workforce, the best interests of the consumer, even national security. The reality is that unfettered free-market economics, much beloved of conservatives, is deeply flawed, as the Tragedy of the Commons and the Prisoners' Dilemma both reveal. The market needs a wider and deeper—in a word, a more liberal—view of its responsibilities. And when it can't or won't, then we must do so. That's we, us, ourselves, the American people, acting through our representatives in the federal, state, or local government. In a democracy, that's what government *is:* not some malign power forced upon us, but we ourselves, collectively organized to turn tragedies and dilemmas into decencies and opportunities.

LIBERALS ARE big on guilt. For many, this is one of their most annoying traits. The parent who says, "Eat your dinner; just think of all the starving children in Ethiopia," is a liberal. Satirist Tom Lehrer defined himself as the kind of liberal who, if shown a photograph of starving people, will send money . . . but who will call the police if a starving person turns up on his own doorstep. Of course, this observation in itself reflects a kind of guilty conscience. Nobody, not even liberals, can take care of all the world's ills.

It has been said that the Calvinist objection to bear-baiting was not based so much on the pain it caused the bear, but the pleasure it provided to the audience. Liberals don't mind when people feel happy, and they certainly have no objection to pleasure. But they are deeply bothered by the pain of others. They lack the blissfully indifferent "serves them right" attitude of conservatives. And so, while conservatives have been

successful with what Christopher Lasch calls the "mobilization of resentment,"[17] liberals—especially white liberals—feel
guilty about our civil rights record, our treatment of Native
Americans, our accumulation of nuclear and chemical weapons, our behavior toward the environment and toward the
Third World, the greenhouse effect. You want to talk about
sports; they want to talk about the destruction of tropical rainforests. Sometimes, liberals are real downers. Their social conscience can be a pain in the ass.

Liberalism's love affair with guilt springs not from resentment, however, but from sensitivity, an awareness of inter-
connections. If we weren't involved with one another, if a
predatory, indifferent society were really our modus vivendi,
so that each of us was separate and disconnected, then there
would be no call for guilt. But if, instead, we see our own role
in someone else's pain, if we recognize that all of us are part
of the tissue of this world, then a feeling of guilt follows almost inevitably. You may eat your dinner or not, but either
way, you darned well *ought* to know that people are in fact
starving in Ethiopia, and you might ask yourself whether that
fact has anything to do with you.

"The true moral test of government," said a renowned liberal, Hubert Humphrey of Minnesota, more than twenty years
ago, "is how it treats those in the dawn of life—the children;
those who are in the twilight of life—the aged; and those who
are in the shadow of life—the sick, the needy, the handicapped."[18] And the true test of a liberal is whether he or she
cares about the outcome, because the real test is of our own
compassion.

Liberals tend to be downright *nice,* so nice, in fact, that even
when kicked around, they are apt to respond with compassion, nonviolence, and an effort to interpret the aggressor's
misdeeds as being a result of his or her benighted upbringing.
Liberals would rather talk than argue, rather understand you
than fight with you.

Traditionally, liberals and especially liberal psychotherapies

---

[17] Christopher Lasch, "Fraternalist Manifesto," *Harpers,* April 1987.
[18] Quoted by David Peterson, in a speech at the JFK School of Government,
March 15, 1989.

have sought to help people overcome a sense of guilt in their private lives—about their "bad thoughts" or their secret, trivial, nasty deeds—while at the same time, paradoxically, encouraging a sense of guilt in their public lives. Martin Luther King, Jr., made a notable advance in American liberal theology when he introduced the concept of "social sin" (originally defined as segregation, then expanded to include war-making and other forms of violence) to go along with the old idea of individual sin. Conservatives reverse the liberal priority, pounding home with evangelical zeal the idea of guilt in our private lives,[19] while favoring blissful indifference to the sins of society.

Instead of blaming themselves, conservatives prefer to blame the victim: Those who are poor must be insufficiently energetic, imbued with inadequate moral fiber, or just plain dumb. Thus, AIDS victims reveal, by their disease, a sinful sexual perversion, for which God is doubtless punishing them. As a result of blaming the victim in this way, conservatives—who loudly proclaim their ethical grounding—in fact achieve a kind of moral vacuum, a guiltless escape from responsibility. If liberals suffer from an excess of guilt, and perhaps they do, I'll take that any day over the conservatives' blissful indifference (mixed on occasion with outright hostility), combined as it is with a guiltfree inclination to do evil.

One of the major successes of liberalism was when it showed people that they did not bear personal responsibility for the Depression, that we were all in it together. Now, we have conservatives telling us once again that we don't have personal responsibility for the ills of society, not because we all share the load, but because it's all government's fault, or the "special interest" groups, or the liberals, or the media, or the communists. For all its worship of rugged individualism, conservatism actually offers an excuse for *diminished* individual responsibility. For all its nostalgia about small-town America, conservatism actually represents a fundamental repudiation of community, of the social contract that unites people and creates meaningful society. Its result: consumption without guilt,

---

[19] Apparently, some of the most energetic of these pounders—such as Jimmy Swaggart and Jim Bakker—had more than their share to be guilty about.

inequality without guilt, self-aggrandizement without guilt, invasion of other countries without guilt, environmental destruction without guilt, militarism without guilt, stepping over prostrate bodies without guilt. Its denial of connectedness is nothing less than a denial of decency . . . without guilt.

Chapter 5 The Secular Trinity: Optimism, Democracy, and the Future

The liberal imagination sits upon a triad of faith: an optimistic approach toward social problems, an orientation toward the future, and a belief in democracy. Not surprisingly, these three attitudes are closely connected. Optimism is a positive stance, a confident anticipation that things will get better and moreover, that they can be *made* better by human action.

By definition, optimism points to the future; it is peculiar, at best, to be optimistic about the past. As to democracy, the ancient Greeks enjoyed a democratic tradition—in fact, they started it. But the fact is that over the last few hundred years, democracy has been a newcomer. Even now, it is struggling to be born, in Central America, Eastern Europe, China, South Africa, and the Soviet Union. Conservatives have always distrusted it—just as they have always distrusted the future itself (such is the nature of pessimism)—and they still do. Liberals, meanwhile, have optimistically looked to a future in which democracy will be triumphant: not only political democracy, but economic and social democracy as well.

In a notable speech to the John F. Kennedy School of Gov-

95

ernment at Harvard University,[1] David Peterson, then liberal premier of the province of Ontario, did a masterful job of summarizing the hopes and aspirations of liberalism. He concluded as follows: "Our horizons are limited only by our vision. Our promise is limited only by our perseverance. And our capacity to make this a better world for ourselves and our children is limited only by our courage and our confidence in our ability to do so."

Let us begin our tour of liberalism's secular trinity with a closer look at optimism.

My CHILDHOOD mnemonic for distinguishing optimist from pessimist was that optimists said *Ah!* whereas pessimists said *Peh!* To some extent, all ideologies have goals that are optimistic, often unrealistically so: Marxism has its classless society, capitalism cherishes the image of a perfectly functioning free market, and liberalism—both classical and modern—places great store in enlightened self-interest and in a kind of beneficence underlying the way people deal with one another. An ideology without optimism is virtually a self-contradiction. But liberals are especially optimistic. They have been saying *Ah!* for a very long time, which is not surprising for a perspective that believes above all in the possibility of improvement, that gave birth to the political activist and the reformer.

Nearly two hundred years ago, the Marquis de Condorcet gave a clear statement of classical liberal optimism:

> No bounds have been fixed to the improvement of the human faculties; . . . the perfectibility of man is absolutely indefinite; . . . the progress of this perfectibility, henceforth above the control of every power that would impede it, has no other limit than the duration of the globe upon which nature has placed us. . . . [Eventually we shall reach] the moment in which the sun will observe in its course free nations only, acknowledging no other master than their reason; in which tyrants and slaves, priests and their . . . instruments, will no longer exist but in history and upon the stage. . . . A period must one day arrive when death will be nothing more than the effect either of extraordinary accidents, or of the slow and gradual decay of the vital powers; and that the duration of the middle space, of the

---

[1] March 15, 1989.

interval between the birth and this decay, will itself have no
assignable limit.[2]

It has not significantly dampened the optimism of subsequent
liberals that Condorcet met his own death on the guillotine
shortly after writing this.

Compare the forward-looking optimism of liberals with the
backward-looking pessimism of conservatives, as revealed in
this passage from William F. Buckley:

> Conservatism is the tacit acknowledgment that all that is finally
> important in human experience is behind us; that the crucial
> explorations have been undertaken, and that it is given to man
> to know what are the great truths that emerged from them.
> Whatever is to come cannot outweigh the importance to man
> of what has gone before.[3]

Given the astonishing liberalization currently in progress
throughout Eastern Europe, it is difficult to fault Condorcet's
enthusiastic anticipation of the "moment in which the sun will
observe in its course free nations only . . ." Clearly, we have
a long way to go, even among Western democracies which
have to some extent been constructed on a foundation of sur-
reptitious human and ecological misery. But the liberal imagination has confidence that we shall get there and maybe even
repair that foundation, while also getting our own house
in order.

To most liberals, change is good because it makes for progress and improvement, set against the ancient and medieval
ideal of no-change, or stasis. (The Renaissance was in a sense
reactionary, yearning as it did for a return to the Golden Age
of antiquity; even among modern-day traditional societies, the
prevailing worldview tends to be that change is more likely to
result in decay than in improvement.) For liberals, by contrast, change came to be identified with progress: social, tech-
nological, political, economic. "Progress is our most important

---

[2]Marquis de Condorcet (Marie-Jean Caritat), *Outline of an Historical View of
the Progress of the Human Mind*, (Baltimore: G. Fryer, 1802).
[3]William F. Buckley, Jr., *Up From Liberalism* (New Rochelle, N.Y.: Arlington
House, 1959).

product," says the General Electric Corporation. The very *idea* of progress, however, was invented by liberals. It was their most important product.

THE NINETEENTH century liberals envisioned a world in which everyone enjoyed a dignified level of material affluence, human rights, civil liberties, mutual respect, and freedom. Their more recent descendants have labored to expand that vision to the international realm as well, giving us the League of Nations, the United Nations, the Universal Declaration of Human Rights, and before that, the Bill of Rights, and the French Declaration of the Rights of Man and of the Citizen.

Communism, like liberalism, has also been optimistic about its goals, although it viewed the route to the ideal society as rather bumpy, marked by conflict and contradiction, a dialectic of dislocation, suffering, and pain.

Conservatives view things differently. They are the champion pessimists, taking a more somber, negative view of the world and its prospects. As columnist George Will writes, conservatives may even derive a perverse joy from such sourness: "When things go badly they have the pleasure of having their beliefs confirmed, and when things go well they enjoy the pleasant surprise."[4] Liberals, by contrast, are the cock-eyed optimists of modern politics, although they do not really believe in the infinite perfectibility of human beings. That is, they see our limitations and our potential to do harm. Unlike conservatives, in fact—whose narrow, blinkered view of good versus evil, us versus them, the saved versus the damned harkens back to a childish view of reality—liberals take a nuanced view of the human prospect. They recognize that most people are not saints, and while many are sinners, virtually none are devils incarnate. Rather, they are just people, trying to make the best of things and of their lives. Liberals leave the melodramatic view of human beings to the conservatives, preferring instead to see life as realistic drama, and only occasionally, comedy or tragedy.

Conservatives also believe that human betterment has defi-

---

[4] *The Washington Post*, April 24, 1986.

nite limits. Rather narrow ones, in fact. Michael Harrington liked to point out that visions of the future (of the sort so appealing to socialists and liberals alike) are inherently utopian; only the present is plausible. Sometimes, liberal optimism even seems a bit naïve, the bright-eyed enthusiasm of those who haven't yet experienced the disappointments and tragedies of life. A neoconservative is a liberal who's been mugged.

Most people, especially young people, tend to be optimistic. When that optimism is thwarted (by cynicism, as after the Vietnam War and the Watergate scandal, or by a reigning conservative ideology that denies the prospects of social cooperation and shared uplift), it doesn't die. Rather, it gets turned inward, to self-centeredness, a hard-eyed pursuit of personal advancement, and various narcissistic, responsibility-denying, feel-good pop therapies and cults; in a word, the conservative politics of self-aggrandizement. The "we" generation becomes the "me" generation. "Power to the people" becomes looking out for "number one."

Novelist Tom Robbins likes to say, "It's never too late to have a happy childhood." For that generation that came to political consciousness in the 1980s and late 1970s, it is still not too late to have ideals, and even to act on them, in one's life as well as in the voting booth. All that is needed is a clear articulation of liberal values.

Liberals tend to be trusting. They are genuinely hurt that people might engage in welfare fraud and they are less likely to believe, for example, that a person or system might want to conquer the world. Conservatives, more distrusting, are inclined to remove the welfare system altogether, thereby punishing the vast majority of responsible but needy people, so intent are they on not being "ripped off." And they are so worried about "enemy" schemes for world domination that they are willing to risk blowing up the world in its "defense."

Jimmy Carter's response to the Soviet invasion of Afghanistan in 1979—personal hurt—was an archetype of the disappointed liberal, mugged by reality. By contrast, George Bush's initial exceedingly cautious and disbelieving attitude toward Soviet disarmament initiatives was characteristic of the profoundly distrustful conservative, so eager to think ill of others that they are themselves ill-suited to deal creatively with great opportunities for progress and betterment. It can similarly be argued that the Bush administration's refusal to explore potential diplomatic solutions to the Persian Gulf crisis, and its determination—almost insistence—on war, further highlights the conservative penchant for seeing the worst in others, thereby closing off creative, nonviolent options.

Liberals are sometimes bedeviled by the accusation that they are naïve, unable to deal effectively with evil. It must be pointed out, however, that there is also a naïveté of distrust. In the case of conservatives, especially when dealing with the poor or, recently, the communists (or, more recently yet, the Middle East), this naïve distrust is a consequence of trying to be excessively "realistic" and "hardheaded," so much so that they wind up being neither.

If liberal optimism is sometimes hard to take, too cheery and unrealistic, conservative pessimism is even worse. This is because along with the expectation that things cannot really be improved and human nature is so fatally flawed that we must lower our expectations, comes an unwillingness to try, and a resistance to creative problem-solving. Or worse yet, in expecting and preparing for the worst, conservatives actually do much to bring it about. Sociologists call this a "self-fulfilling prophecy," whereby we create reality by our expectations. Thus, for example, picture a legislator who is convinced that public education is doomed to failure. Then ask yourself: Is this person likely to favor appropriating more money, or less, for public education? And what effect is this likely to have on our schools? Or, imagine the president who is convinced that the U.S.S.R. wants nothing more than to blow us up, and who therefore insists on building a vast nuclear arsenal, and pointing it at the Soviets, so as to "deter" them. What effect is this likely to have on Soviet intentions, and on their perceptions of us? (And of course, when the U.S.S.R. dutifully responds by building its own vast nuclear arsenal, and pointing it at us, fellow conservatives can self-righteously point to this fact as "proof" that their original pessimistic assessment was correct.)

To liberals, evil is the result of a bad social order; people are fundamentally well-meaning (so long as they are secure, and thus unlikely to fall prey to unreason and resort to violence). This confidence in rationality is one of the hallmarks of liberals, both classical and modern. By contrast, conservatives are more comfortable with a Calvinist perspective, in which people are fundamentally evil creatures, born into sin and virtually irredeemable. With such impossible beasts as *Homo* not-so-very *sapiens*, the best one can hope for is occasional remission, obtained only by fear and the constant threat of punishment, underpinned by authoritarian rule. Suffused with original sin, we are inherently incapable of becoming good until we are eventually reunited with God in heaven. As Calvin put it:

> Even infants themselves, as they bring their condemnation into the world with them, are rendered subject to punishment of their own sinfulness . . . for though they have not yet produced the fruits of their iniquity, yet they have had the seed of it in them. Their whole nature is, as it were, a seed of sin and therefore cannot but be odious and abominable to God.[5]

Because of our innate human sinfulness, we were cast out of the Garden of Eden and doomed to death. We deserve—in fact, we require—to be treated sternly and punished as soon as we get out of line. In fact, maybe we should be punished regardless of our behavior, because we probably were at least thinking sinful thoughts! Some students of human behavior have concluded that much human misery, including the continuing cycle of child abuse and possibly even war itself, is the consequence of such extreme conservatism, which results in the abuse and mistreatment of children.[6]

This is not to say that conservatives are necessarily child abusers. But there is undeniably an abusive strain in an ideology so convinced of human imperfection that it justifies harshness and violence . . . and often generates harshness and violence in return.

The liberal answer to conservative insistence on original sin

---

[5] John Calvin, *On God and Man*, ed. F. W. Strothmann (New York: Frederick Ungar, 1956).
[6] Alice Miller, *For Your Own Good* (New York: Farrar, Straus & Giroux, 1984); Andrew Bard Schmookler, *Out of Weakness* (New York: Bantam, 1988).

and innate human depravity can be framed in equally theological terms: salvation via good works. And most liberals have confidence in this approach because they have confidence in people. Conservatives' distrust of other human beings is matched only by their lack of concern for them (except if they are captives of communism, in which case they are infinitely worthy—even trade unions!). Consider the confident, optimistic liberal sentiments expressed by Thomas Jefferson in one of his many letters to John Adams. In it, Jefferson explained his belief that the human being is "a rational animal, endowed by nature with rights, and with an innate sense of justice; and that he could be restrained from wrong and protected in right, by moderate powers, confided to persons of his own choice, and held to their duties by dependencies on his own will."[7]

One of the trickier aspects of liberalism is the way it combines Jefferson's confidence in rationality along with the expectation of a Condorcet or Mill that things can and will be made better, with a critical view of the way things actually *are*. As a result, liberals often seem more pessimistic than conservatives; but this isn't really pessimism, and in fact it is motivated by a core of optimism, since it insists on identifying problems in order to solve them. Unfortunately, people would rather hear good news than bad; they'd even rather hear that everything is just fine—that is, a shortsighted, insular, conservative-style optimism—than a genuinely optimistic message: that our world has a lot of rough edges, which can be repaired if we get to work. Real optimism is sizing up the world honestly, warts and all, and then concluding that it can be made good, or at least, better.

On the other hand, it is a whole lot easier to maintain the conservative stance that nothing much can be done, or should be, if you also claim that nothing much *needs* to be done. "If it ain't broke," Americans like to say, "don't fix it." Fair enough, but conservatives take this maxim further yet, hoping that if they say it ain't broke, they won't have to fix it . . . or even try.

They don't want to know about the consequences of prenatal malnutrition, rusting bridges, the national debt, the dan-

---

[7] Quoted in Gottfried Dietze, *Liberalism Proper and Proper Liberalism* (Baltimore: Johns Hopkins University Press, 1985).

gers of nuclear war, the costs of Third World interventionism, air and water pollution, and the increasingly precarious state of our natural environment. See no evil, hear no evil, and speak no evil add up—in conservative strategy—to an excuse for doing nothing. "What, me worry?" would be a suitable slogan for the conservative indifference to national and global problems.[8] But such self-deception should never be taken for true optimism, because, in fact, it is just the opposite. As we have seen, Ronald Reagan's brand of "optimism" was very selfishly personal in its construction and appeal. There may even have been a genuine inability to see the nation's problems, a true blindness to racial injustice and poverty, a gut-level indifference to environmental or social horrors. In any event, it took six years, for example, to get Mr. Reagan even to utter the word *AIDS*. Behind the seeming optimism of Reaganism lurked a deep, dark pessimism: that we can't solve problems *as a community*. But it was wrapped in a crass, base, and wholly selfish brand of pseudo-optimism: that we have unlimited prospects *as individuals*. Each of us can go first class on the *Titanic*. So long as we go alone.

LIBERALS BELIEVE in the "efficacy of purposive social action."[9] As FDR once put it, "It is common sense to take a method and try it. If it fails, admit it frankly and try another. But above all, try something." But even this "common sense" assumes that it is possible, and desirable, to get somewhere, that in addition to the risk of failure, there is also the prospect of success. It assumes what has cynically been called the "liberal lie," that righting wrongs creates justice or that the world can ever be just at all. It is often true that injustice persists even after certain wrongs are righted. But the alternative is to accommodate to injustice, even to learn to love it, just as Winston Smith, in Orwell's *1984*, learned to love Big Brother. And of course, the expectation is that people won't struggle against what they love.

Conservatives claim that certain problems—racism, pov-

---

[8]During the 1988 presidential election, in fact, George Bush adopted, "Don't Worry, Be Happy" as his campaign song, until Bobby McFerrin, who wrote and sang it, objected.
[9]Benjamin DeMott, "Rediscovering Complexity," *The Atlantic*, September 1988, pp. 67–74.

erty, war, environmental deterioration—either don't exist or don't warrant government involvement. Ostensibly, they point to a "solution," namely a kind of benign neglect while something analogous to the free market supposedly works things out. But in fact, it is more likely that underneath the posturing, most conservatives really don't want these problems solved, or—at best—don't care.

Sadly, there may be some truth in the "liberal lie." Maybe the world never can be altogether just. Maybe the forces of unfairness are simply too strong, and human strength too puny. Maybe the world is just so uncaring and indeed, nasty, that resistance is useless and hope, a mockery. There are two liberal rejoinders to this. For one, there is the view most eloquently expressed by the French existentialist Albert Camus, that in the face of a cold and uncaring universe, it is the responsibility of each of us to affirm and indeed, to *define* our humanness by struggling for a better world. Benjamin DeMott writes: "Nothing can be done to ease injustice or oppression except wth the aid of the flexible intelligence, the mobile imagination, and the will to self-sacrifice."[10] But this is a far cry from saying that nothing can be done, period. Or that nothing should.

In fact, liberals are preeminently willing to work and work hard, even to sacrifice. It was John F. Kennedy who said that we would "pay any price, bear any burden, to assure the survival and success of liberty."[11]

The simple fact remains that whereas much remains to be done, much has already been accomplished, most of it by liberals: It is a better world because slavery has been abolished, and child labor, and because people don't starve on the streets of America. It would be better yet if the homeless had places to live, if the hungry were adequately fed, if our schools taught more, and if our environment were better protected. The operative word is *better*. We haven't created heaven on earth, and never shall. But liberals in particular have much to be proud of. They have made this world a *better* place, and they are still working at it.

---

[10] Ibid.
[11] Inaugural Address, 1961.

Conservatives, on the other hand, are not only pessimistic about the possibility of social betterment, they also resent the fact that liberals are so eager to try. Michael Oakeshott, a renowned English conservative political philosopher, complained:

> To some people, [i.e., liberals, who apparently don't even deserve to be identified] "government" appears as a vast reservoir of power which inspires them to dream of what uses might be made of it. They have favorite projects, of various dimensions, which they sincerely believe are for the benefit of mankind, and to capture this source of power, if necessary to increase it, and to use it for imposing their favorite projects upon their fellows, is what they understand as the adventure of governing men.[12]

From this it follows, Mr. Oakeshott goes on to claim, that liberals necessarily must rely on the basest of human sentiments—emotion—in order to govern: "They are, thus, disposed to recognize government as an instrument of passion: the art of politics is to inflame and direct desire." By contrast, the conservative, true child of the enlightenment, is supposed to be calm, cool, and judicious in all ways:

> Now, the disposition to be conservative in respect of politics reflects a quite different view of the activity of governing. The man of this disposition understands it to be the business of a government not to inflame passion and give it new objects to feed upon; but to inject into the activities of already too passionate men an ingredient of moderation; to restrain, to deflate, to pacify and to reconcile; not to stoke the fires of desire, but to damp them down. And all this, not because passion is vice and moderation virtue, but because moderation is indispensable if passionate men are to escape being locked in an encounter of mutual frustration.

Mr. Oakeshott's goal—and the goal of conservatives generally—is indeed "to restrain, to deflate, to pacify and to reconcile," to damp the fires of dissatisfaction and discontent, to becloud the self-awareness of the downtrodden and disaf-

---

[12]Michael Oakeshott, *Rationalism in Politics* (New York: Barnes and Noble, 1962).

fected, to restrain them from bettering themselves, to deflate movements for social justice and change, to pacify the angry and the dispossessed, to reconcile the have-nots to their station in life, and above all, to keep things cool, calm, and comfortable for those whose interests are best served—at least in the short run—by a continuation of business as usual. No wonder they begrudge the liberal's love of change and the politics of passion.

More correctly, they oppose passionate indignation on the part of the impoverished or excluded. Conservatives have no problem stirring up their own brand of emotion: flag-waving, Bible-beating, or dripping with a schmaltzy nostalgia for small-town America with the wholesome "family values" of a Norman Rockwell illustration for Kellogg's Corn Flakes. Consider George Bush's empty but passionate endorsement of the Pledge of Allegiance, or his voice, cracking with emotion (whether real or simulated) when, during the 1988 presidential campaign, he reminded an audience of veterans that Dan Quayle "sure as hell never burned the American flag."[13]

Mr. Oakeshott notwithstanding, the truth is that liberalism generally does not value emotion very highly. It is primarily interested in rationality, efficiency, effectiveness, and the solving of problems, although "happiness" may paradoxically be placed at the center of human goals, and compassion is valued for its own sake as well as the impetus it provides for positive social programs. Michael Dukakis was in many ways the perfect liberal embodiment: cool, cerebral, unemotional. (Columnist Robert Novak called him "Zorba the Clerk.")

It is sometimes thought that liberalism is too practical, that it lacks a rhapsodic sense, a messianic goal. But in fact, for all their belief in rationality, liberals can indeed be passionate. Leonard Bernstein, for example, wrote the following, in the heat of the 1988 presidential campaign:

> Who fought to free the slaves? Liberals. Who succeeded in abolishing the poll tax? Liberals. Who fought for women's rights, civil rights, free public education? Liberals. Who stood guard

---

[13] Apparently, his failing to have burned the flag constituted Mr. Quayle's major political asset, just as in Edwin Meese's case, the fact that while attorney general, he was not actually indicted for his transgressions.

and still stands guard against sweatshops, child labor, racism, bigotry? Lovers of freedom and enemies of tyranny: Liberals.[14]

Clearly liberals can be emotional, particularly when they have been attacked. Mr. Bernstein also bespoke the optimism of his ideology when he added that "A liberal is a man or woman or child who looks forward to a better day, a more tranquil night and a bright, infinite future."

Liberal passions are not reserved only for the underdogs and the dispossessed. Walter Lippmann, supreme political columnist of his day, maintained:

> Underlying all the specific projects which men espouse who think of themselves as Liberals there is always, it seems to me, a deeper concern. It is fixed upon the importance of remaining free in mind and action before changing circumstances. This is why Liberalism has always been associated with a passionate interest in freedom of thought and freedom of speech, in scientific research, in experiment, in the liberty of teaching, in an independent and unbiased press, in the right of men to differ in their opinions and to be different in their conduct.[15]

Among those interests, democracy ranks especially high.

If we examine the writings of conservative gurus such as William F. Buckley, Jr., we find a revealing connection: Liberalism is equated with democracy and democracy, in turn, is disparaged as a trifling aberration, a peculiar insistence of misguided do-gooders, not worth much in its own right. After all, it is liberals who promote a populist skepticism of private power, just as conservatives are skeptical of public power. Take this last phrase literally, because conservatives have a horror of power wielded by and for the public; that is, you and me, we the people.

This visceral conservative distrust of democracy goes beyond an eagerness to restrict voting rights and otherwise to limit the political participation of the nonrich majority. Conservatives tend to evaluate social policies through a withhold-

---

[14] *The New York Times*, October 30, 1989.
[15] Walter Lippmann, *The Essential Lippmann: A Political Philosophy for Liberal Democracy* (New York: Random House, 1963).

ing, Scrooge-like lens of narrow-minded skepticism about human beings themselves: This is the consistent thread behind conservative opposition to abortion rights, obsession with welfare chiselers, and enthusiasm for drug-testing in the workplace or in schools. By contrast, Douglas Wilder, a moderate liberal, won a governorship in 1989 in part because of his proabortion stance, and his assertion that unlike his conservative opponent, he "trusts the women of Virginia" to make their own decisions.

According to Mr. Buckley, liberalism and democracy also fail in the most crucial test of all: their ability to go toe-to-toe with The Communist Menace. Thus, "Liberalism is no match for Communism," according to Buckley, "because it is not a redemptive creed." All that it has to offer is democracy—highly suspect in conservative eyes—and foolish, if not dangerous, claptrap about social and economic justice. By contrast, as Buckley sees it:

> The Communists' program is capable (at least for a period of time, until the illusion wears off) of being wholly satisfactory, emotionally and intellectually, to large numbers of people. The reason for this is that Communist dogma is eschatologically conceived. Communism promises the elimination of poverty, war, inequality, insecurity. Communism offers a view of human history, holds out a millennial vision, indicates the means (revolution) of effecting this millennium . . . Democracy, by contrast, talks a wholly different language. *In fact, democracy is nothing more than a procedural device aimed at institutionalizing political liberty. It has no program. It cannot say to its supporters: do thus, and ye shall arrive at the promised land. Far from being capable of defining the millennium, democracy's first commitment is to guarantee that 50 percent plus one of the people may put an end to any dalliance with a previously acknowledged millennium.* Thus it cannot, alone, provide the faith, the opiate, or the stimulant.[16] [italics added]

Try telling that to the people of Eastern Europe, or to those who struggle against apartheid in South Africa, or to the martyred students of Tiananmen Square in China: that democracy is nothing more than a pallid procedural device. Democracy is

---

[16] William F. Buckley, op. cit.

even more than the best political system yet devised (by liberals, in case you've forgotten); it is the essential one. "Man's capacity for justice makes democracy possible," wrote Reinhold Niebuhr, "but man's inclination to injustice makes democracy necessary."[17]

Although conservatives are quick to seize upon the human capacity for injustice (as part of their pessimistic view of human nature more generally), they are much less impressed with the need to do anything about it. They have consistently resisted civil rights legislation and enforcement within the United States, for example. A good example is Buckley's patronizing attitude toward voting rights for blacks: "The problem of the South is not how to get the vote for the Negro, but how to train the Negro—and a great many whites—to cast a thoughtful vote."[18] The problem has actually been quite different: how to get conservatives out of the way of democracy, for blacks and whites.

Democracy is not only unique in promising to respect the rights—and to demand responsibilities—of every person, it also offers this remarkable testament: Whereas democracies have shown themselves quite willing and able to make war, *they have never gone to war against other democracies*. Thus, of all liberal ideals, it may well be that democracy is the one that is most needed, around the world, and as soon as possible.

ONE OF the defining traits of conservatism is a reverence for the past. This was well expressed by one of the most notable classically trained scholars of political philosophy, Leo C. Strauss:

> The greatest enemies of civilization in civilized countries are those who squander their heritage because they look down on it or on the past; civilization is much less endangered by narrow but loyal preservers than by the shallow and glib futurists who, being themselves rootless, try to destroy all roots and thus do everything in their power in order to bring back the initial chaos and promiscuity.[19]

---

[17] Reinhold Niebuhr, *The Children of Light and the Children of Darkness* (New York: Scribner's, 1944).

[18] William F. Buckley, Jr., op. cit.

[19] Leo Strauss, *Liberalism Ancient and Modern* (New York: Basic Books, 1968).

For Strauss and other conservatives, the solution is clear: "The first duty of civilized man is . . . to respect his past."

Our past is certainly of more than passing interest or importance. It is the repository of our accumulated wisdom and the record of the route we have trodden, without which we would not know where we are. It must not lightly be cast aside. But the past is also the fossilized consequences of long-ago abuses and neglect, and often it is a heavy weight that threatens to drag down the future. In defending the past and yearning for its preservation, conservatives may be defending some of our noblest accomplishments, but at the risk of inhibiting the best of what might otherwise be.

In a radio address in 1939, Franklin Roosevelt spoke to the conservatives' fondness for the past and discomfort with the future. "A conservative," he said, "is a man with two perfectly good legs who, however, has never learned how to walk forward."

Liberals, on the other hand, are inclined to run . . . or at least, to jog. The liberal conception of the human condition sees the future as something to be created, not blindly continued from the past. From its inception, liberalism has prided itself on being free of tradition, superstition, and taboo. The liberal is likely to be rational, goal-oriented, pragmatic, participating, and possessing a kind of psychic mobility that is open to new ideas and new prospects for society. The *Oxford English Dictionary* defines liberal as "free from unreasonable prejudice in favour of traditional opinions or established institutions," and thus "open to the reception of new ideas or proposals for reform." This echoes the earlier opinion of John Stuart Mill, that the "Liberal looks forward while the Tory [i.e., the conservative] looks back."

The transition is a natural one: from an aspect of personal character (open-mindedness), to a social and political outlook that is receptive to reforming ideas and not especially partial to the present situation . . . which, after all, is simply the most recent manifestation of the past. Rephrasing Ambrose Bierce, we might say that conservatives are enamored of the way things are and have been, while liberals are hopeful about what they can be. Conservatives are far more likely to be enamored of existing evils, especially if those evils are usually visited upon someone else; liberals, as noted previously, are less inclined to make the distinction between "someone else" and themselves.

Probably more than any people on earth, Americans are fond of the "new" and profess to be in love with the future. Advertisers have long known that "new and improved" and "bigger and better" are magic phrases. "We have to adapt to a world in the making," said conservative French president Valéry Giscard d'Estaing, "and not try to remain adapted to a world that is fading."[20] But the truth is that Deputy Secretary of State Lawrence Eagleburger was closer to conservative sentiment when he commented nostagically in a speech early in 1989 that the Cold War was at least "characterized by a set of predictable relations" between East and West. Uncertainty makes the future troublesome enough, even for liberals. For conservatives, it is something to be avoided at all costs.

Liberals, as we have seen, are far more likely than conservatives to identify problems, and to entertain solutions. Not surprisingly, these solutions may be diverse, sometimes "all over the map." When asked why liberals so often speak with many voices whereas conservatives seem united, FDR replied, "There are many ways of going forward, but there's only one way of standing still."[21] (There is another reason as well: The conservative tradition is one of hierarchy, authoritarianism, and discipline, all of which are consistent with the conservative attitude toward the past, and which also tend to discourage the rowdy contentiousness that characterizes liberal politics.)

Along with their greater diversity and overall "liberality," liberals are also more willing to consider that their worldview may be ethnocentric, and to try walking a mile in someone else's shoes. It is primarily conservatives, for example, who bemoan the loss of "traditional Western values," not only at home but also in the educational curriculum.[22] They call for a return to the "classics" and a far more rigid intellectual envi-

---

[20] Interview in *Paris Match*, 1980.
[21] Quoted in Milton Viorst, *Liberalism: A Guide to its Past, Present, and Future in American Politics* (New York: Avon, 1963).
[22] Alan Bloom, *The Closing of the American Mind*, (New York: Simon and Schuster, 1987). This book was a widely read conservative complaint that Americans haven't been paying sufficient attention to their intellectual ancestors, notably such establishment men as Plato, Dante, and Chaucer. By contrast, liberals are more willing to expand the "basic curriculum" to include women and Third World contributors.

ronment, one that subordinates problem-solving to lock-step learning and rote memory, with its trappings of obedience to hierarchy . . . and often, patriarchy as well.

Don't misunderstand: Liberals aren't inevitably in favor of change, and conservatives don't always cling to the past or the present. Liberals can be downright "conservative" in defending liberal programs—Social Security, education and health benefits, labor protection, environmental legislation—against the right-wing meat-ax. And conservatives can be liberal, indeed, radical, when they try to roll back liberal accomplishments. "In the matter of beliefs," wrote William James, "we are all extreme conservatives."[23] But there is nonetheless a strain of consistency here; the ideas of conservatives essentially reflect the bygone (and largely imaginary) glories of an America dominated by the rugged, two-gun-sheriff individualist, for whom—as the bumper sticker suggests—"Gun control is a steady trigger finger." By contrast, liberals are less comfortable with violence, less tolerant of injustice, and far more adapted than conservatives to a progressive stance, looking ahead to a future (whether realistically attainable or not) in which we get the best of both worlds: economic and political rights as well as social and ecological responsibilities.

The likelihood is that history will look on the Reagan years not as a truly conservative period but as a wildly permissive one, open to gross excesses of private greed and selfishness. Was it a time of conserving resources or of exploiting them? Of making sound investments in America or of taking the money and running? Nonetheless, Reagan was a revolutionary of sorts, although less an activist than a reactivist. George Bush, by contrast, is more genuinely conservative (although less ideologically right wing). And so, he is incapable of inspiring the country with a vision of change, of challenge, largely because—like most conservatives—he is too wary of doing anything that might upset anyone, especially those who are now relatively comfortable and oblivious of any need for change.

Liberals, on the other hand, entertain great hopes, and with them, sometimes great disappointments. Perhaps the purist

---

[23] William James, *Pragmatism* (New York: Longmans, Green, 1908).

version of liberal optimism for the future was expressed by Thomas Paine, in his *The Rights of Man*, written during 1791–1792. This was a time of immense liberal enthusiasm, coming on the heels of the American and French Revolutions. Paine noted:

> Government of the old system is an assumption of power, for the aggrandizement of itself; on the new, a delegation of power for the common benefit of society. The former supports itself by keeping up a system of war; the latter promotes a system of peace, as the true means of enriching a nation. . . . What Athens was in miniature, America will be in magnitude. The one was the wonder of the Ancient World. The other is becoming the admiration of the present.[24]

Paine's rosy view of the future may seem naïve today, but it is also beautiful, inspiring, and possibly even accurate. Certainly it is likely to lead to far more positive, humane, and inspired behavior than its conservative alternative.

When Paine suggested that "Man is not the enemy of man but through the medium of a false system of government," he spoke for attempts to improve the human condition, attempts far more likely to bear fruit than a pessimistic, past-oriented conservatism that gives up on our potential for happiness, betterment, or brotherhood. And when he thrilled to the dawning of liberty in the modern world, Thomas Paine spoke for an eternal flame of hope that drives the liberal dream:

> There is a morning of reason rising upon man on the subject of government, that has not appeared before. As the barbarism of the present old governments expires, the moral condition of nations with respect to each other will be changed. Man will not be brought up with the savage idea of considering his species his enemy.[25]

Let us therefore turn next to the question of governments, and their role in the liberal scheme of things.

---

[24] Thomas Paine, *The Rights of Man* (Buffalo, N.Y.: Prometheus, 1987).
[25] Ibid.

Chapter 6 Government: Affirmative or Conservative?

WE AMERICANS pride ourselves in being antigovernment, or at least, anti-Big Government. We cherish an image of the primordial "American," part Daniel Boone, Davy Crockett, and Paul Revere, with a touch of Betsy Ross thrown in—hearty frontier types with no interest in or patience with pettifogging bureaucrats or fancy-talking "govmint" types. Or alternatively, there is the *Mr. Smith Goes to Washington* version, the noble, straight-thinking and incorruptible salt-of-the-earth, just-generally-wonderful common guy, who battles corruption and government (which are typically seen as merely different versions of the same thing.)

Liberalism, too, originated as opposition to Big Government,[1] although it eventually has become associated with certain aspects of Big Government itself, and for good reasons. But to some extent, the modern liberal fondness for government—contrasting as it does with the myth of antigovernment Americanism—has been a troubling development for the continuing acceptance of liberalism.

---

[1] An opposition that was much more real than the American frontier myth.

114

Myths aside, there are two powerful conservative strains running through the political consciousness of the United States: For one, there is no other developed country in the world—not in Europe, Latin America, Africa or Asia—that is so deeply distrustful of itself, that is, of the very idea of the state. For another, we are more hesitant than any other country about committing ourselves to cooperative social goals, so long as that commitment is expressly to be achieved via government policies. We are the only major industrialized society on earth, for example, that does not have a nationalized system of health insurance.

It is because of our deep distrust of Big Government that George Bush struck so responsive a chord during the 1988 presidential campaign when he said with mock horror (and to appreciative laughter), "We can see it now when the government agent from the Fund to Rebuild America comes to your door with the most feared words in the land: 'We're from the government and we're here to help.'"

And yet, there are countervailing realities to each of these strains. Despite its visceral distrust of the state, the United States is in fact the most powerful country in the world, and despite its discomfort with social cooperation, the United States cherishes its self-image as a nation of caring, compassionate, fair-minded people. We even have a distinguished history of pulling together for the common good, so long as we don't label it "socialism" (and, increasingly, so long as we avoid the "liberal" designation as well).

One of our earliest political traditions, "Jacksonian democracy," was notable for beginning the shift from classical liberalism to its modern incarnation. As we have seen, the difference between these two is that classical liberalism defines freedom as the State leaving the individual alone, whereas modern liberalism defines it as the State *helping* the individual. During the administration of Old Hickory, the United States government struggled to become modern; for the first time it began to govern consciously and successfully in the interest of the people . . . meaning the lower and middle classes instead of the wealthy.

For conservatives, "equality" is the equal opportunity to compete freely. The key difficulty, however, is that such opportunity is never truly equal. Clearly, "free competition" is to the advantage of those who start with inherited money, education, family contacts, etc. The idea that government should act affirmatively, in the interests of its people, is not entirely foreign even to conservatives. Thus, arch-conservative Edmund Burke wrote in his *Reflections on the French Revolution* that "Government is a contrivance of human wisdom to provide for human wants. Men have a right that these wants should be provided for by this wisdom." Burke meant the "wisdom" of the ruling class, not of the public as a whole, but it was a start.

In going a step further and actually seeking to govern on behalf of the nonrich, Andrew Jackson expanded the powers of the federal government. As historian Arthur M. Schlesinger, Jr., sees it, Jackson had no alternative. The Industrial Revolution had overrun Jefferson's dream of a nation of small farmers and artisans, and the development of large corporations

> began to impersonalize the economic order. It removed the economy, in other words, from the control of a personal code and delivered it to agencies with neither bodies to be kicked nor souls to be damned. Impersonality produced an irresponsibility which was chilling the lifeblood of society. The state consequently had to expand its authority in order to preserve the ties which hold society together. *The history of governmental intervention has been the history of the growing ineffectiveness of the private conscience as a means of social control. The only alternative is the growth of the public conscience, whose natural expression is the democratic government.*[2] [italics added]

But that growth was painfully slow. In 1819, the United States experienced the first of what was to be a continuing string of economic depressions, at twenty-year intervals.[3] "Distress is the universal cry of the people," noted Senator Thomas Hart Benton at the time, "relief, the universal demand thundered at the doors of all legislatures, State and Federal."[4] But no

---

[2] Arthur M. Schlesinger, Jr., *The Vital Center.* (Boston: Houghton Mifflin, 1949).
[3] During the nineteenth century, depressions occurred in 1819, 1837, 1857, 1873, and 1893.
[4] Quoted in Arthur M. Schlesinger, Jr., *The Cycles of American History* (Boston: Houghton Mifflin, 1986).

relief was sent. Indeed, during the depression of 1893, Grover Cleveland warned during his second inaugural address that people should not "expect from the operation of the Government especial and direct individual advantages." President Cleveland even announced—apparently with a straight face— that "While the people should patriotically and cheerfully support their Government, its [that is, government's] functions do not include support of the people." The relationship of people to their government, in the age of the great robber barons, was to be a one-way street.

It was the duty of Americans to give patriotism and support (in other words, votes and taxes, and, if the military so demands, their lives) but not to ask anything in return. At best, government would promise to keep out of certain aspects of our lives, leaving us to the tender mercies of economic cycles and the altruistic corporate kindnesses of John D. Rockefeller, Andrew Mellon, Andrew Carnegie, and company.

But as we have already seen, a current of dissent had been brewing within the free market, classical liberal tradition of the nineteenth century. Self-interest alone, it was increasingly felt, was an inadequate guiding principle for the American social order, and was unlikely, by itself, to create an enlightened and rational state. Government would have to step in, to direct and organize socioeconomic realities, not simply submit to them. After all, the liberal tradition had long considered that the future was ours to invent; what better time to do so than when things were bad?

Teddy Roosevelt finally became the first American president to do something about an economic depression. The federal government expanded the currency supply and lowered interest rates during the banking panic of 1907. The state had come to be seen less as a potential tyrant than as a needed protector of the individual citizen. But the means were not strictly Hamiltonian: whereas Alexander Hamilton had distrusted democracy, the new apostles of affirmative government believed in it . . . and still do.

Nonetheless, the road to affirmative government has been bumpy, strewn with conservative potholes. In his 1978 State of the Union address, for example, the not-very-liberal Jimmy Carter said that "Government cannot solve our problems. It cannot set our goals. It cannot define our vision. Government cannot eliminate poverty, or provide a bountiful economy, or reduce inflation, or save our cities, or cure illiteracy or provide energy."

And nearly fifty years earlier, when the Great Depression was at its worst, President Herbert Hoover hid behind this highly conservative statement of government incapacity: "The sole function of government is to bring about a condition of affairs favorable to the beneficial development of private enterprise."

Arthur M. Schlesinger, Jr., points out that in the same year that Hoover was restricting government's role to feathering the beds of the already comfortable, the governor of New York, one Franklin Delano Roosevelt, expressed a very different belief: "I assert that modern society, acting through its government, owes the definite obligation to prevent the starvation or the dire want of any of its fellow men and women who try to maintain themselves and cannot."[5] In short, the liberal vision is that society (via government) should help care for the weak and the poor; the healthy and the wealthy can take care of themselves.

In time, basic liberal policies were accepted even by conservatives: legality of labor unions, farm price supports, housing subsidies, a social safety net, education grants, arms control, attempts at environmental protection.

Big Government has its problems, to be sure. It is slow, inefficient, often impersonal, and its functionaries and their interminable regulations can be frustrating in the extreme. Moreover, as bureaucracy expands, so does the potential for abuse. But compared to the selfishness and recklessness of big business, modern liberal government is a veritable fairy godmother. The growth of federal influence and management in the United States has resulted in our shared greatness and wealth, as well as our dignity and freedom as individuals. Sometimes government programs fail. The same happens in the private sector. But no one argues that because entrepreneurs occasionally go belly-up, private enterprise ought to be

---

[5]Quoted in Arthur M. Schlesinger, Jr., "Is Liberalism Dead?," *The New York Times Magazine*, March 30, 1980.

abolished, or even cut back. Quite the opposite: The cry goes up for more inventiveness, better thinking and planning, even various schemes for protecting venture capital. The public sector deserves at least the same respect.

In fact, the argument can be made that public endeavors deserve, if anything, greater latitude and support. For one thing, public enterprise, in a democratic society, has a conscience. Business does not. Ronald Reagan can prate on about volunteerism, and George Bush can wax pseudo-mystical about "a thousand points of light," but the fact remains that—once again, in a democracy—government is *us*. If we have a conscience writ large, it is to be found in the programs initiated by our people as an organized society; that is, in the institutions of our government. Otherwise, there is nothing but a thousand black holes, spawned in the darkness of corporate greed.

As CONGRESSMAN Henry A. Waxman put it, for conservatives, "no problem is so big that it cannot be ignored." (Except for communism, of course, which can always use a bit of threat inflation.) "Just say NO" to drugs, or maybe "YES" to military interdiction, or, according to former Drug Czar William Bennett, "YES" to beheading drug dealers. But don't say anything whatever about underlying social or economic causes. Self-discipline is laudable, and the disciplining of others may be good politics (with or without the beheading), but neither is likely to be a cure-all. The conservatives' answer almost always falls short of the problem, as in this vignette: A drowning man is flailing about in the water, fifty feet from shore. The conservative response is to throw him twenty-five feet of rope, and order him to swim to it! (The liberal, meanwhile, tries to throw him a seventy-five-foot rope . . . and sometimes gets tangled in the excess.)

The free market is in many ways wondrously powerful and efficient at distributing resources over the short run. It has two notable weaknesses, however: For one, it lacks a heart. Efficiency may be a virtue, but it is not the only one. It says much about our time that compassion has gotten a bad name. Second, the free market lacks vision. It cannot plan for the long-term and it has no awareness of "externalities," those diffuse costs that are borne by everyone but typically are not reflected in product costs or corporate profits. As a result of the first weakness, the free market does a poor job when it comes to social fairness and economic justice. And as a result of the second, it is equally inept on environmental issues. Starvation, civic unrest, gross inequities in wealth and opportunity, global warming (the greenhouse effect), a devastating loss of species diversity, irreplaceable soil erosion, demolition of the rain forests: All this will be upon us long before the free market rouses itself to respond, if indeed, it ever will. Indeed, they are upon us right now.

These problems are especially acute for so-called step functions, those that give relatively little warning, and then—after conditions cross a threshold—change suddenly by a quantum leap, like taking a sudden step onto a new level rather than sliding smoothly up a continuous inclined plane. In some cases, the market is marvelously capable of adjusting; for example, if petroleum prices go up, demand will decline somewhat, and alternative fuels may be found. But if the change is abrupt, as threatens to be the case with global warming or violent social upheaval, we are in danger of stubbing our toes on the step or—more likely—stumbling over a cliff.

For many decades after 1949, conservatives had a battle cry of sorts: "Unleash Chiang!"[6] For modern conservatives, the cry is, "Unleash private enterprise!" But in fact, when it comes to educating our people, providing good-quality low-cost health care, rebuilding our roads, establishing consumer safety standards or gun control, rebuilding bridges and tunnels, or protecting our environment, private enterprise is as toothless as old Chiang Kai-shek ever was.

A fundamental philosophical question, and one that distinguishes liberals from conservatives, is simply this: What are governments for? Why do we have them? One possibility is that governments are instituted primarily to protect people from themselves, to maintain order within the society and to defend its members from other societies. This is the Hobbesian, conservative view, driven by a pessimistic sense that people are inclined toward evil. Hence, conservatives are comfortable

---

[6]Nationalist Chinese leader Chiang Kai-shek, who was defeated by Mao and his followers and subsequently took refuge on Formosa.

spending money on law enforcement and the military, but not on social betterment or environmental protection.

Hobbes emphasized what government and people should *not* do: "Do not that to another, which thou wouldest not have done to thyself." This is a classically conservative maxim, telling us to refrain from misdeeds toward others. Compare it with the Golden Rule, namely, "Do unto others as you would have others do unto you." This is a liberal, do-gooder's credo, urging us not simply to avoid evil, but to go out of our way to do good.

Beyond the right-wing view of government as inhibitor lies the liberal perspective, that the reason for government is to help people, to make things better, to enable its citizens to achieve in community what eludes them as individuals. The presumption here is a deeply liberal one, that people are fundamentally good, and that the world can be made better. Government as naysayer and defender does not necessarily preclude government as helper, but the difference in focus is important.

The liberal's goal is not only to make things better but also to keep them from getting worse, to anticipate difficulties and avoid disasters. It seeks not to replace capitalism but to supplement it. It also aims to use government on behalf of all of us, to overcome the blindness and excess of laissez-faire, to assure that we really are an "opportunity society," and not just for those wanting an opportunity to take advantage of their fellows and their environment, or those already guaranteed an opportunity by fatness of wallet or fortune of birth; in short, to move from trickle-down to open-up.

DEMOCRATIC GOVERNMENT *means* the fulfillment of community aspirations. (As we have seen, this is one reason why conservatives find democracy itself so distasteful.) There is abundant evidence that even in the seemingly conservative America of the 1980s, public aspirations were identical with the liberal agenda; that is, in favor of an activist, affirmative government. In 1989, according to a Harris survey,[7] 78 percent of the public gave high priority to government activism in

---

[7]Reported at "FDR and the Future of Liberalism" conference, Hyde Park, N.Y., October 1989.

controlling AIDS, 71 percent for alleviating the plight of the homeless, 84 percent for protecting the environment, 73 percent for making the United States more competitive abroad, 61 percent for making abortions available on demand, and 69 percent for a federally run system of national health insurance. Not surprisingly, the overwhelming majority in all these cases clearly aligns itself with the shared well-being of America, while conservatives increasingly reveal themselves to be opposed to the public interest. (Actually, sometimes they don't honestly reveal themselves; in 1990, for example, George Bush congratulated himself for an education budget which reached "another record high," without mentioning that it failed even to keep pace with inflation. Such misrepresentation is tacit acknowledgment that liberal programs such as education are popular with the American people.)

George Bush indirectly confirms the underlying popularity of liberal ideas by talking like a liberal—telling people what they want to hear—then governing like a conservative. For example, after campaigning in favor of a bill that would have allowed employees to take unpaid leave when a family member was ill, he proceeded to veto it. Similarly with civil rights: After meeting with the leadership of the NAACP and (unlike Ronald Reagan) making it seem at least that the White House was sympathetic to black concerns, Bush became in 1990 the first president since the Civil War to veto civil rights legislation . . . which, incidentally, would have benefited Latinos, gays, and women no less than blacks.

The great majority of Americans don't follow public affairs very closely, and don't have a coherent political philosophy. Most are unable to define *liberal* or *conservative*. Most people cannot even name their member of Congress. But most do know how they feel about what government should or should not be doing. Furthermore, polls have consistently shown that the three most popular presidents of the century were FDR, JFK, and HST[8]—all of them liberals. Americans have come to

---

[8]"We have rejected the discredited theory that the fortunes of the nation should be in the hands of a privileged few," said Truman. "Instead, we believe that our economic system should rest on a democratic foundation and that wealth should be created for the benefit of all. . . . Every segment of our population and every individual has a right to expect from his government a fair deal."

distrust the L label, but they like the L presidents, and their L programs.[9]

In an important book on the political beliefs of Americans, Hadley Cantril and Lloyd A. Free[10] distinguished between the "ideological spectrum" and the "operational spectrum." American's ideological spectrum—their theoretical beliefs—tended toward the conservative. But their operational spectrum—the specific programs that they favored—were overwhelmingly liberal. Thus, whereas the majority of Americans liked and admired Ronald Reagan, they opposed most of his policies. They are conservatives in principle, liberals in practice.

More recently, Americans have shown a tendency to elect liberal, Democratic members of Congress to get them what they want, and Republican presidents to protect them from other people's liberal, Democratic members of Congress.

Conservative myth-makers have in some cases succeeded in making it appear that when it comes to liberal doctrine, the whole is smaller than the sum of its parts. Thus, people admire the parts (that is, the specific programs), often clinging to them tenaciously, even while they simultaneously reject the term *liberal*. Liberals, meanwhile, have been all too quick to accept conservative criticism about the "failed policies of the past," whereas in fact, liberal programs have by and large worked, and impressively.

One of the more influential critiques of modern liberal social programs was penned by a previously little-known conservative named Charles Murray.[11] Right-wingers found Mr. Murray's argument immensely attractive because he claimed that social programs were actually detrimental to the poor. Greed, you see, may be privately seductive, but it is less than appealing as a public philosophy. Imagine the conservatives' delight, therefore, when, courtesy of Mr. Murray, they were able to claim that the welfare state should be dismantled, not for the benefit of the wealthy, but to help the poor! It is possible—likely, in fact—that some worthy programs actually have

---

[9] When it comes to Social Security, for example, virtually every politician is a liberal.

[10] Hadley Cantril and Lloyd A. Free, *The Political Beliefs of Americans* (New York: Simon and Schuster, 1968).

[11] Charles Murray, *Losing Ground* (New York: Basic Books, 1984).

backfired, and that in some cases, they have engendered dependency rather than self-reliance. But these arguments are largely based on selective statistics, misleadingly applied.

This is not the place to go into detailed analyses, but in fact, the War on Poverty and Great Society programs were, for the most part, substantial successes.[12] Consider total life expectancy: For whites, this sensitive measure of overall health increased just 1.9 years during the 15 years prior to 1960, as opposed to 3.4 years during the period 1965–1980; improvements in nonwhite life expectancy went up from 3.3 years to 5.4. The elderly were in a sorry plight during the early 1960s; today, they are immeasurably better off, thanks to such liberal programs as Medicare, Medicaid, and the indexing of Social Security to inflation via cost of living allowances.

The young also benefited by various supposedly "failed" liberal programs. For example, there was a dramatic decline in infant mortality, from 2.3 percent for whites in 1960 to 1.1 percent in 1980, and from 4.4 percent for blacks (1960) to 2.2 percent (by 1980). In some regions of Appalachia, infant mortality fell by 50 percent within a few years of the initiation of government medical and nutrition programs.[13] The Head Start program has been another success story, resulting in a net increase of 3.5 points in average IQ of participants. But the 1980s, on balance, were especially hard on children. In real terms (that is, corrected for inflation), Aid to Families with Dependent Children payments declined fully 25 percent from 1977 to 1988.

Unions were also hard hit: The unionized share of labor dropped from 24 percent to 18 percent—the lowest in the in-

---

[12] John E. Schwarz, *America's Hidden Success: a Reassessment of Twenty-Years of Public Policy* (New York: Norton, 1983).

[13] And in 1990, the Agriculture Department has even admitted to having doctored a study to examine whether the department's Supplemental Food Program for Women, Infants, and Children had benefited the health of pregnant women and boosted the IQ of their children. The study, by nutritionist David Rush, actually found among other things that the program substantially reduced fetal mortality; it was butchered because conservative officials apparently wanted lawmakers to think that the program was unsuccessful. By 1989, WIC was reaching only 40 percent of those formerly eligible—not because it wasn't working, but because the Reaganites had succeeded in falsifying the evidence of its effectiveness.

dustrialized Western world—between 1980 and 1985. During the relatively liberal 1960s and 1970s, the percentage of Americans below the poverty line decreased from about 15–20 percent in 1960, to less than 10 percent in 1980. Then, under conservative government, poverty actually *increased*, by 3.5 percent during the 1980s.

In all, real wages either stagnated or actually went down for the bottom 60 percent of the American population during the 1980s, while they rose sharply for the top 20 percent. The upper ½₀ enjoyed an 11.5 percent leap. Consider another aspect of economic redistribution, conservative-style: Interest payments of the national debt literally quadrupled during the 1980s. We now pay fully $200 billion per year just to service the national debt. And to whom do these payments go? Overwhelmingly, to those wealthy enough to buy U.S. Treasury securities in minimum amounts of $5,000 and $10,000. More than half of all such bonds are owned by the wealthiest ½ of 1 percent of the population. Ninety-three percent of all bonds are held by the richest 10 percent. Thanks to conservative economic policies, in short, wealthy people have been granted a reliable (and taxfree) return on their investment. At the same time, corporations have been paying substantially less than their share: In 1952, taxes paid by corporations represented more than 32 percent of federal receipts; by 1983, this figure had plummetted to 6.2 percent. The highest rate on capital gains was effectively reduced to 20 percent, down from 49 percent in 1978.

Government income was enhanced especially by a Social Security tax increase in the early 1980s. This tax is applied as a constant percentage of income, across the board. As a result of these regressive and illiberal policies, as Senator Daniel Moynihan pointed out, the United States has come to lead the world in taking money from its relatively hardworking low- and middle-income people, whose incomes derive largely from salaries, while demanding remarkably little from its wealthy citizens, much of whose hefty incomes are "unearned," coming from investments, rents, dividends, and so forth. And as if this hasn't been enough, according to the Joint Committee on Taxation, George Bush's 1991 proposal for a capital-gains tax cut was tilted even more strongly toward the rich: More than 83 percent of the direct benefit would go to those whose incomes exceed $100,000 a year.[14]

Conservatives argue that goodies for the rich will eventually create benefits—such as jobs—for everyone else. In fact, goodies for the rich create more goodies for the rich, and virtually nothing else. Satirist Calvin Trillin called it "Economics, with Power Steering":

> The Bush economists say folks with gobs
> Should not be taxed (the gospel of the eighties)
> So they'll invest the money and make jobs.
> But that neglects the role of the Mercedes.
>
> That's why this reinvestment talk is cant:
> The man who makes a bunch of money lends
> No start-up fund to some new widget plant.
> Instead, he buys a white Mercedes-Benz.
>
> And if you let him keep more of his pay
> He won't finance a new assembly line.
> He'll simply buy another one in gray.
> The rich stay rich. The Germans like it fine.[15]

Defenders of Reagan-era, favor-the-rich policies like to point out that wealthy Americans are providing a larger proportion of American tax revenues than ever before, but this is in fact a misleading trick of statistics. (There are three kinds of lies, said Mark Twain: regular lies, damned lies, and statistics.) The wealthy have in fact been paying more in taxes, but only because they are making much, much more than ever before, while enjoying tax rates lower than ever before.

When Michael Dukakis proposed increased enforcement of our Internal Revenue laws, as a way of enhancing the federal treasury, candidate George Bush countered, "I don't agree with his vision of America where the government has a hand in every pocket and a tax agent in every kitchen." Instead, the conservative vision is for government to work hand-in-glove with the wealthy, while socking it to the rest of us.

---

[14] In an unintentionally comical speech in 1959, Nelson Rockefeller said, "Take the average guy earning $100,000 per year . . ." No one seems to remember what came next, since it was drowned in snickers.

[15] Calvin Trillin, *The Nation*, November 19, 1990.

Supply-side economics is a perfect example of such destructive flimflammery, with its claim that we need simply encourage the supply side of production—in short, tax breaks for wealthy individuals and for corporations. By contrast, liberals would have us put the horse back where it belongs, in front of the cart. This horse is called demand, notably consumer demand. Liberals recognize that for economies—and families and countries—to be productive, the citizenry must be well educated, healthy, motivated, and adequately paid. Then, they not only produce things, they also buy them, and build them, while building their own lives as well. In a very real sense, sound liberal policies kill two birds with one stone: Government practices that benefit people in turn rebound positively by stimulating demand and creating a solid economy which in turn benefits those people for whom the economy and the government are supposed to exist.

The reagan administration—operating from a hallowed conservative tradition in this regard—gave us government by and for the rich, which has widened the gap between them and the poor. Most social programs have been seriously gutted, leaving a "safety net" that is tattered at best. Federal funding for day-care programs, for example, was slashed by 25 percent from 1981 to 1986. The 1980s generally exaggerated the "hourglass society": creating an economic profile that is bigger at the top and the bottom, and smaller in the middle. Among black families, for example, those in the middle class (earning $25,000 to $50,000 per year) actually fell from better than 30 percent in 1976 to 26.7 percent in 1988.[16] Prosperity at the top expanded at the same time: Those earning $50,000 or more increased from 7.7 percent to 12.6 percent, whereas those in deep poverty, earning $5,000 or less, increased as well, from 6.7 percent to 11.9 percent. In 1979, there were thirty million persons without any form of health insurance; by 1986, their numbers had swollen to thirty-eight million. Numbers, however, are numbing. It must be emphasized that these are not simply dry data, or mere examples of inequity, anonymous

---

[16] Adjusted for inflation; these data reported in *Money* magazine, December 1989.

injuries to our sense of justice. They are real, suffering people, millions and millions of individuals, the facts of human tragedy, weakening *our* society, and thus, ourselves.

The eight Reagan years were the first since FDR in which there was no increase in the minimum wage. While wages stagnated relative to inflation, the return on capital (investments, dividends, rents, capital gains—aptly termed "unearned income" by the IRS) skyrocketed. Yes, average family income increased, as did per capita income, but this was because increasing numbers of women joined the workforce, seeking to make up for the fact that per-worker income had actually gone *down*.[17]

Meanwhile, federal appropriations for public housing were cut by two-thirds. Can this possibly have anything to do with the horror and national shame of homelessness, a social problem that was virtually nonexistent before? And the Reagan administration gave us, simultaneously, an immense scandal at the Department of Housing and Urban Development (HUD), in which hundreds of millions of dollars were spent to fatten the wallets of political cronies. The underlying cause is clear, and worth understanding: For the first time in American history, a major branch of government was peopled by appointees who were ideologically opposed to the institution they were supposed to be monitoring and whose work they were supposed to carry out. Combine this with personal venality and a lack of presidential oversight or even interest, and small wonder the result was dereliction of duty as well as outright corruption.

Moreover, in addition to the misdirection of funds ostensibly intended for social betterment, actual spending on human resources went down, from 28 percent of federal outlays to 22 percent, while during the same period, the military fed high on the hog, enjoying an increase from 23 percent to 28 percent. When talking about hundreds of billions of dollars, incidentally, a percentage point or two represents a vast difference.

---

[17] Take note that per capita income goes up if a woman who had previously stayed home takes a job. But per-*worker* income goes down if her job, and that of her husband, pay lower wages.

Civil rights comprised another sorry spectacle during the 1980s. Conservatives who had opposed the landmark (and liberal) civil rights Acts of 1964 and 1965 suddenly claimed to be wholeheartedly in favor of a "color blind society," that is, one in which government did nothing to alter the status quo . . . and which therefore opposed affirmative action and the righting of past wrongs. Deregulation—another leading conservative heartthrob—has caused great problems in the airlines, the telephone system, banking, consumer protection, workplace safety, the securities markets, and nuclear weapons production and waste storage. On the environment, George Bush has not been able to bring himself to use federal authority to reduce acid rain or the emission of greenhouse gases, to support protection of rain forests, or the acquisition of wilderness areas. His 1990 budget even included a $400-million *reduction* in Ronald Reagan's abysmally low allocations for pollution control.

But, you might say, perhaps this conservative reluctance to take an activist role simply reflects a greater commitment to economic growth, if necessary at the expense of social justice and environmental protection. Robert S. McElvaine, professor of history at Millsaps College in Jackson, Mississippi, compared national economic growth when Republicans and Democrats were in control of the presidency between 1930 and 1984. Of these fifty-four years, thirty-one were Democratic and twenty-three were Republican, close enough to make a comparison. Using impartial data from the Bureau of the Census and the Commerce Department's Bureau of Economic Analysis, McElvaine discovered a startling fact: During Democratic administrations, growth averaged 5.11 percent per year as compared with 0.80 percent when Republicans were in power. The GNP grew, on average, more than six times faster when Democratic presidents occupied the White House.[18] This suggests that even at the crude level of economic growth, liberal policies haven't been failures; rather, conservative ones have been. And also, it confirms the common-sense proposition that the politics of common good are good for all of us, whether our concerns revolve especially around fairness or money.

---

[18] Robert S. McElvaine, *The Coming End of the Conservative Era*, (New York: Arbor House, 1987).

Certainly, there was some prosperity during the Reagan years, but as Kevin Phillips documents in great detail,[19] it was prosperity for a limited segment of the population, notably the already-rich. And even for this privileged few, much of the wealth created during the 1980s was based on artifice and reshuffling of existing assets, as opposed to the creation of anything new and real. While agriculture (especially family farms), mining, forestry, and heavy manufacturing languished, the money poured in for the latest "captains of industry," whose ships typically never left the dock. Rather, they made fortunes refinancing and moving money, repackaging various debt instruments, and raiding each other's corporations . . . making profits, but nothing else.

At the same time as junk-bond king Michael Milken, for example, was making more than five hundred million dollars *in one year* (more than John D. Rockefeller at his peak), American competitiveness declined internationally, the United States became the world's biggest debtor, and our inner cities deteriorated inexcusably, buried under an avalanche of despair, drugs, and violent street crime. Speaking for American liberals, Elliott Currie, of the Institute for the Study of Social Change, at the University of California at Berkeley, noted:

> It was not on our watch that this accelerating public emergency was met not by a corresponding deployment of public resources but by their deliberate reduction; more recently, by the steadfast refusal to raise new revenues in the face of new and terrifyingly urgent needs. Liberals should forcefully point out that the conservative failure to carry out these essential public tasks is hardly accidental, for they have similarly failed to deliver on every other fundamental public obligation government owes to ordinary working Americans. The same people who fail to assure decent health care for all; who have failed to increase the supply of affordable housing and indeed allowed the dream of homeownership to skyrocket out of reach; who have permitted the fouling of the air we breathe and the dumping of frightening chemicals in our backyards; who won't fix the subways or clean up the parks or pave the potholes in the streets or come up with enough money for someone to care for our children while we work to put that decreasingly affordable roof

---

[19] Kevin Phillips, *The Politics of Rich and Poor* (New York: Random House, 1990).

over our heads; are the same people who talk "tough" about crime and drugs, but somehow can't find enough money to put enough police on the street to chase away the dealers from our doorsteps or to help the addicted—but *can* come up with $20 billion in six weeks to begin bailing out the savings and loan industry.

A liberal anticrime, antidrug strategy must accordingly aim to restore—and to enhance—the cities' capacity to nurture and socialize their children; to police their streets; to help the addicted; to care for the troubled; to provide a contributive future for the young.[20]

English journalist and writer G. K. Chesterton once observed about Christianity that it hasn't been tried and found wanting, rather, it has been found difficult and left untried. We might say that liberalism hasn't seriously been tried since LBJ's Great Society was overwhelmed by Vietnam . . . and that it's high time to try once again. Chesterton believed that we needed to put Christ back in Christianity; we would certainly do well to put liberalism back in government.

At about the same time as Chesterton, a renowned sociologist wrote a famous paper titled, "The Unanticipated Consequences of Purposive Social Action," in which he showed how good plans sometimes go astray. But unlike the nefarious Charles Murray, who likes to blame poverty on our efforts to help the poor, this social scientist—Robert K. Merton—concluded that "genuine failure consists only in the lessening of ambition."[21] Such failure is a hallmark of American conservatism.

By contrast, it was liberal ambition, on the part of Lyndon Johnson and his cohorts, that gave us the Great Society programs, most of which are still in existence and still benefiting millions of Americans: community action grants, Foster Grandparents, the Job Corps, Upward Bound, legal services for the poor, community health centers, VISTA, college work-study programs, and Head Start. And it was during liberal

---

[20] Elliott Currie, "Crime and Drugs: Reclaiming a Liberal Issue," paper presented at "FDR and the Future of Liberalism" conference, Hyde Park, N.Y., October 1989.
[21] Robert K. Merton, *Social Theory and Social Structure*, (Glencoe, Ill.: Free Press, 1949).

ascendancy that the civil rights movement made its greatest advances, with the nonviolent campaigns in the streets led by Martin Luther King, Jr., and the legislative campaigns culminating in the Civil Rights Act of 1964 and the Voting Rights Act of 1965.

In summary, there is no reason for liberals to be on the defensive. It is conservatives, instead, who should cringe when being called to account for their all-too-genuine failures, and their egregious combination of heightened personal greed with lessened social ambition.

CONSERVATISM WAS undeniably successful in the 1980s. But its success was in politics, in getting conservatives elected, not in governing. Conservatives claim credit for three particular advances, but each of them is questionable. First, inflation was indeed brought under control, but only because of several mighty assists, none of which came from Reagan conservatives: good harvests, the disarray of OPEC, and stringent policies on the part of the Federal Reserve (whose chairman was appointed by Jimmy Carter). Second, the Cold War has finally ended, and conservatives vociferously claim the credit; as we shall see, however, there is equally good reason to believe the precise opposite: that the Cold War has crumbled *in spite of* conservative American policies, not because of them. Third is a resurgence of national pride, a sense that the United States is "standing tall" once again. It is curious that the successful invasion of fourth-rate countries should induce such a feeling, and highly questionable whether it is, after all, a healthy one.

On the other hand, by running up a monumental national debt—larger than all of his predecessors combined—the conservative 1980s of Ronald Reagan has hardly gotten government off the backs of the American people. Just the opposite: We'll be paying off the debts of Reaganomics for many years to come, possibly for generations. Historically, it was conservatives who were critical of liberals' penchant for accruing a national debt, contemptuous of the Keynesian sleight of hand whereby, for example, FDR's brain-trusters promoted the notion that since we owe the national debt to ourselves, it isn't so troublesome. Now, Reaganomics has made that molehill of debt into a genuine mountain . . . and instead of owing it to ourselves, we owe it increasingly to the Japanese!

If that weren't bad enough, it will also take $200 billion and more to clean up the inexcusable mess that has been allowed to accumulate at America's nuclear weapons plants, another $500 billion to bail out the greedy, incompetent, and inadequately regulated Savings and Loan Associations, $100 billion or so to clean up our toxic dumpsites, unknown billions to make up for the HUD scandal, the Pentagon procurement scandal, and the mess at the farm credit system. Not to mention many billions more for waging war on Iraq. As the late Senator Everett M. Dirksen (himself a leading conservative) put it, "a billion here, a billion there; pretty soon it adds up to real money."

And real problems.

In historian Arthur M. Schlesinger, Jr.'s view, this mess is the predictable result of national leadership that "gave the pursuit of self-interest moral priority and crippled the machinery of regulation in the public interest."[22] Such disasters occur, Schlesinger notes, when "mindless deregulation is combined with boundless greed."

Conservatives claim that they dislike government, by which they mean the prosocial, affirmative aspects of government. (They retain a great fondness for its more secret and repressive components, such as the FBI, CIA, and the military generally.) Because of conservative priorities during the 1980s, the United States has been crippled and terribly restricted in its potential scope. We must ask, accordingly, whether it is really in the interests of conservatives, or any American, for government to be so weakened and discredited. In a miserable default of leadership, for example, we have been consuming about 3 percent annually more than we have been producing; this simply is not sustainable.

By combining tax cuts for the wealthy with an enormous increase in military spending, conservativism has saddled us with an immense national debt, in the process achieving a

---

[22] Arthur M. Schlesinger, Jr., "Liberalism: What It Was, Where It Is," paper presented at "FDR and the Future of Liberalism" conference, Hyde Park, N.Y., October 1989.

fundamental conservative goal: making us unable to undertake great things at home. Can you imagine the United States,
in its present financial straits and frame of mind, building another Panama Canal, establishing a national highway system,
or creating a massive network of land-grant universities? Do
we have the resources, for example, to combat AIDS? The Cold
War began with Soviet domination of Eastern Europe; it is now
ending with their withdrawal, but we have scarcely any resources to help stiffen the spine and take some of the sting
out of the costly but crucial transition to democracy and capitalism in these long-suffering nations.

It is often said—correctly—that the crushing national debt
accumulated during eight years of Reagan conservatism is a
devastating burden that we shall bequeath to our children and
grandchildren. Often overlooked is the fact that we are also
suffering, right here and now, from this same burden. Servicing the debt is now the third largest category of federal expenditures.[23] (The Red Queen would understand: We have to run
like crazy just to pay the interest on our debts and stay where
we are; to get anywhere with domestic or foreign programs,
we will have to go even faster . . . that is, pay even more.)

Our massive debt is due not only to conservative insistence
on combining tax cuts with massive military spending, but also,
in large part, because of conservative success in weakening
the fundamental and crucially important infrastructure of government itself. Thus, in 1984, Federal Home Loan Bank Board
Chairman Edwin Gray begged President Reagan to hire 750
new S&L examiners; he was told that such requests went
counter to conservative philosophy, which called for a reduction in the number of examiners, not an increase. In Texas
alone, fifty-four examiners in 1981 were cut to twelve in 1985—
and not coincidentally, Texas along with Oklahoma accounted
for over 50 percent of failed S&L property subsequently re-

---

[23]Senator Paul Simon has pointed out to me that even this is misleading,
obtained only if—as the Bush administration insists—we first *reduce* the debt
burden by adding the interest earned by surpluses in the Social Security
and other trust fund accounts. Looked at honestly, by contrast, servicing
our national debt was in fact the second largest budget category in Fiscal
Year 1991, and for 1992, it is the largest expenditure of the federal government, for the first time in the nation's history.

purchased (by the American taxpayers), when their investments went sour.

Throughout the 1980s, the Reagan administration, following conservative doctrine, cut deeply into the bone and muscle of government. Once-proud agencies such as the Food and Drug Administration, the Fish and Wildlife Service, and the Environmental Protection Agency, were made almost as inefficient and ineffective as their conservative critics had long claimed.[24] And by gutting these and other crucial branches of government, conservatives set the stage for an extraordinary flourishing of white-collar crime. We "saved" millions of dollars in civil service salaries, while incurring resultant costs in the hundreds of *billions*, through S&L and HUD losses alone. In most of the critical social agencies, conservative policies have created a hollow shell of inadequate government, often overseen by bureaucrats who are downright antagonistic to the mission of their own agencies.

In the 1980s we experienced a kind of crackpot conservatism. Solid conservatives,[25] from Alexander Hamilton to Winston Churchill, would never have countenanced such diminution in the strength of public institutions. They also would have understood the importance of investing in a nation's growth and future. The sad truth is that we have been impoverished by conservative rule, not so much in money as in spirit. As a proportion of GNP, our national debt—huge though it is—is actually lower now than it was in the 1940s and early 1950s. Yet, we cannot "afford" to do many of the things that need to be done. In his first State of the Union address in 1989, George Bush lamely declared that our goodwill is deeper than our wallets. In fact, our greatest deficit is not financial but precisely in our will, in the conservatives' understanding of what goodwill means, and how much is appropriate.

In the summer of 1990, for example, an unnamed senior Bush administration official was widely quoted as having announced that the federal government would not be initiating any antipoverty programs. Instead, the official—most as-

---

[24]Walter Williams, *Mismanaging America* (Lawrence, Kans.: University Press of Kansas, 1990).
[25]Yes, there have been a few, and perhaps there still are, somewhere.

suredly not impoverished himself—suggested cheerfully that the Bush administration will "keep playing with the same toys. But let's paint them a little shinier."

The real cost of 1980s conservatism may well be the shriveling of the American spirit of community, kindness, and of generous possibility. We "stand tall" with our arms, but not our hearts . . . or even our heads.

It is ironic that an ideology so closely allied with a "can-do" spirit of rugged individualism is also the purveyor of so narrow, selfish, and crabbed a view of human potentiality. But so it is. The greater irony is that a worldview informed by a horror of Hobbesian man—competitive, nasty, and brutish— should be a self-fulfilling prophecy, whose very policies threaten to make us more competitive, nasty, and brutish.

There are other ironies as well. Thus, both Richard Nixon and Ronald Reagan did conservatives' work in ways they did not intend. Notably, they succeeded in tarnishing the image of the federal government and in diminishing the public's faith in its own institutions. Nixon's Watergate scandal added a substantial legacy of cynicism about government, already well advanced by the Vietnam War. And Reagan's Iran-Contra fiasco, along with the HUD and Pentagon contract debacles, the S&L scandal, and the widespread, distasteful "sleaze factor" of Reagan Attorney General Edwin Meese, Environmental Protection Agency head Anne Burford, Labor Secretary Raymond Donovan, presidential confidant Michael Deaver, and others—not to mention the president's own inattentiveness and indifference to facts—has gone a long way toward undoing the traditional optimism on which liberalism thrives. Insofar as Big Government has gotten a bad name, it is far less because of liberal programs that have misfired than because of conservatives who got caught.

INFRINGEMENTS ON personal freedom, and on the sanctity of private property: Here is the bedrock of conservative gripes about liberal-sponsored government programs. Personal freedom is undeniably diminished when a proportion of someone's money is taken away, in the form of taxes, and then used for purposes of which he or she might not approve. But in a democracy, these decisions are made by the public. (Remember "No taxation without representation"? We won that struggle, more than two hundred years ago, and if the people—through their sovereign representatives—decide upon taxation, that is precisely our system in operation. News analyst Daniel Schorr likes to tell of the irate citizen, complaining about the cost of the S&L bailout, who suggested in exasperation that the money shouldn't come from the taxpayers, but from "the government.")

And what about the infringement on the freedom of those persons forced to suffer alone because of infirmity, racism, or accident of birth? Freedom to spend all of our money as we please—that is, freedom from taxes—must be balanced against freedom of opportunity, and the freedom provided by a just society. What about forcible redistribution? Is that unethical? Robin Hood was a hero in theory, in myth, in the popular imagination. But in practice? The truth is that we look to government to be a sort of Robin Hood, although to conservatives, government feels more like Bad King John. (Good King Richard, you see, when he returns from the Crusades, will institutionalize a kind of Robin Hoodism and make things right . . . thus proving to be not just Lion-Hearted but also Kind-Hearted.) We have a form of Robin Hoodism right now; it is called the progressive income tax, and it is the product of the Progressives—that is, the liberals of their day.[26]

Those who worry that affirmative government will lead to tyranny need to be reminded of the lessons of history. Tyrants arise from the weakness of inept governments, not from the successes of effective ones. Thus, Lenin and Stalin came to power in the Soviet Union largely because the last czar, Nicholas II, was rather bumbling and ineffectual, unable or unwilling to initiate the reforms that might have saved his regime. And the same can be said for Aleksandr Kerensky, who briefly headed an interim, "Menshivik" government after the czar was

---

[26]To no one's surprise, the various conservative Bad King Johns—notably Ronald Reagan and his cronies—consider the progressive income tax to be a great evil. They seek constantly to equalize the tax rate regardless of income, or (better yet from their perspective) make it truly *regressive*: a fixed amount regardless of income. Margaret Thatcher successfully instituted such a "poll tax" in Great Britain, whereupon this triumph of conservative regressivism rebounded substantially to her undoing.

ousted but before Bolshevism triumphed. Similarly, Hitler's rise to power was a direct result of the incompetence and inadequacy of the democratic Weimar government that preceded him. Mussolini, for his part, would never have become *Il Duce* if the post–World War I Italian government had been effective and if it had had the best interests of the Italian people at heart.

But the reality is that most conservatives are not really worried that liberalism will degenerate into dictatorship. Rather, they resent the fact that liberals threaten to diminish one very limited aspect of their freedom: Freedom to spend their money as they choose. Paradoxically, the road to freedom is paved with restrictions on personal liberty. We accept all sorts of legal infringements on our behavior and liberty, of which the loss of total freedom over the disbursement of our money is but one. Most of these are rules and regulations concerning what we *cannot* do: We cannot murder, or steal, or blackmail, or engage in fraud. Interestingly, there are no comparably affirmative injunctions: We can be prevented from taking our clothes off in public, but we may not be forced to wear clothes of a particular sort. We can be prohibited from libel, but we cannot be forced to say something nice about another person (even a politician).

Does this mean that government—or more positively, society—may only prevent and not require actions? Hardly. We may be forced to serve in the armed forces, and in fact, conservatives are particularly enthusiastic when it comes to demanding such service. Is there a difference, then, between society requisitioning one's body for the military and one's money for social programs? The former is ostensibly a response to some threat to society's existence and freedom; so too is the latter. It is just that in the case of the military, the threat is external, whereas in the case of social difficulties, it is internal. Was the war in Vietnam, for example, more crucial to our national security than the war on poverty? And has "fighting" the Cold War helped us more than would a fight against greenhouse warming?

On balance, the tax collector asks far less than the draft board; it is much less demanding to have some of our money conscripted than all of our body, if only because we might lose all of the latter, whereas in the former case—at least, when liberals have their way—governments are careful to take amounts only from those who have large amounts to give. Like Nathan Hale, each of us has only one life to give for our country, but some have lots of money! (Not that we must render up our taxes with giddy patriotic enthusiasm; even Mr. Hale presumably would have preferred to itemize deductions, or even to file late if he had the option.)

A favorite conservative barb is that liberals want nothing more than to "tax and tax, spend and spend." This phrase was actually initiated by FDR's superassistant and adviser, Harry Hopkins, although Reagan and Bush always leave out Hopkins's conclusion, "elect and elect." The point is that when government provides services that people appreciate, they respond not only with their gratitude, but with their votes. Liberals are without doubt more inclined toward taxation, so long as it is progressive: that is, if those better able to absorb the costs are asked to do so, not only by establishing a tax rate (percentage of income) rather than a fixed amount for everybody, but also by establishing gradations in that rate, with those at the top paying a higher percentage. The result is a far cry from the Marxists' goal of "from each according to his ability, to each according to his need." It also differs substantially from the ideal of conservatives, in which government would threaten the commies abroad and other miscreants at home, but aside from these "security" provisions, presumably no one would pay any taxes. In this conservative nirvana, the rich would purchase private educations for their own children, contract privately for garbage collection and other services (and of course, take care of their own medical needs and retirement), while the poor and the environment could go to hell.

Liberals see things differently. They recognize that we have problems, but that even though we experience these problems personally, as individuals, they are in fact shared. And moreover, they recognize that shared problems demand shared solutions. They also recognize—with William Leuchtenberg, biographer of Roosevelt and Truman—that government is "not part of the problem, it is part of the answer."[27]

---

[27] Quoted in Robert Kuttner, *The Life of the Party* (New York: Viking, 1987).

Chapter 7 Civil Liberties and Other "Values"

LIBERALS ARE the preeminent defenders of civil liberties . . . occasionally to a fault, at least in the eyes of some voters in recent years. Thus, liberals have been criticized as being more concerned about the rights of criminals than of their victims, more worried about avoiding a straitjacket of authoritarianism than establishing discipline and self-reliance, more permissive than directive.

They also have a kind of moral humility. Thus, whereas liberals may be anything but humble in criticizing the moral imperialism of others—they can be fierce in defending the ideal of freedom—when it comes to what should be going on within people's minds or homes or bedrooms, liberals lack the strident certainty of the right wing. The great legal theorist Montesquieu ushered in modern legislation and was seen in his time as shocking and revolutionary for his view that law must be relative, that there are few if any moral absolutes. "Liberty," wrote Montesquieu, with more than a touch of irony, "is the right to do whatever the law permits." The challenge, therefore, is to create laws that permit and encourage behavior that accords with our sense of liberty.

140

Although flexibility and open-mindedness are strengths of liberalism and among its most defining qualities, they also make the liberal seemingly weak-kneed and lacking in conviction as compared with his or her conservative counterparts.

Conservatives are not shy about seeking to impose their particular brand of social morality on others:

> They [the Moral Majority and its ilk] know what kind of sex is bad, which books are fit for public libraries, what place religion should have in education and family life, when human life begins, that contraception is sin, and that abortion is capital sin. They think the rest of us should be forced to practice what they preach.[1]

Conservatives always seem to be worrying that some social policy or innovation will lead to the imminent moral collapse of society. Liberals, by contrast, worry less about other people's morality and more about their actual well-being; their inclination is to let each of us watch out for his or her own morality. Take, for example, the following episode: A study conducted by the National Academy of Science concluded in 1986 that the increase in black teenaged pregnancy could best be controlled by increasing the availability of condoms, birth control pills, and abortions. *The Wall Street Journal*—a premier conservative mouthpiece—was outraged. Editorially, the *Journal* contrasted the conservative and liberal view: Liberals misguidedly seek to "develop programs whose implementation will ameliorate a social problem within a given class of people" (as though that is a bad thing!), while conservatives are rightfully concerned with fostering "individual responsibility," including "implied responsibility for one's failings or personal inadequacies."[2]

In short, poor young blacks—as individuals—should simply shape up. But what about the individual responsibility of rich white men, of the sort who regularly read *The Wall Street Journal*? What a neat way to discharge this responsibility, to wag their collective fingers at those having unwanted babies, lecturing them to improve their private morality rather than dig-

---

[1] Ronald Dworkin, "Why Liberals Should Believe in Equality," *New York Review of Books*, February 1983.
[2] *The Wall Street Journal*, December 15, 1986.

ging into their pockets to help provide real assistance. In fact, liberals are all in favor of private morality and self-discipline, but they also believe in the additional private morality that mandates socially responsible behavior not only on the part of the underclass, but the upperclass as well. And moreover, liberals are appropriately hesitant about telling anyone what to do with their private sex lives.

The Wall Street Journal went on to complain that "condoms and abortions aren't social policy. They are mechanical devices masquerading as social policy." But making birth control available is in fact highly enlightened social policy; a benighted one, on the other hand, would be to forbid its availability or fail to make it accessible to people who desperately need it. For "social policy" conservatives, the ideal family-planning program would probably consist of a chorus of young black women, singing "Just say NO," or perhaps a return to the Puritans' public stocks as punishment for the morally lax. They might also look kindly on bedroom police and other infringements on personal freedom and privacy. In fact, conservatives have never been comfortable with sex, deriving as they do from a repressed, authoritarian tradition immersed in images of human sin and depravity, and, more often than not, dripping with excesses of their own personal guilt.

THE AMERICAN Civil Liberties Union—very definitely a liberal organization although one that is nonpartisan—came under withering attack during the 1988 presidential campaign. Nonetheless, Americans have consistently come down on the side of civil liberties once the issues are clearly laid out. During four remarkable months in the summer of 1987, for example, the American people looked at the somber face of a scuzzy-bearded judge and law professor, and discovered within themselves a strong dose of liberalism. (Although they preferred to call it something else, like "respect for privacy," or for "individual rights.") Judge Robert Bork had been nominated by Ronald Reagan for a seat on the Supreme Court. He believed that constitutional rights were only those intended by the framers of the Constitution, two hundred years ago, plus the various amendments—narrowly interpreted—that have been passed.

The Fourteenth Amendment, for example, calls for equal

protection under the laws for all persons. When passed, it was intended to apply to blacks and not—according to conservative advocates of "strict constructionism"—to gender discrimination. Similarly, it was Judge Bork's view that since the Constitution never specified a "right" to abortion, none could be derived from it. As recently as 1965, the dissemination of contraceptives was illegal in Connecticut, and an official with Planned Parenthood was actually convicted of prescribing a diaphragm for a married woman. The case was appealed to the Supreme Court, which overturned the conviction, finding that there existed an unwritten series of "zones of privacy," including birth control by a married couple. Writing in a law journal in 1967, Bork condemned this decision. Twenty years later, Harvard law professor Laurence Tribe correctly pointed out, on a Sunday news talk program, that Judge Bork "would not allow the Constitution to be used to protect even the right to use birth control." Judge Bork had in fact rejected the claim of a "right to privacy." During his confirmation hearings, Bork asked rhetorically, "Privacy to do what, Senator? . . . privacy to use cocaine in private? Privacy for business to fix prices in a hotel room?" But Americans believed (and still believe) overwhelmingly in personal privacy, so long as the public welfare is not threatened, and Mr. Bork was rejected.[3]

For all their concern for class, group, and community, for social solutions to social problems, liberals maintain a core belief in the inviolability of the individual. Each of us is surrounded, essentially, by a bubble, a private sphere into which government must not intrude. It is a tradition that can be traced directly to the German philosopher Immanuel Kant, and to numerous Greek philosophers long before. More recently, John Rawls, one of the most influential liberal political philosphers, has written: "Each person possesses an inviolability founded on justice that even the welfare of society as a whole cannot override . . . the rights secured by justice are not subject to political bargaining or to the calculus of social interests."[4]

There are two trends within modern-day conservatism, which

---

[3] Instead, we got Anthony Kennedy as well as Antonin Scalia, who may well be worse!

[4] John Rawls, *A Theory of Social Justice* (New York: Oxford University Press, 1971).

exist in uneasy alliance with each other: economic individualism, in the style of Milton Friedman, and personal moralism,
à la Jerry Falwell. The issue of abortion, along with fundamentalists' headstrong insistence on universal acceptance of their
moral vision, threatens this coalition of economic yuppies and
the religious right. Liberals, by contrast, believe that government should protect rights, not promote private virtue. They
are not at all sure that they received the one revealed truth,
like Moses returning from the mountain. On the other hand,
moralists and religious fundamentalists have no such doubts:
They are right and everyone else is wrong. Where liberals fear
to tread, they rush in with the certainty of the True Believer.

When it comes to our personal privacy and individual rights,
there is a lot to be said for watching our step. Despite their
rhetoric of individual freedom, it is actually conservatives who
favor restrictions on our personal liberties: loyalty oaths, censorship, drug and lie-detector tests, prohibitions on abortion,
nosy intervention into our private sexual practices. "Where
liberalism wants to regulate corporations and liberate individuals," notes Arthur M. Schlesinger, Jr., conservatism "wants
to liberate corporations and regulate individuals."[5]

According to conservative intellectuals such as Norman
Podhoretz, liberals are hopeless "relativists," whereas conservatives are rock-solid moralists, with the courage to say forthrightly that "some things are right and some things are wrong."
Unfortunately, this "courage" extends to an intrusive arro-
gance when it comes to issues that belong within the realm of
personal privacy. It is also ironic that conservatives accuse liberals of being soft on morality: It is precisely liberalism that
holds that morality belongs in government policy. Conservatives would abandon the major ethical responsibilities of government, just as they have shown a marked tendency—when
in government themselves—to abandon personal ethics as well.
It is actually the liberals who proclaim forthrightly that some
things are wrong: notably, conservative efforts to make us into
an uncaring society, and to dilute our precious civil liberties.

The 1980s gave us a searing vision of conservative values,
or, as Laurence Shames summed it up, a lack of values:

---

[5] Arthur M. Schlesinger, Jr., *The Cycles of American History* (Boston: Houghton Mifflin, 1986).

Consumption without excuses and without the need of justification—the beauty part was that it finessed the irksome question of values and of purpose. During the past decade, many people came to believe there didn't have to *be* a purpose. The mechanism didn't require it. Consumption kept the workers working, which kept the paychecks coming, which kept the people spending, which kept inventors inventing and investors investing, which meant there was more to consume. The system, properly understood, was independent of values and needed no philosophy to prop it up. It was a perfect circle, complete in itself—and empty in the middle.[6]

I prefer to look at it differently: Few people really lack values, and that even includes conservatives. The rapist, for example, has values: He values raping. Charles Keating, Michael Milken, and Ivan Boesky have values: They value money, and the exploitation of the poor, the weak, and the ethical. None of these folks lacks values; it is just that their values stink. The 1980s were preeminently a decade of values: lousy, right-wing values of greed, selfishness, and shortsightedness. We can do better.

ECONOMIC AND social issues raise substantial moral questions. Liberals recognize, for example, that the pursuit of self-interest does not deserve moral priority. It may be a right—so long as others are not harmed, as by robbing a bank, engaging in fraud, etc.—but no amount of conservative self-congratulations can make it a laudable enterprise. Even George Bush recognized this, in his inaugural address:

> What is the end purpose of this economic growth? Is it just to be rich? What a shallow ambition. Is there really any satisfaction to be had in being the fattest country? . . . What will they say of us, the Americans of the latter part of the twentieth century? That we were fat and happy? I hope not.

But then, George Bush was never really a 100 percent bona fide conservative. (It is difficult to say what George Bush really is, since his career appears to be singularly devoid of any sincere attachment to principle, other than his own personal advancement.)

---

[6]Laurence Shames, *The Hunger for More* (New York: Times Books, 1989).

Liberals would do everyone a favor if they backed off a bit on the guilt-mongering. There is nothing wrong with success and people shouldn't be made to feel guilty about wanting to succeed, or about feeling pride and pleasure in having done so. But if that is all they desire, if their life's boundaries are set by personal ambition, then they *ought* to feel guilty. Self-reliance can be distinguished from selfishness.

Whereas conservatives agitate about certain narrowly defined rights to be enjoyed by the few, liberals concern themselves with the wrongs suffered by the many. Hunger, illiteracy, drug abuse, teenage pregnancy, environmental destruction: These are not problems that simply demand our sympathy. Rather, they speak to all of us; they are legitimate matters of public as well as private conscience. And how we respond says something about our values, our moral worth as individuals and as a society. What do such problems portend for each of us, as members of a deteriorating and decreasingly competitive nation? The liberal recognition of community is crucial here, stating a morality that includes personal self-interest, but that also goes beyond it.

Conservative opposition to such liberal programs as day care, equal pay for equal work, abortion services, family leave—all this is couched in "moral" terms, as valiant efforts to defend traditional family values. But such opposition is largely due, in fact, to a deeper and typically unstated agenda: to keep women in "their place," that is, at home, barefoot and pregnant. This is a social issue, and also a profoundly moral one.

Conservatives claim to represent the ideology of personal responsibility, and they berate liberals for trying to get something for nothing, for denying the role of individual morality, the virtues of sacrifice and hard work, and so on. What a scam! In fact, the conservatives surrounding Ronald Reagan, for example, were the primo con artists of recent American history, smilingly assuring us that the United States could "have it all," without pain—indeed, without even paying for it. They promised to lower taxes, spend additional hundreds of billions of dollars on the military, and balance the budget at the same time! We'd get everything we've ever wanted and wouldn't even have to pay for it. Ronald Reagan and his conservative colleagues were masters at avoiding precisely what they claim to stand for: responsibility (fiscal as well as personal).

One of the secrets of FDR's appeal wasn't so much the New Deal itself—after all, it wasn't the New Deal but World War II that finally ended the Depression—as his ability to communicate to people that their problems were largely attributable to social forces beyond their control, not to their own shortcomings. He, like Ronald Reagan, reassured and encouraged people with the message that they should stop blaming themselves.

Fundamental to capitalist, free-market ideology is that you get what you deserve. The liberal message has historically softened this notion, explaining that personal failings should not be blamed when in fact larger social processes are at fault. Carried too far, this equates to a denial of responsibility: Rapists are simply misunderstood; homicidal thugs aren't to blame for their criminality, rather, they just didn't get hugged enough, watched too many violent cartoons, or ate too many Twinkies.

In the 1980s, conservatives spoke to the pain of those experiencing social difficulties such as drugs, crises within their families, the absence of a secure sense of community, by blaming their problems on others, notably liberal permisiveness, the Supreme Court, feminists, environmental activists, and gays, just as in foreign affairs they blamed all our troubles on the communists.

That is what the "Teflon" presidency was all about. First, claim that nothing is wrong, and if that doesn't work, don't let the fault stick to you, blame someone else. Budget deficits? That's Congress's fault. Unrest in the Third World? Communist agitators. (Or Libya, or Castro, or the "liberal media.") Crime is up? The liberals. The economy a mess? Jimmy Carter. Harry Truman had a sign on his desk in the Oval Office, saying "The buck stops here." Conservatives seem to prefer one reading, "What, me worry?" Or "The excuses start here."

WE HAVE encountered the so-called liberal lie; now it is time to meet the conservative calumny, that liberals are soft on communism, weak on defense, permissive on crime, antagonistic to religion, lacking in patriotism, and morally spineless. This was the implication behind George Bush's rather smug assertion that America shared his "values," and not those of his liberal opponent. These values were never spelled out, although the conservative calumny was clear. Bush's success with the Pledge of Allegiance and in blaming liberals such as Michael Dukakis for the criminality of black rapist Willie Horton—detestable and unfair as this tactic was—emphasized the liberals' dilemma of becoming alienated from what is a major part of their natural constituency: the nonrich, socially conservative, hard-hat voters who are proudly patriotic and honestly fearful of crime.

There is some basis for this alienation. Compared to conservatives, liberals are in fact less obsessed with a military response to communism, less inclined to throw money at the Pentagon, more likely to modulate a rigid law-and-order approach to crime with concern for its social and economic causes, less likely to be religious fundamentalists or windbag superpatriots, and more likely to feel that when it comes to personal morality, each of us should be his or her own boss.

Representative Barney Frank notes that liberals have been hurt by a kind of self-imposed censorship. Thus, liberals aren't "supposed to say that the free enterprise system is wonderful and has worked better than any other. You're not supposed to say that in our era . . . communism has been by far the worst form of government in the world, or that most people who are in prison are bad people."[7] In their eagerness to be open-minded, liberals sometimes reverse the conservatives' error, and equate an anticrime stance with being anti-black, religious convictions with being a fundamentalist loony, and patriotism with being a myopic jingoist whose knuckles drag on the ground. By treating crime, religion,and patriotism as vulgar concerns, many liberals have come to seem elitist, and distant from the worries and interests of "normal" folks. When George Bush the campaigner referred to his "values," he spoke to the deep need of Middle America to have not only a materially satisfying life, but also to have its religion, its patriotism, its family, validated and legitimated. In such cases, condescension is not appreciated.

It is not surprising that so many liberal positions have been widely misunderstood, even without conservative exaggera-

---

[7]Barney Frank, *The New York Times*, December 22, 1988.

tion and misrepresentation. Thus, it is far easier to express an ideology that simplifies—like conservatism—than one, like liberalism, that by definition considers things to be complex and subtle. Sometimes, even open-minded liberals envy the clarity and simplicity, the freedom from serious thought, that comes from seeing the world through the rigid lens of conservatism, where everything is neatly arranged and blame is readily apportioned: right versus wrong, good guy versus bad guy, honest taxpayers versus welfare cheats, God versus the devil, Us versus Them.

Because liberalism is in fact an ideology of relativism rather than absolutes, many liberals have come to worry that the public has gotten the wrong impression of just what are the moral guideposts of liberalism. For example, Jesse Jackson recognized that liberalism's emphasis on freedom during the 1960s and 1970s was mistakenly equated with personal irresponsibility, and a lack of values: "It became free speech turned into license for obscenity, pornography, abortion, smoking pot. The liberal movement got trapped with all the decadent fallout and no values."[8] And according to Martin Peretz, publisher of *The New Republic,* who has been leading that once-proud liberal flagship down dark avenues of conservative villainy, outside the economic sphere liberal ideology has increasingly become "the dogma of those who want to do as they damn well please."[9]

No one, least of all liberals, believes that people should do as they damn well please, even under the guise of freedom. "The only freedom which deserves the name is that of pursuing our own good in our own way," wrote John Stuart Mill, "so long as we do not attempt to deprive others of theirs, or impede their efforts to obtain it."[10] Thus, "freedom," for a slave, can mean emancipation; for the master, it can mean the right to keep slaves! My freedom to swing my arm ends where your nose begins.

But liberty and freedom are not this simple. In the wake of

---

[8]Quoted in Robert S. McElvaine, *The End of the Conservative Era* (New York: Arbor House, 1987).

[9]*The New Republic,* November 28, 1988.

[10]John Stuart Mill, *On Liberty* (New York: W. W. Norton and Company, 1975).

personal freedom—even when that freedom does not directly
injure someone else—there often comes inequality. And while
liberals value liberty, they also cherish equality. Historians Will
and Ariel Durant recognized the fundamental tensions between liberty and equality:

> Since practical ability differs from person to person, the major-
> ity of such abilities, in nearly all societies, is gathered in a mi-
> nority of men. The concentration of wealth is a natural result
> of this concentration of ability and regularly recurs in history.
> The rate of concentration varies . . . with the economic free-
> dom permitted by morals and the laws. Despotism may for a
> time retard the concentration; democracy, allowing the most
> liberty, accelerates it.[11]

The Durants conclude that "liberty and equality are like buck-
ets in a well. When one goes up, the other goes down." For
conservatives, this is scarcely a problem, since they are comfortable with social inequalities that are anathema to basic liberal values.

Conservatives claim to be profreedom, but in reality they
are proauthoritarian and antiequality. The only form of freedom that they really cherish is *economic* freedom.[12] Otherwise,
conservatives are quite unconcerned when personal freedom
is abridged, for example by discriminatory qualifications for
voting registration. And their enthusiasm is boundless for such
intrusions on personal freedom as restrictions on the availability of abortions, dulling the separation of Church and State,
tightening the options of accused and convicted criminals, restricting access to information under the guise of "national security," or enforcing conscription.

Conservatives also claim to support "traditional values," and
to be "profamily." And yet, their policies are precisely antifamily, especially since the traditional "Ozzie and Harriet–Leave
It to Beaver" American family hardly exists today except in
the nostalgic imagination of conservatives. In most modern

---

[11] Will and Ariel Durant, *The Lessons of History* (New York: Simon and Schuster, 1968).
[12] Even the freedom to "keep and bear arms" is primarily a matter of the
right to a special kind of property, and, incidentally, one intended to apply
to state militias, not individuals.

families, both husband and wife work; as a result, day care has become a deeply "profamily" institution. More than one quarter of American families are headed by a single parent, and 95 percent of these are women. Seventy percent of mothers with school-age children work outside the home. Given these realities, it is virtually obscene for conservatives to oppose day-care financing, and ludicrous for them to call liberals "antifamily" for doing so. The entire liberal agenda is marked by a profamily theme, from job training, assistance to family farms, tax reform for the lower and middle class, education and health benefits, maternal and child health programs, to the goal of full employment. With our needs so great, conservatives simply cannot simultaneously be profamily and anti-government.

Liberals hold firmly to the belief that restrictions on personal freedom are especially justified in matters of potential harm to others, and particularly unjustified in matters of personal expression. Conservatives reverse these priorities. Thus, conservatives are likely to interpret the Second Amendment broadly, and to oppose any restrictions on gun ownership; liberals, by contrast, are willing to restrict this aspect of our "freedom" in order to achieve greater freedom for society: freedom from avoidable accidents and homicides. On the other hand, the liberal/conservative positions tend to switch on the First Amendment. Liberal supporters (and by far, the most fervent First Amendment supporters are liberals) defend the right of people to assemble peacefully, to practice their own preferred religion, and to "speak" as freely as possible, with speech defined broadly to include just about any form of self-expression.

Such as burning the flag. On this one, even conservatives such as Antonin Scalia and Anthony Kennedy agreed with noted liberal Justice William Brennan that "the bedrock principle behind the First Amendment is that government may not prohibit the expression of an idea simply because society finds the idea itself offensive or disagreeable." In short, if we are to be free to wave the flag, we must also be free to burn it.

Unlike conservatives, liberals will vigorously defend what they oppose; for example, pornography, the right of the Ku

Klux Klan and neo-Nazis to hold rallies. Conservatives respond by exploiting this principled (and often, politically unpopular) position. "Social liberalism"—opposition to the death penalty, vigorous and unflagging defense of the Bill of Rights—has consistently been less popular than economic liberalism: protecting the little guy from the abuses of corporate power and the awful coldness of an indifferent universe.

In a time when many in the middle class have become increasingly self-satisfied and intolerant themselves, conservatives have been quick to capitalize on the politics of resentment and shortsightedness. Thus, they have increasingly jettisoned civil liberties and sought to brand the ACLU and similar groups as the "criminals' lobby," and in other ways "out of the mainstream" of American political life. In doing so, they show themselves to be opportunists rather than true conservatives. And they obscure the distinction between defending the right to a practice and endorsing that practice. In defending the rights of unpleasant minorities, or of people to express unpopular ideas or to do distasteful but nonharmful things, liberals are in good company. They are keeping faith with the sage advice of Thomas Jefferson's first inaugural: "If there be any among us who wish to dissolve this union, or to change its republican form, let them stand undisturbed, as monuments to the safety with which error of opinion may be tolerated where reason is left free to combat it."

Conservatives, by contrast, are much less willing or able to tolerate erroneous opinions. They claim that to permit, say, flag-burning as an exercise of free speech is to support desecration of our national symbol, or that opposition to school prayer is to oppose religion in general and prayer in particular, or that only extremists defend the rights of fascists (or communists).

In their own defense, liberals sometimes argue that morality ought not be legislated. This is a slippery slope, however; once started down, the brakes are difficult to apply. Thus, the next step is a kind of moral relativism: "Who is to say what is right?" But if values aren't worth defending, then what about the values of tolerance, fairness, liberty, diversity, rationality, etc.?—that is, the basic tenets of liberalism itself. Clearly, there are decent, humane values that warrant being legislated and enforced. No one ever said that defending these values—against conservatives—was going to be easy.

Liberalism stands accused, by conservatives, of weakening social, family, and national bonds. During the 1930s, Nazi thinkers excoriated liberals for exalting the atomistic individual at the expense of the organic, romantic "state" and "people." They hated liberalism's belief in the primacy of rights. Zealots of the far right and left are similar in romanticizing a tight little world in which everyone agrees: either with the Party line, or with the State and about the nature of God. Liberals are different. They believe in diversity, in the privitization of morality. They detest moral imperialism. They believe (of course) that they are correct, but like Voltaire, they will defend their neighbor's right to disagree with them.

Liberals, for example, generally favor a woman's right to an abortion, believing that this procedure should be the private concern of a patient and her doctor. They oppose attempts to restrict or limit this right. But liberal journals are filled with soul-searching debate about the personal implications—moral, physical, psychological—of this position. Conservatives are generally opposed to abortion rights, but unlike their liberal colleagues, conservatives seem to have very few qualms about such a stance. While liberals examine and debate, always trying to see every side of every question, conservatives are serenely convinced that there is only one correct answer: theirs.

Liberals may admire the confidence that such certainty must generate. But they cannot share it . . . not because they are more likely to be wrong, but because their own way of thinking precludes such comforting (and potentially dangerous) absolutism.

Take crime. Some liberals have had a tendency to minimize the problem, to see it as hysteria, a cover for repression of minorities and dissidents. And so, they emphasized protection for the accused, restrictions on police, and so forth. Conservative zealousness for law enforcement did—and still does, in fact—constitute a real threat to civil liberties (consider the excesses of Attorney General John Mitchell during the Nixon years), but crime also posed such a threat, and still does. By combining suppression of legitimate political gatherings and dissent with a general call for "law and order," conservatives linked street crime with the free expression of constitutional rights. So liberals, in defending the latter, found themselves accused of being soft on the former.

Government does have an obligation to ensure public safety; this is legitimately part of a liberal social agenda no less than a conservative one. In fact, since the poor and disadvantaged are disproportionately the victims of crime, their advocates have if anything greater reason to be concerned. Yet, liberals can seem elitist, insofar as they are relatively well-off, living in areas where street crime is much less frequent. And so, liberals tended to opt out of what should have been their role in the 1980s; they should have raised holy hell over the Reagan Administration's phony "war" on drugs and crime, and its continuation by George Bush. This feeble and misguided "war" focuses on enforcement, and not very much of that, while leaving the inner cities painfully vulnerable to crime by skimping on social supports, drug treatment, and delinquincy prevention programs.

A balanced liberal approach would recognize the need for a more effective criminal justice system. It would also continue recognizing that the rights of criminals are real, as are the rights of accused criminals, who—let us remember—are innocent until proven guilty. (Reagan's attorney general, Edwin Meese, once made the extraordinary statement that people wouldn't be suspects unless they were guilty; accused of personal wrongdoing himself, Mr. Meese subsequently discovered the wisdom of the presumption of innocence.)

Most important, as the crime commission formed by Lyndon Johnson in 1966 put it, crime is a very difficult problem, but one that can be reduced: "Society must seek to prevent crime before it happens by assuring all Americans a stake in the benefits and responsibilities of American life." The liberal view of crime considers it in the context of families, of repeat offenders, of alienated and hopeless youth, not just by reflexly calling for more jails and more hanging judges. Liberal anticrime thinking is based on this fundamental wisdom, as W. H. Auden put it: "What all schoolchildren learn,/Those to whom evil is done/Do evil in return."

Elliott Currie, of the Institute for the Study of Social Change, at the University of California at Berkeley, identifies three kinds of liberal responses to crime: retreatism, minimalism, and realism. Those who call us to retreat wish to emulate the conservatives: Proclaim our devotion to law and order, and demand tougher sentencing and more enforcement. Who cares that it doesn't work—the important thing for the retreatists is that a tough stance against crime is often politically popular, especially in an era that has allowed itself to believe that liberal anticrime programs have failed. Shockingly few serious rehabilitation efforts are now underway in the United States; most prisons and so-called reformatories do little more than warehouse criminals until their release. And upon release, ex-convicts find themselves lacking job skills and in a socially toxic environment, made in large part by conservative opposition to various social-betterment programs. Yet it is precisely these liberal anticrime programs that get the blame when recidivism rates remain high, along with crime rates themselves. It is as though we build a reasonably good airplane but fail to construct an adequate runway; then, when the plane crashes upon landing, after bumping into boulders and careening down ravines, the aircraft designers are blamed, and the conclusion drawn that airplanes obviously will never work!

The liberal minimalist view has also caused trouble. It minimizes the problem, simply preferring to talk about something else. Some liberals worry that crime, like welfare fraud, gives conservatives ammunition to twist and distort the facts as well as manipulate public emotion. Minimizers are also prone to see worry about crime—especially street crime—as racism in disguise. But law enforcement isn't for conservatives alone; for liberals, too, government has an obligation to provide for public safety.

Finally, the liberal realist position offers the most hope. It looks unblinkingly at the problem and tries to solve it, through social betterment as well as evenhanded enforcement. Liberal realism requires money, however, as well as patience. By the late 1960s, serious efforts at reconstructing the inner cities became yet another casualty of the Vietnam War. Conservatives, by contrast, at least had a certain rhetorical simplicity and verbal boldness, even bellicosity: hang 'em high, or lock 'em up and throw away the key. Nonetheless, liberals can empha-

size—over and over—that it was during conservative administrations that the drug epidemic, for example, has multiplied.

Republicans have controlled the White House for eighteen
of the past twenty-two years. They have made every Supreme
Court appointment of the last twenty-four years. Yet we have
a huge and growing crime problem. The two-part conservative "anticrime strategy" has been in place since the mid-1970s:
(1) deny an affirmative role for government in bettering the
lot of those most at risk for crime, along with (2) increased
incarceration. The results? Crime rates are up, along with the
prison census. Our prison inmate population has more than
tripled in fifteen years; at present, there are more than a million Americans behind bars and new prison beds are needed
at a rate of one thousand per week. It is not softhearted judges
and woolly-brained liberals who produce furlough and work-
release programs, but budget restrictions and local community
resistance to more jails, along with the shameful neglect of
America's underclass by the country's conservative leadership. In the face of terrifying new problems, public resources
were deliberately withdrawn, especially from the inner cities
where the crime rate is the highest. And who gets the blame?
Liberals . . . for a crime epidemic that has if anything been
exacerbated by conservative mean-spiritedness, shortsightedness, and neglect.

MODERN-DAY LIBERALS most assuredly have a fondness
for government, not as an end in itself, but, as we have seen,
as an affirmative expression of collective goodwill and in pursuit of social betterment, widely shared. Of course, there is
always the possibility of excess, Big Government could become Big Brother. But in fact, more than any other political
creed, liberalism is a friend of civil liberties. Our fundamental
freedoms—of expression, of assembly, of religion—the entire
pantheon of America's cherished democratic and civil rights,
are valued and defended more by liberals than by anyone else.
These rights have very definitely been under attack in the past,
sometimes by the United States government itself, most often
under the auspices of a conservative administration or legislator. And most often liberals—along with those farther to the
left—were the victims.

The wretched excesses of McCarthyism are the most important recent example, when the unscrupulous, megalomaniacal Republican senator from Wisconsin conducted his singular version of anticommunist witch-hunts during the early 1950s. But Joe McCarthy was only one in a series of homegrown threats to American civil liberties, all of which, interestingly, were carried out by a federal government grown too big for its britches, too intolerant of dissent, and controlled by conservatives.

The Alien and Sedition Acts, for example. They came in the wake of the first Cold War in American history, a time of undeclared hostilities against France in 1798. The Sedition Act was particularly abominable: It made it illegal to publish anything that was seriously critical of the president or Congress. Ten people were actually convicted under this law, which clearly overstepped the Bill of Rights:

> A New Jersey editor, for example, was fined $100 for hoping in print that the wad of a cannon fired in a presidential salute might hit President John Adams on the seat of his pants. A Vermont Jeffersonian, who accused the President in a campaign speech of "unbounded thirst for ridiculous pomp, foolish adulation, and a selfish avarice," received a thousand-dollar fine and four months in jail.[13]

Fortunately, Adams was defeated in the next election, and the offending laws were repealed.

Perhaps the greatest offenses against American liberty were the notorious Palmer raids, named for Attorney General A. Mitchell Palmer, toward the end of World War I, and for two years afterward. Unlike the Second World War, the First was not a particularly "good" war: Although we were supposedly fighting to "make the world safe for democracy," our allies included czarist Russia, for example, which was the most absolutist and nondemocratic country of the Old World, if not the Whole World. Moreover, the "Great War" was fought for no particularly good reason, but rather because of massive blunders, stupidity, and stubbornness. As a result, unlike World War II, which was widely supported by the American people,

---

[13] Arthur M. Schlesinger, Jr., *The Vital Center* (Boston: Houghton Mifflin; 1949).

World War I was unpopular, generating antiwar protests which
led in turn to an episode of repression that most Americans
would rather ignore, and which is rarely taught in high school
civics classes, but which we had better not forget. Over forty
years ago, historian Arthur M. Schlesinger, Jr., recounted the
horror of those times:

> The Espionage Act of 1917 and the Alien Act of 1918 had given
> the Government broad powers to arrest persons whose of-
> fenses might range all the way from treason down to grum-
> bling. During the war these laws were applied, to put it mildly,
> with sternness. Rose Pastor Stokes, for example, received a ten-
> year jail sentence for writing in a letter, "I am for the people,
> and the government is for the profiteers." Men were thrown
> in jail for hot words overheard in trains, in hotel lobbies or
> even around the dinner table in the boarding house.
>
> But the forces of repression were just warming up. By 1919,
> with the war over, A. Mitchell Palmer saw the opportunity of
> making a political career out of post-war anxieties. While Wil-
> son lay ill in the White House, Palmer detonated the famous
> Red Scare. As the Attorney General, struggling in the grip of
> metaphor, described the situation a few months later, "Like a
> prairie-fire, the blaze of revolution was sweeping over every
> American institution of law and order a year ago. It was eating
> its way into the homes of the American workman, its sharp
> tongues of revolutionary heat were licking the altars of the
> churches, leaping into the belfry of the school bell, crawling
> into the sacred corners of American homes, seeking to replace
> marriage vows with libertine laws, burning up the foundations
> of society."
>
> It is hard to do justice in brief space to the permutations and
> vagaries of the Palmer terror. He liked to work in large mag-
> nitudes, and scorned what he called the "nice distinctions drawn
> between the theoretical ideals of the radicals and their actual
> violations of our national laws." Unpopular ideas were his tar-
> get, not illegal acts. At one moment in 1919, he herded to-
> gether 249 aliens, without benefit of court trial, and shipped
> them off summarily to Russia. On New Year's Day, 1920, he
> conducted simultaneous raids on radical centers through the
> country, sent his agents into homes, with or without warrants,
> to seize persons and property, and crowded the jails with the
> desperate characters trapped in his dragnet.
>
> The mass raid hardly lived up to advance notices. Palmer
> captured over four thousand presumably sinister individuals,
> but only three revolvers and no dynamite at all—not quite the
> raw material for the great conspiracy. Yet his alarming noises

did succeed in spreading a contagion of fear. In Hartford, Connecticut, for example, all visitors at the jail inquiring after friends caught in the raid were themselves arrested on the ground that this solicitude was prima facie evidence of Communist affiliation. The result through the country was the rise of vigilantism—that is, of minor officials or private persons bent on assuming for themselves the prerogatives of trying, convicting and punishing unpopular characters. In the trail of Palmer came months of panic, intolerance and repression.[14]

The point is worth repeating: Big Government poses certain dangers, particularly suppression of dissent, but this danger is much more likely to be wielded by conservatives, against liberals and other noncomformists of the left, than by liberals against anyone.

There is simply no question about it: Our civil liberties are far safer in the hands of liberals. This is because liberals cherish them, both because they are central to liberal thinking and because liberals themselves lack the certainty and inclination toward authoritarianism that is so characteristic of conservatives, and so dangerous to civil liberties. Conservatives are far more prone to the demagoguery of an A. Mitchell Palmer or Joseph McCarthy, than are liberals, who are almost anatomically unsuited to behaving repressively: They are too wedded to intellectual freedom and convinced that most truths are relative.

Conservatives traditionally have been comfortable employing the machinery of government to stifle dissent. Recall Nixon's "enemies list," the whole mind-set leading to Watergate, Ronald Reagan's efforts to smear and red-bait the nuclear-freeze movement, efforts to gut the Freedom of Information Act, unleashing of the FBI against groups opposed to American complicity with South African apartheid, and others such as CISPES (Committee in Solidarity with the People of El Salvador), which have struggled against interventionism in Central America. In *The New York Times* of October 26, 1988, a group of prominent liberals (including John Kenneth Galbraith, George Kennan, and Arthur M. Schlesinger, Jr.,) purchased space to publish "A Reaffirmation of Principle," in which they noted that "lib-

---

[14] Ibid.

eral principles—freedom, tolerance, and the protection of the rights of every citizen—are timeless." They also noted that liberalism seeks "the institutional defense of decency," not just a personal defense, but an *institutional* defense; that is, it labors to enroll the institutions of government on behalf of civil liberties, and a higher morality than that of the unbridled marketplace, thought police, or bedroom patrollers.

Barbara Ehrenreich points out that the 1980s saw a return to at least one grouping of so-called traditional values: "bigotry, greed, and belligerence."[15] But there are other traditional values as well, all of them deeply American and quintessentially liberal: dissent, compassion, fairness.

Anyone who thinks that our civil liberties are safer and our values better defended by conservatives would do well to think again.

---

[15] Barbara Ehrenreich, *The Worst Years of Our Lives* (New York: Pantheon, 1990).

Chapter 8 Vital Center or Wishy-Washy Middle?

Like the great Tao of Chinese wisdom, liberalism is the middle way. It is neither here nor there, but rather, somewhere in between. It recoils equally from the hypernationalistic, grotesquely individualistic, and often theocratic far right, as well as from the superstatist, freedom-denying, and rigidly authoritarian far left. It advocates reason and compromise, tolerance and civil liberties, a mixed economy that takes the best from capitalism and social democracy without toadying to either. Liberalism not only defies the extremes of right and left, to a great degree it *defines* those extremes. Right-wing extremists can be identified by how far they are willing to depart from the social responsibility that is imbedded in modern liberal ideals, and left-wing extremists, by their departure from the liberal commitment to civil liberties. In Eastern Europe today, it seems likely that people will be seeking a comparable middle way, between the oppression of the right—which they knew all too well under Nazism—and that of the post–World War II left, from which they are finally emerging. (On the other hand, it would not be surprising if countries such as Poland and Hungary experiment first with a rather doctrinaire ver-

161

sion of free-market capitalism. And then, after the shocks of unemployment, unaffordable goods, homelessness, and a sudden loss of medical and educational benefits, watch for these states to grope toward a system that is "kinder and gentler"—that is, more liberal.)

In the absence of a genuine, credible, homegrown left in the United States, liberalism has often seemed left wing. But in fact, it is only mildly left of center, espousing a mixed system that blends the best of right and left. American liberalism received its modern form during the 1930s, after the shock of the Great Depression. As Arthur M. Schlesinger, Jr., describes it:

> When FDR became President at the depths of the Great Depression, many said he had only two choices: the laissez-faire alternative—political freedom combined with economic collapse; or the totalitarian alternative—economic security (it was supposed) combined with political tyranny. Against this grim either/or choice Roosevelt offered a third possibility: a mixed system that would give the state the power to expand economic and social opportunity without giving it the power to suppress political opposition and civil freedom.[1]

The result, at least in theory, is the best of both worlds. And this seems to hold in practice as well. But at the same time, being in the middle means that you can be attacked from both sides. This also has been the case.

Liberals have been criticized, for example, for failures of patriotism (not enough) and of citizenship as well (too much). They do not shy away from patriotism or from citizenship; their conception of the former is simply more positive (love of country) than negative (hatred of others). As a result, they often come across—unfairly—as lacking in resolve. Similarly, their view of citizenship is social rather than isolated, of community rather than solitary achievement. Once again, it is positive (helping, caring, making things better), rather than negative.

---

[1] Arthur M. Schlesinger, Jr., "Liberalism: What It Was, Where It Is," paper delivered at "FDR and the Future of Liberalism" conference, Hyde Park, N.Y., October 1989.

Liberals are to capitalism what arms controllers are to the nuclear arms race: Their highest goal is to manage it. In this sense, they do not aim terribly high. As Richard Hofstadter put it, liberals in the United States sought "first to broaden the numbers of those who could benefit from the American bonanza and then to help humanize its workings and help heal its casualties." They do not aim to end capitalism altogether, or to replace it with something else, but rather, to smooth out its rough edges and make it operate more smoothly and safely (and profitably, too). Their goal: capitalism with a human face. No wonder they are scorned by critics on the left. Like arms controllers, the liberals' goal is stability, whereas more radical opponents want to *de*stabilize the system—whether nuclear or capitalist—and make it over.

A similar condition holds for social patterns, such as women's rights. John Stuart Mill, for example, extended the defense of the individual to include women, proposing complete equality of the sexes, to be enforced by law. For the liberal Mr. Mill, status should not in any way be defined by birth; thus, he advocated the elimination of any "birthright" distinctions between men and women. Although his proposed methods were moderate enough—legislation—his goals were seen as radical at the time. Those same goals, and methods, remain attractive and appropriate for liberals today.

Radicals see things differently. Whereas liberals seek to use the existing machinery of government to redress social problems, radicals consider that these problems themselves lie too deep for any law, any mere tinkering, to reach. We need surgery, they argue: radical surgery. We can extend property rights to women, they maintain, but if marriage itself is still a relationship of domination and ownership, then nothing fundamental will have changed. If the existing arrangements need changing, then it won't do simply to integrate women (or blacks, for that matter) into these arrangements, any more than it is acceptable to "live with" nuclear weapons by incorporating them into our "defense" establishment.

To many radicals of the left, therefore, liberals simply don't allow themselves to dream as imaginatively as they might, or to act as boldly as they should. They are too quick to accept things as they are, too ready to be apologists for the establishment too happy to be cheerful tinkerers. They are willing, even eager, to obtain social freedom for women, or minorities, or to legislate medical, educational, and other entitlements. But there is a radical viewpoint—one worth listening to—that questions the very granting of freedom as opposed to the *winning* of it. According to this approach:

> All freedom is essentially self-liberation—I can have only as much freedom as I procure for myself . . . If they [i.e., the liberals] nevertheless give you freedom, they are simply knaves who give more than they have. For then they give you nothing of their own, but stolen wares: they give you your own freedom, the freedom that you must take for yourselves; and they *give* it to you only that you may not take it and call the thieves and cheats to account to boot. In their slyness they know well that given (chartered) freedom is not freedom, since only the freedom one *takes* for himself, therefore the egoist's freedom, rides with full sails. Donated freedom strikes its sails as soon as there comes a storm—or calm; it requires always a gentle and moderate breeze.[2]

A gentle and moderate breeze is precisely the climate that liberalism handles best. It spreads too much sail for the gusty winds of fundamental discontent: Liberal policies may well capsize in stormy seas. And liberalism lacks the power to propel its craft when the winds are very light. It is too easily becalmed in quiet seas of indifference and apathy. But then again, for the moderate breezes that governments most often experience—and that the overwhelming majority of their citizens ardently desire—liberalism may well be the best possible ship of state.

RADICALS ENSHRINE the struggle no less than the end product. "In the battle for freedom," wrote Emma Goldman," . . . it is the struggle for, not so much the attainment of, liberty, that develops all that is strongest, sturdiest, and finest in human character."[3] Liberals would not agree; they would rather succeed than fight. Even if the success is modest.

At the same time as radicals of the left criticize liberals for

---

[2]Max Stirner, *The Ego and Its Own* (London: The Trinity Press, 1971).
[3]Emma Goldman, *Red Emma Speaks* (New York: Vintage, 1972).

being too timid, too compromising, too eager to sign on to what they see as a fundamentally oppressive society, radicals of the right are equally negative, if not more so. To dyed-in-the-wool conservatives, liberals are incessantly dissatisfied, woolly-headed do-gooders who have a naïve faith in human nature (and in democracy), inadequate appreciation for the dangers of the welfare state, and are too quick to see problems or even to encourage discontent when in fact, our best course is to leave things alone. Most conservatives have disdain for the liberal's inclination to rock the boat . . . especially because conservatives, by and large, are likely to be happy with things as they are. Most conservatives—even those of the far right—generally acknowledge that liberals are patriotic (or at least not overtly traitorous), but feel that liberals' concern with social equality is itself enough to make them suspect. Moreover, misguided trusting souls that they are, liberals may well be "innocent dupes" of socialism . . . or worse.

The extremes of left and right take a unidimensional view of the human being in society.[4] To rightists, the magic of the free market will solve everything: Society is that which the market ordains. To leftists, a classless society will solve everything: Society is that which the Party ordains. In either conception, individual human beings don't count for much. Certainly, they don't exist importantly in relationship to others. Both these views are simple, appealing, and altogether wrong. Contrary to the title of Helen Gurley Brown's best seller, *Having it All*,[5] the truth is that we can't. And no one else can, either.

Liberty and equality often conflict. Under conditions of liberty for all, equality is likely to be trampled upon, since liberty might well be taken to include permission to take "liberties" with someone else's rights or possessions. How can you keep me from trampling on you without in some sense restricting my "freedom"? We often assume that all the good things of

---

[4] And not surprisingly, both extremes tend to be wrong. Before the democratic revolutions in Eastern Europe, the far left claimed that people living under Stalinist-style communism weren't really unhappy, whereas those of the far right maintained that such totalitarian regimes would never reform themselves.

[5] Helen Gurley Brown, *Having It All* (New York: Linden, 1982).

democracy and freedom automatically come together once we are fortunate enough to have gotten it (that is, them). Happiness, we like to think, is a package deal. But liberty and equality often conflict, and when they do, liberals tend to emphasize equality, and conservatives, liberty. In short, promoting equality requires some limits on liberty. Left-wing radicals favor even more equality and, if necessary, less liberty, while the right worships liberty and disdains equality. The result is that liberals, once again, are in-between, and both the radicals and the conservatives seem comparatively forthright, even courageous, while liberals come across as wishy-washy and indecisive.

Financial liberty does in fact run counter to certain social benefits that are attainable only via taxation; maximizing competitiveness requires trade-offs in entrepreneurial liberty; protecting the environment requires trade-offs in economic growth; and so forth. Liberalism, more than any other political philosophy, recognizes this. Along with its apparent ambivalence, liberalism also gives rise to what is fundamentally a tragic view of society, that everything is a compromise.[6] As Reinhold Niebuhr used to emphasize, any action in the political realm is filled with moral ambiguity. Our every act casts ethical shadows.

The "Vienna School" of superconservative economics, expressed notably by the likes of Friedrich von Hayek and Ludwig von Mises, claimed that free enterprise was not only exquisitely effective in allocating resources, but also that it was morally blessed, because it was intimately connected with political freedom. There has also been an influential "Chicago School," composed chiefly of Milton Friedman and George Stigler, which among other things, exemplified their special branch of right-wing economic morality by providing extensive advice to Chile's neofascist and repressive General Augusto Pinochet. Notable about such schools is that they are about as certain as they are hurtful.

Life as melodrama is an easy concept, sometimes elating and sometimes depressing, but always cathartic. Asked to

---

[6]This tragic view should not, however, be construed as morose, or even pessimistic.

choose between good and evil, most of us have no trouble. Extremists of the left and right give themselves the luxury of living in such a world, one of evil empires and welfare queens, or malevolent bourgeoisie and noble proletarians. But life as tragedy—life as the liberal sees it—is another story: Asked to choose between good and good (or bad and bad), with the addition that you must choose, you can't have them both, that by choosing one you lose the other, we find ourselves in a *genuine* quandary. Genuine, because there is literally no way out. And not surprisingly, many people resent the choice, preferring the simple certainties of one melodramatic extreme or the other.

As we have seen, classical liberalism had only a negative conception of liberty: freedom *from* the state. Later, it developed a deeper sense of liberty: freedom *to*, to develop one's self, to experience an enriching environment, and so forth. But often, we must choose between competing goals and contending limitations. Inherent in the obligation to make such a choice is a recognition (often, an unspoken one) that society is foreign, alien, antagonistic to the individual. Otherwise, the individual wouldn't need protection; there would be no anguish. And yet, the act of governing requires doing things on the level of society. Tragedy, again.

But don't get the wrong idea. Just because liberalism is sensitive to the nuances and complexities of life, and just because of its awareness of the inherent need for compromise in our social and personal lives, and just because liberalism identifies government as closer to tragedy than to melodrama does not mean that the liberal outlook is necessarily glum. Quite the opposite. As we have seen, the liberal view is essentially optimistic, based on a positive view of human potential, especially if our problems are faced honestly and with decent purpose.

Facing these problems, liberals advocate a mixed economy, a partnership between government, labor, and the private sector. Not surprisingly, they draw fire from both political extremes. To critics on the far left, such a partnership is "corporatism," a blatant cave-in to big business. To those on the far right, the liberal agenda represents statism and cryptosocialism in disguise. Liberalism struggles not only to defend itself, but to avoid the Scylla of a smothering, too-powerful (or at minimum, frustrating and inefficient) Big-Brotherish state, and the Charybdis of excessive freedom, which can spawn greed, suffering, and a chaotic blend of entrepreneurial piracy and a dangerously curtailed social contract. Threat to freedom or engine of equality: Will the real liberalism please stand up? In fact, it is neither. It is a navigational aid, an effort at steering a middle course between the great rocks of modern society. Conservatism offers an image of stability, but one that is false because it has actually run aground on the shoals of selfishness and militarism; seeking to avoid disorder, it teeters even now in the ferocious whirlpools of the religious right and of problems unaddressed when not actually exacerbated. The radical left, for its part, proposes to lead us directly onto its own rocks, hoping thereby to shake things up a bit. Liberalism, by contrast, is moderate and cautious. When navigating a fast stream with dangerous rapids, keeping to a middle way is by far the best course. It can even be exhilarating.

YEATS DESCRIBED the dilemma of the moderate liberal faced with extremists on either side: "The best lack all conviction, while the worst are full of passionate intensity." Except that liberals do not really lack conviction. Rather, their convictions are themselves moderate: Liberals believe in rationality, in freedom of thought and expression, in civil liberties for all (even those with whom they disagree), and in a social conception of citizenship and of society. Liberals also seem lacking in conviction because, ironically, one of their most strongly held convictions is that no one has a monopoly on the truth. Hence, liberal beliefs are tempered with a humility that is unknown to the radicals of right or left. According to Bertrand Russell:

> The essence of the Liberal outlook lies not in *what* opinions are held, but in *how* they are held: instead of being held dogmatically, they are held tentatively, and with a consciousness that new evidence may at any moment lead to their abandonment. This is the way opinions are held in science, as opposed to the way in which they are held in theology.[7]

---

[7] Bertrand Russell, *Unpopular Essays* (New York: Simon and Schuster, 1950).

Herein is a bit of a dilemma: how to arouse popular enthusiasm for so careful, muted, and virtually bloodless a philosophy? Sometimes, the tentativeness of liberalism may be mistaken for a lack of determination or of courage. But it is more like the tentativeness of the agnostic confronted with the fundamentalist. While the fundamentalist knows that he knows the nature of God, and what people should do about it, the agnostic knows—and with equal certainty, and probably a good deal more accuracy—that he does *not* know. The difference is that whereas the radical fundamentalist will have no hesitation in prescribing what everyone else must do, the liberal agnostic will be much more circumspect . . . although he or she will likely be equally definite that in the face of such fundamental uncertainty, humility is a deep virtue, and that certainty—which includes an eagerness to dictate to others—is a vice.

Significantly, liberalism appears to have developed historically in association with trade and commerce, the free exchange of people, goods, and ideas. Periclean Athens became liberal as soon as it became a center of commerce, as also occurred, for a time, among the early Renaissance city-states of Italy, and in upstart Holland and England, not to mention the United States a few centuries later. "The reasons for the connection of commerce with Liberalism" are, according to Russell:

> Trade brings men into contact with tribal customs different from their own, and in so doing destroys the dogmatism of the untravelled. The relation of buyer and seller is one of negotiation between two parties who are both free; it is more profitable when the buyer and seller is able to understand the point of view of the other party.[8]

As we have seen, the liberal outlook was also closely related to the emergence of capitalism and free enterprise, as the appropriate perspective for free spirits ready to sally forth into the world and make their fortunes.

In our brief exploration of the history of liberalism, we noted the important role of the eighteenth-century philosopher, John

---

[8] Ibid.

Locke. Locke also developed the philosophy of "empiricism," which emphasized the importance of facts and of experience—as opposed to arbitrary ideals—in determining our view of the world. Since empirical "truths" are likely to differ somewhat from experience to experience, and from person to person, it stands to reason that these truths are meant to be taken with a grain of salt. Thus, liberalism at its very core stands in marked contrast to dogmatic assertions of fundamental Truths that must never be challenged.

There is an underlying similarity here between the intellectual approaches of liberalism and of science, since both rely upon the consensual agreement of freely thinking individuals, rather than obeisance to received Law. Russell, again: "Scientific theories are accepted as useful hypotheses to suggest further research, and as having some element of truth in virtue of which they are able to collate existing observations; but no sensible person regards them as immutably perfect."[9] And not surprisingly, as we have seen, the Lockean, liberal, scientific approach is also highly compatible with democracy, which represents the collective will of an informed majority.

The fanatic, the zealot, the witch-hunter, book-burner, Islamic fundamentalist, Bible-beating evangelical Christian, superorthodox Jew, Marxist hard-liner, and neofascist Neanderthal—what all these people have in common is just this: They know Truth, with utter certainty and no doubts. This is what makes them dangerous. And, most assuredly, they are not liberals.

Since so much of this discussion has relied on the thought and writings of Bertrand Russell, let us close this section with some more words from England's greatest twentieth-century mathematician/philosopher:

> Dogma demands authority, rather than intelligent thought, as the source of opinion; it requires persecution of heretics and hostility to unbelievers; it asks of its disciples that they should inhibit natural kindliness in favor of systematic hatred. Since argument is not recognized as a means of arriving at truth, adherents of rival dogmas have no method except war by means

---

[9] Ibid.

of which to reach a decision. And war, in our scientific age, means, sooner or later, universal death.

I conclude that, in our day as in the time of Locke, empiricist Liberalism . . . is the only philosophy that can be adopted by a man who, on the one hand, demands some scientific evidence for his beliefs, and, on the other hand, desires human happiness more than the prevalence of this or that party or creed. Our confused and difficult world needs various things if it is to escape disaster, and among these one of the most necessary is that, in the nations which still uphold Liberal beliefs, these beliefs should be wholehearted and profound, not apologetic towards dogmatisms of the right and of the left, but deeply persuaded of the value of liberty, scientific freedom, and mutual forbearance. For without these beliefs life on our politically divided but technically unified planet will hardly continue to be possible.[10]

Is THE moderation of liberals a sign of their virtue, or of a failure of nerve? Arthur M. Schlesinger, Jr., called liberalism the "vital center." Critics, on the other hand, think of liberals as occupying a kind of flabby, invertebrate middle. And during the 1988 campaign, when for months Michael Dukakis refused to acknowledge his liberalness—never mind campaign on it—this negative perception of liberals as lacking in the courage of their convictions was reinforced.

It hasn't always been this way. The middle has often been a good place to be in American politics. Thus, Harry Truman experienced secessions from both the right and left in 1948, when the left wing of the Democratic Party split off to form the Progressive Party, nominating FDR's former vice president Henry A. Wallace (seeking a less virulent anticommunism), while a group of southerners, led by South Carolina's Governor (later Senator) Strom Thurmond (trying to halt progress on civil rights), split off on the right. It didn't stop Truman from being elected, however, largely because Truman himself had the good sense to stand up for what he believed, and because liberals had something tangible to offer the American people.

They still do. It seems likely, for example, that the environment will be the next great national and global issue. Yet, as

---

[10] Ibid.

measured by their regard for the natural environment, and their track records on environmental protection and achieving a sustainable way of life, both capitalism and communism have been dismal flops. Under capitalism, it may be concluded, people exploit people, whereas under communism . . . it's the other way around. Either way, it is the environment that is endangered. Communist environmentalists look longingly at capitalism, arguing that if people only owned their own land, they would be likely to care for it; capitalist environmentalists, in turn, look longingly at socialism, thinking that if land were only owned by the people as a whole, they would not be inclined to rape and pillage it, selling its resources to the highest bidder, extracting short-term profits at the cost of long-term degradation. The grass appears greener (an appropriate environmental hue) on the other side of the ideological fence. A compromise between private and public ownership—that is, a mixed economy designed along liberal themes—would doubtless offer the best prospects for ecological harmony.

But in the United States most especially, people fear state-sponsored solutions. We have often been inclined to see the state as a regrettable burden, an unfortunate imposition on our free-roaming frontier spirit. Following World War II in particular, and at the same time that we found ourselves maintaining a larger and more activist federal government than ever before (and also benefiting from it more than ever before), the United States developed a healthy distrust of the state, largely because of the chilling examples of far-rightist Germany, Italy, Japan, and the far-leftist Soviet Union. And so, from the mid-1940s onward, liberals have striven especially to avoid being heavy-handed, to manage—or at least, guide—the economy indirectly, without the federal government ostentatiously imposing itself by fiscal or monetary mechanisms. The liberal state seeks to be effective, but without being either seen or heard. When it is really successful, liberal policies may even be so inconspicuous that we fail to give them the credit that is their due. The result is that conservatives have begun getting away with blaming liberalism for not solving *all* our problems, while ignoring those substantial accomplishments that it has achieved.

We generally don't like extremists. Rose Bird lost her position as head of the Supreme Court in California for being too liberal (that is, not tough enough) on crime, while Robert Bork lost his bid for a seat on the Supreme Court of the United States for being too conservative (especially on issues of personal privacy). Even "extremism in the defense of liberty," as Barry Goldwater found out to his sorrow, is indeed widely perceived as a vice. And well it should be.

On the other hand, there is a difference between moderation as a principled intellectual stance based on a conviction that beliefs themselves should be held with a grain of salt and a dose of humility, and a much less principled refusal to take a firm stand on matters of social policy. In this regard, the middle ground has a good deal less to recommend it. As Jim Hightower, former agriculture commissioner of Texas,[11] likes to say, only two things are found in the middle of the road— yellow lines and squashed armadillos.

There was nothing middle of the road about John Kennedy's call for Americans to "pay any price, bear any burden, to assure the survival and success of liberty." And there is nothing wishy-washy about committing one's self, and one's country, to peace, to saving the environment, to civil liberties, and to social justice. Politics isn't really about power, or image, or compromise, but about human problems and achieving results in solving those problems. That's where successful politicians (and successful political ideologies) must be: with policies that work, that solve problems. To former Senator Wayne Morse,

Liberalism cannot be defined in the abstract in any helpful way. Liberalism in politics can best be defined in terms of specific issues. Political liberalism should also be defined in terms of objectives. A major objective is the protection of the economic weak and doing it within the framework of a private-property economy. The liberal, emphasizing the civil and property rights of the individual, insists that the individual must remain so supreme as to make the state his servant.[12]

---

[11] He prefers to call himself *progressive* or *populist*, but the policies are what really count.

[12] Wayne Morse, "Morse on Minority Rule," *The New Republic*, July 22, 1946.

By focusing on the underlying reason for government—to help us solve our problems—liberalism can rightfully claim its place of preeminent leadership, even as liberals themselves continue to be appropriately tentative, even deferential, about matters of dogma and certitude. In this respect, the best have every reason to be full of passionate intensity.

IF THE goals of liberalism have been outstanding, its means have been modest. Some say that its goal has been to achieve liberal ends with conservative means. There can be no doubt, for example, that New Deal liberalism saved capitalism (and perhaps democracy) in the United States, by moderating its excesses, guaranteeing a minimum quality of life to most Americans and giving most of us a legitimate stake in the nation's survival. But it stopped short of any fundamental restructuring of the social or economic system. Was this a failing of liberalism or of the American people themselves, since it seems clear that the great majority of us did not want (or, to put a more positive gloss on systemic change), were not ready for, more radical departures? Or was liberalism doing well what it does best, expressing in moderate tones a realistic pathway for expanding the human spirit?

Liberalism was (and still is) an attempt to rescue capitalism from the capitalists. Before FDR's liberalism, the rule of the conscience-free rich had brought the United States to the brink of collapse. We had no unemployment compensation, no farm price supports, no guarantee of bank-deposit safety, no social security, no federal regulation of securities. We used to have a serious depression about every twenty years, a depressing cycle that has been eliminated because of the controls erected by—you guessed it—liberals.

Liberalism places the individual at the center of its concern. But true to form, it does even that in a balanced, modulated way. It recoils from the selfish, me-first glorification of the individual found in Ayn Rand's "objectivism," from the enshrinement of personal greed or the phony-nostalgic "old-fashioned values" so beloved by Ronald Reagan and the mythic American heroes from Davy Crockett to Rambo. Rather, liberalism satisfies itself with a more subtle, more consuming yet more balanced celebration of the individual as special, unique, irreplaceable and unconquerable, yet also firmly embedded in society.[13] Immanuel Kant was a true liberal (in the modern sense) when he wrote, "No one could compel me to be happy in accordance with his conception of the welfare of others."[14]

This book has generalized about "liberals" and "liberalism," although of course there are as many different styles of liberalism as there are individual liberals. As we have seen, liberals often disagree; indeed, because of their lesser inclination toward authoritarianism, they are a much more fractious lot than are conservatives. For an example of liberal controversy, consider the question of equality. On the one hand, liberals of a more conservative persuasion acknowledge the validity of equal opportunities, and seek as their goal a society in which government doesn't discriminate, and neither does objective circumstance. On the other, liberals of a more leftist stripe prefer to go somewhat further toward equality: not just equal opportunity but equal *outcome*.

Classical liberalism developed around the notion of freedom. Then, it had to confront the problem of what to do when freedom goes too far, as in laissez-faire capitalism. Modern liberals agree that in such cases, capitalism must be modified, whereas radicals would opt to discard it, and conservatives would prefer to keep it as "pure" and unmodified as possible. This key notion of modern liberalism—retain the system, but modify it—may be valid and indeed, wise, but at the risk of seeming flabby compared with its more headstrong alternatives, the hidebound stubbornness of conservatism and the helter-skelter, potentially anarchic disruptiveness of radicalism. Critics have enjoyed sniping away at liberalism, always doing so from a position securely entrenched within a fortress whose foundations were constructed by liberalism itself. As a matter of fact, the one thing on which the extreme right and extreme left seem to agree is hostility to liberalism; it is not clear which ideology does more heaping of scorn. But if those underpinnings ever begin to sway, extremists of either stripe

---

[13] If this dissatisfies, and you want simple dichotomies and distinctions, try extremists of either right or left; liberalism is for those with a taste for the nuanced and complex.

[14] Immanuel Kant, *Foundations of the Metaphysics of Morals,* trans. Lewis White Beck (Indianapolis: Library of Liberal Arts, 1969).

had best beware what they wish for, because (as the Chinese say) they just might get it. And then their wishes may well change rapidly, to something distinctly liberal.

Any way you slice it, the liberal ideal is a modulated concept of human individuality: (1) admire distinct personhood, but persist in developing a basis for shared public life and legitimate social authority, (2) promote protection of the individual, but in a context of democracy, in which the public will is supreme, although minority rights are also respected, and (3) recognize the importance of private property and market economics as part of individual liberty, but temper the worst excesses of laissez-faire with a carefully orchestrated welfare state. Liberals understand that individuals cannot flourish unless excessive concentrations of power are minimized, whether this power is in private hands or exercised by the state.

Against this background, it is ironic that liberals were blamed for the excesses of the 1960s. If liberals are guilty of excess, it was—and still is—an excess of moderation.

We are supposed to believe that conservatives believe in the virtues of competition, tooth and nail, dog eat dog, and may the best man (in the conservative's ideal world, the competitors are in fact men) win. But do they really believe in such a free-for-all? Consider the Lockheed and Savings and Loan bailouts, or the various and numerous forms of "corporate socialism" whereby government provides special benefits and tax breaks to large corporations, especially those engaged in military contracting. What conservatives really prefer is competition among the nonrich, the wage earners, the smaller and less well established . . . especially since out of this competitive fray generally come lower wages and a more docile workforce.

Beyond this, we can inquire whether competition is all that wonderful anyway. Ostensibly, it brings out the best in us, but what does this mean? The clearest case would be athletics, in which, for example, a runner is likely to do better if he or she is "paced" by another, thereby evoking a higher level of effort and a better overall performance. But in morality, sensitivity, and cooperativeness, it seems clear that competition can be a pernicious force.

Psychologists have long known that a moderate level of stress results in the best mental functioning: too high and people get jangled and confused, too low and their attention is apt to wander. Similarly, biologists have found that high levels of stress among animals correlates with high levels of mortality, and interestingly, that very low levels of stress are also not entirely healthful: If living things have it too easy, their immune systems are likely to become as flabby as their muscles. Once again, a kind of Platonic "golden mean" seems best. And by the same token, the liberal penchant for moderation may be precisely the best prescription, not only for individuals but also for societies.

Chapter 9 War and Peace

LIBERALS AND conservatives have very different views about the causes of war and, therefore, about how to maintain peace. They also relate differently—although, sad to tell, not *that* differently—to the Cold War. And they even have different views about the very meaning of warfare. Not even I would claim that conservatives prefer war over peace; however, there can be no doubt that our conservative brethren[1] have long been more favorable to it, seeing war as unavoidable and often the lesser of evils. As we have seen, conservatism originates with a very severe, pessimistic view of human nature. As far back as the seventeenth century, Thomas Hobbes warned that primitive life consists of *"bellum omnium contra omnes"* ("war of all against each") because our species is inherently sinful, competitive, and altogether nasty. This, in turn, opens the door—in conservative thinking—to stringent hard-nosed government authority, the "night watchman state," which does virtually nothing for its own people other than keep them from damaging their fellows, while also holding other like-minded and unpleasant folks at bay.

---

[1] And sisters, too (would that be *sistern*?).

Even before Hobbes, the conservative view was reflected by Plato, who concluded from the Peloponnesian War that since the world was violent and unruly, and war inevitable, states must be tightly organized for survival. Christianity, with its emphasis on original sin, was a worthy successor to such gloominess, which in turn provided further conceptual underpinnings for a conservative view of the causes of war, and thus, of the best way to secure peace: through military strength and the willingness to use it.

By extension, strong moral and governmental controls are also necessary if peace is to be maintained. For conservatives, war occurs because we are aggressive animals by nature, and because of breakdown in the social order: which is to say, when the riffraff get uppity. In short, wars—whether of revolution or of conquest—take place when people cease to know their place. Since social groups are seen as basically irrational and unstable, peace can be assured only by appropriate organization and management of power and order. For Hobbes, virtually nothing could justify the overthrow of a monarch, because the "state of nature"—to which the rabble would doubtless regress if royalty is ever discarded—is so abominable.[2] Even Hobbes, however, recognized that states interact with other states in what is essentially a comparable state of nature. "The state of Commonwealths considered in themselves is natural, that is to say, hostile," Hobbes wrote in *The Citizen.* "Neither if they cease from fighting, is it therefore to be called peace; but rather a breathing time."

According to conservative doctrine, there should be little cause for war so long as power is properly and securely held—assuming, of course, that those holding said power aren't Bad Guys, like the Sandinistas, or communists. (It's OK if they're right-wing military dictators or if they practice apartheid.) In the conservative view war may be acceptable, even laudable, if it serves to prevent civic breakdown, especially if that break-

---

[2] It is noteworthy that no midground (that is to say, democracy) was envisioned between anarchic chaos and rigid despotism. Modern conservatives often suffer from a similar tunnel vision. Consider, for example, Ronald Reagan's assertion during the 1984 presidential debate that we must continue supporting Filipino dictator Ferdinand Marcos because the only alternative would be a communist takeover. Two years later, Corazón Aquino, aided by "people power," was popularly elected and replaced Marcos.

down threatens the existing social hierarchy. For example, in *The Early History of Rome,* the Roman historian Livy (59 B.C.– A.D. 17) wrote approvingly that the Senate had "ordered an immediate raising of troops and a general mobilization on the largest possible scale" . . . in the hope that the revolutionary proposals which the tribunes were bringing forth might be forgotten in the bustle and excitement of three imminent military campaigns. The Roman general Vegetius is first credited with the phrase, *"vis pacem, para bellum"* ("if you want peace, prepare for war"), and in more recent times, the doctrines of "balance of power" and "peace through strength" have continued this trend of conservative thought.

Probably the most articulate spokesperson of conservative peace was the English orator and statesman Edmund Burke (1729–1797). Burke reflected conservative doctrine in stressing the importance of preserving the existing institutional order and skepticism about the perfectibility of We the People. At heart, this philosophy has long been motivated by disbelief in the potential of human beings and a deep suspicion of democracy. For conservatives, as we have seen, the traditions of the past must at all costs be respected. According to Burke, society is a partnership "not only between those who are living, but between those who are living, those who are dead, and those who are to be born."

Social cement is seen to come from reverence, respect, and deference (which is why Confucius is also considered to be a conservative social philosopher). Authority and, typically, patriarchy, are valued over change, equality, and spontaneity. Social hierarchies have long been admired by conservative political philosophers, as providing necessary reference points and stability.

Not surprisingly, conservatives have traditionally been especially opposed to the threat of disorder coming from abroad. Writing of the traumatic event of his day, the French Revolution, Burke observed: "It is a war between the partisans of the ancient, civil, moral and political order of Europe [the monarchy] against a set of fanatical and ambitious atheists which means to change them all." Burke anticipated the attitude of present-day ideological conservatives when he wrote the following, which could also stand for Ronald Reagan's attitude toward the Sandinistas of Nicaragua:

I never thought we could make peace with the [French revolutionary] system; because it was not for the sake of an object we pursued in rivalry with each other, but with the system itself that we were at war. As I understood the matter, we were at war, not with its conduct, but with its existence, convinced that its existence and its hostility were the same.[3]

The goal, for Burke no less than for Reagan, was to establish a kind of peace by making an unruly and troublesome system say "uncle."

We HAVE seen how classical liberalism was closely allied with capitalism, the industrial revolution, and the rise of the middle class. In their classical phase, liberals argued that a warm, cozy blanket of worldwide economic self-interest would smother the flames of war. As recently as 1914, liberal theorist Norman Angell claimed that capitalists were necessarily peace-loving: "The capitalist has no country, and he knows . . . that arms and conquests and juggling with frontiers serve no ends of his and may very well defeat them, through the great destruction that such wars will generate."[4]

Another major strand in liberal thought about peace also argues from economics, especially international trade and connectedness. In *The Spirit of Laws*, Montesquieu had proposed that international trade and commerce will naturally tend to promote peace: "Two nations which trade with each other become reciprocally dependent; if it is to the advantage of one to buy, it is to the advantage of the other to sell; and all unions are founded on mutual needs." He also argued that trade leads to an improvement in manners and basic civility: "It is almost a general rule that wherever there are tender manners, there is commerce, and wherever there is commerce, there are tender manners."

John Stuart Mill similarly maintained:

It is commerce which is rapidly rendering war obsolete, by strengthening and multiplying the personal interests which act in natural opposition to it. And it may be said without exaggeration that the great extent and rapid increase of interna-

---

[3] Edmund Burke, *Reflections on the Revolution in France*, (New York: Doubleday, 1961).
[4] Norman Angell, *The Great Illusion* (London: Heinemann, 1914).

tional trade, in being the principal guarantee of the peace of
the world, is the great permanent security for the uninter-
rupted progress of the ideas, the institutions, and the character
of the human race.[5]

This view became a major part of the liberal antiwar credo:
By spreading commerce and the political power of capitalism,
as well as working on public opinion, war would be made
obsolete. Englishmen Richard Cobden (1804–1865) and John
Bright (1811–1889), for example, led the so-called Manchester
school, which opposed foreign interventionism and maintained that maximum free trade among nations would serve
to make war not only unnecessary but also impossible.

They meant well, these nineteenth-century liberals, but they
were clearly wrong. This is not to say that international trade
and communication isn't potentially useful in preventing war,
just that they aren't sufficient to do so.

Just as liberals have long held that war could be prevented
by certain actions—trade, communication, good government—they have been unimpressed with the claim that failing
such activities, human beings will naturally slide into war, like
a rock acted upon by gravity. Thus, liberals have not bought
the argument that war is caused by human sinfulness. They
also hold little with innate nastiness, depravity, and free-float-
ing evil. Instead, liberals tend to emphasize the excessive power
of political states, psychological "state of mind" theories as
well as the role of misunderstandings, and the undue influence of a military/economic/political elite. For many liberals,
wars are often analogous to automobile accidents: Most people do not willingly drive their cars into one another. Rather,
if they come to grief it is because they were driving too fast,
or because of faulty brakes, poor road conditions, insufficient
attentiveness, or bad judgment (by oneself or an oncoming
driver).

Liberals are likely, therefore, to emphasize the potential
dangers of war by accident or misunderstanding. They also
tend to be acutely aware that when countries try to achieve
security through military force, the results are often unin-

---

[5]John Stuart Mill, *Considerations on Representative Government* (New York: The
Liberal Arts Press, 1958).

tended, and disastrous. Liberals have been preeminent in identifying the so-called security dilemma, in which a country—seeking security for itself—makes others insecure, which in turn produces tension and often an arms race, ultimately making everyone less secure than ever . . . and sometimes even leading to war.

This is consistent with several liberal traits, which we have already identified: sensitivity to others, a capacity for empathy, and an inclination to see truth as relative and not exclusively the property of one side or the other. Conservatives, by contrast, have very little hesitation about proclaiming that they are right and the other side, wrong (that is, left). Thus, Richard Nixon: "It may seem melodramatic to say that the United States and Russia represent Good and Evil, Light and Darkness, God and the Devil. But if we think of it that way, it helps to clarify our perspective of the world struggle."[6] And of course, Ronald Reagan:

> I urge you to beware the temptation of pride—the temptation blithely to declare yourselves above it all and label both sides equally at fault, to ignore the facts of history and the aggressive impulses of an evil empire, to simply call the arms race a giant misunderstanding and thereby remove yourselves from the struggle between right and wrong, good and evil.[7]

Things are more complicated when we abandon the simplistic good guy versus bad guy rhetoric (as, to his credit, Reagan finally did), and look instead at the role of errors, miscalculations, misunderstandings, and of so-called mirror-image factors—in which each side perceives the other as a reflected pattern of its nastiest self, which in turn drives a vicious circle of increasing hostility and suspicion.

In a much-quoted passage in his memoirs, Sir Edward Grey, British foreign secretary during the fateful days leading up to World War I, gave voice to one of the notable liberal perceptions of the relationship of arms races to war:

---

[6] Richard Nixon, "America Has Slipped to Number Two," *Parade*, October 5, 1980, p. 7.
[7] Ronald Reagan, speech to the National Association of Evangelicals, Orlando, Florida, March 1983.

> Great armaments lead inevitably to war. The increase of arma-
> ments . . . produces a consciousness of the strength of other
> nations and a sense of fear. Fear begets suspicion and distrust
> and evil imaginings of all sorts, till each Government feels it
> would be criminal and a betrayal of its country not to take every
> precaution, while every Government regards the precautions
> of every other Government as evidence of hostile intent.[8]

Not surprisingly, World War I is the war that liberals like to
point to, the one that we must learn from and never repeat.
The First World War was the "war no one wanted," precipi-
tated by blunders and misperceptions, arms races that unne-
cessarily aggravated international tensions, and rigid
mobilization schedules that restricted the decision-making
flexibility of national leaders. And liberals worry—for good
reason—that in the Nuclear Age, a repeat of World War I would
be both possible and catastrophic.

Even Henry Kissinger has been known to analyze events
this way:

> The superpowers often behave like two heavily armed blind
> men feeling their way around a room, each believing himself
> in mortal peril from the other whom he assumes to have per-
> fect vision. Each side should know that frequently uncertainty,
> compromise, and incoherence are the essence of policy-mak-
> ing. Yet each tends to ascribe to the other a consistency, fore-
> sight, and coherence that its own experience belies. Of course,
> over time, even two blind men can do enormous damage to
> each other, not to speak of the room.[9]

The liberal emphasis on error over evil seems generally to
be valid, but it must also be admitted that in the past it may
have led to excessive "psychologizing" and an occasional tendency to ignore wrongdoing, thereby sometimes making war
more likely rather than less. For example, noted liberal pacifist
Philip Lothian wrote[10] in 1935, "In some degree the brutality
of National Socialists [Nazis] is the reaction to the treatment

---

[8] Edward Grey, *Twenty-Five Years, 1892–1916* (New York: Frederick A. Stokes, 1925).
[9] Henry Kissinger, *White House Years* (Boston: Little, Brown, 1979).
[10] Quoted in Martin Gilbert, *Britain and Germany Between the Wars* (London: Longmans, 1964).

given to Germany herself since the war," and that "the best way of restoring reasonable rights to the Jews in Germany is not to counter hate with hate, but to undermine the source of the evil aspects of National Socialism by giving Germany her rightful place in Europe." (Nonetheless, it was mainly the conservatives, in Britain and France, who appeased Nazism, at least in part because of their greater fear of communism, and their hope that Hitler might help destroy European communism, and especially the Soviet Union.)

Conservatives are so quick to rail against "Munich"—by which they mean appeasing an aggressor—that they have succeeded in twisting some important history. Thus, it was British liberals who favored war, if need be, against Italy in support of the League of Nations when Mussolini invaded Ethiopia in 1935. And it was conservatives—worried about antagonizing the Italian dictator and hoping to curry his favor against Hitler—who won out, as a result of which the League of Nations went down the drain. Then, we "lost" Mussolini, who allied with Hitler after all, and almost the eventual war against the Axis as well, in part because those same conservatives couldn't bring themselves to ally with the Soviet Union against Nazism until after World War II actually started.

Nonetheless, while liberals point to World War I, conservatives point to World War II, which may well have been prevented if the Western democracies had seen Hitler for the monster he was and responded more firmly. Ironically, World War I, for its part, might have been avoided if the West had been as flexible and compromising in 1914 as it sought to be in the mid-1930s, just as World War II might have been avoided if the West had been as rigid and intransigent when Hitler remilitarized the Rhineland, or sought to annex Austria and then Czechoslovakia, as it had been toward Austria and Germany in 1914. On the other hand, there do not seem to be any Hitlers on the world stage today (although President Bush repeatedly, and unconvincingly, compared Iraq's Saddam Hussein to the Nazi leader). In a world of nuclear weapons— and a Soviet Union that seeks accommodation rather than confrontation—the greater danger seems to be a nuclear Sarajevo rather than another Munich.

After World War I, the growth of fascism caught liberals,

pacifists, and the more radical socialists by surprise, unprepared for its combination of populism, nationalism, and authoritarianism, its overtly militaristic tendencies and distaste for peace. The liberal perspective has had difficulty coming to terms with highly aggressive individuals, cultures, and ideologies generally; today, conservative critics never tire of accusing liberals of being insufficiently attuned to the ruthlessness and ambition of world communism. (Even though what we used to call the "Soviet bloc" has essentially disintegrated.) Liberals, in turn, criticize conservatives for taking a narrow, us-versus-them view of foreign events, one that verges on inflammatory warmongering, and that often employs a double standard in embracing right-wing—even fascist—regimes so long as they pronounce themselves to be anticommunist. Many conservatives were so fond of the Cold War that they are having a terrible time admitting that it is over.

Among most liberals, arms control—and, more rarely, disarmament—is a prominent goal, and much hope and respect tends to be invested in international organizations such as the United Nations, as well as international law more generally. Liberals are also much more inclined than conservatives to be enthusiastic about nonviolence.

However, liberalism has also, on occasion, embraced specific wars. The Spanish Civil War, for example, was initially seen by the left as an unambiguously just war: a democratic, popularly elected government was under attack by reactionary forces aided by fascist dictatorships (Italy and Germany). Liberals and others of the political left sought (although unsuccessfully) to involve Britain, France, and the United States in the Spanish Civil War, while conservatives preferred noninvolvement. By the 1980s, that situation had reversed: Reagan conservatives were urging greater United States involvement in wars in Nicaragua, El Salvador, Afghanistan, Cambodia, and Angola, just as a decade earlier, conservatives had urged vigorous prosecution of the war in Vietnam, one that was—to their great shame—started by liberals.

The ultimate factor that decides liberal-versus-conservative attitudes toward any particular war seems to have less to do with general ideological preferences for peace than with the question of whom the war would be against: Liberals are likely to condone, even support, wars that oppose right-wing despotisms, whereas conservatives respond similarly to wars against governments of the far left. In summary, neither liberals nor conservatives have a monopoly on opposing war and supporting peace, although the liberal view—flawed though it sometimes has been—seems a better guideline for the future.

CONSERVATIVES UNBLUSHINGLY beat the drum for a narrow definition of national security (that is, military power), and for the aggressive pursuit of what they see as American goals in the world (that is, anticommunism and free markets). Significantly, a recently established conservative magazine toward that end is titled *The National Interest*. A comparable liberal magazine might be called *The International Interest*, or rather, it would recognize that our national interest is intertwined with and indistinguishable from global interests. Liberals would redefine national security as a subset of global security, and they would protect the environment and maximize human well-being with at least the same fervor that conservatives exhibit for protecting their investments and maximizing their profits.

"Liberal internationalism" has a long and distinguished history, with its claim that a more peaceful world can be constructed by international cooperation of various sorts, and that the United States should take the lead in doing so. Its more recent legacies include the United Nations, the Organization of American States, the World Bank, the North Atlantic Treaty Organization, the International Monetary Fund, and the General Agreement on Tariffs and Trade. Liberal internationalists, both in the United States and worldwide, are also responsible for the entity known as international law. Unlike conservatives, liberals take international law seriously. This means that they are willing to accept limitations on unbridled national sovereignty, recognizing that in the long run such restrictions are in everyone's interest. (The conservative passion for nationalistic, occasionally xenophobic insistence on going it alone—outside the United Nations, indifferent to international law—is actually a continuation of conservative domestic preferences: idealization of the self, and of private enterprise. Similarly, the liberal penchant for internationalism is consistent with modern liberalism's inclination toward social rather than individual solutions to problems.)

Far more than conservatives, liberals were unhappy with

the American invasions of Grenada (1983) and Panama (1989), our support for government terrorism in El Salvador, and our undeclared war against Nicaragua. It was a conservative United States government that mined Managua harbor, and then ignored the World Court ruling that this action was illegal. Such flagrant disregard for international law is especially hypocritical for conservatives who ostensibly value "law and order," but only when it supports their political beliefs.

It is easy to favor freedom of speech when everyone who wants to talk agrees with you. The trick is to support the First Amendment when racists, fascists, or other unsavory zealots want to be heard. Similarly, it is easy to favor noninterventionism and respect for international law when the issue is whether the U.S.S.R. has the right to intervene and crush democratic reforms in Hungary or Czechoslovakia . . . or even, in Lithuania, Latvia, Georgia, or the Ukraine. The trick is to be consistent when people like Manuel Noriega are at issue. We failed that one, and even many liberals went along with George Bush on what proved to be a popular transgression of international law.

The eminent English military historian Sir Michael Howard described such acts beautifully as "aggression in the pursuit of self-interest under the cloak of hyprocisy."[11] And he notes that this is "always likely to be the case when a party makes a unilateral statement of its interpretation of the legal position and proceeds to enforce it."[12] The liberal view recognizes the existence of an international morality and endeavors to function within it.

Professor Howard also defined "liberal" with respect to international affairs as those who "believe the world to be profoundly other than it should be, and who have faith in the power of human reason and human action so to change it that the inner potential of all human beings can be more fully realised."[13] Consistent with this approach, the various international peace movements beginning in the nineteenth century

---

[11] Michael Howard, *War and the Liberal Conscience* (New Brunswick, N.J.: Rutgers University Press, 1978).
[12] Ibid.
[13] Ibid.

were all liberal creations, trying by agitation, education, and organization to increase understanding and international co-operation, and to abolish war.

After World War I, Woodrow Wilson was far more liberal than the U.S. Senate, but the conservative isolationists were more powerful, and America stayed out of the League of Nations. Its demise, then, was not a failure of liberalism, but of not enough liberalism. And much the same can be said of the United Nations. It has had some notable successes; when it has failed, it is because a narrowly defined, conservative vision of national interest and state sovereignty has prevailed over the more encompassing vision of liberal internationalism.

Nonetheless, liberal internationalism has been criticized—as usual—from both right and left. One of the more interesting critiques comes from Leo Tolstoy, who so embraced Christian principles during his later years that he is sometimes referred to as the thirteenth apostle. In his writings on nonviolence, Tolstoy emphasized the responsibility of individuals, not only in their personal relationships, but also in their refusal to participate in violence organized by the state. He had contempt for such traditional liberal responses to war as the convening of meetings, the passing of resolutions, even attempts to establish and invoke international law. Rather, Tolstoy[14] believed that the abolition of war—even more crucial, in his view, than the establishment of social justice—fundamentally required a decision by individuals to say *NO*, and to say it unequivocally. He argued that governments themselves reveal what kind of antiwar actions are most threatening to the state-sponsored system of war:

> Liberals entangled in their much talking, socialists, and other so-called advanced people may think that their speeches in Parliament and at meetings, their unions, strikes, and pamphlets are of great importance; while the refusals of military service by private individuals are unimportant occurrences not worthy of attention. The governments, however, know very well what is important to them and what is not. And the governments readily allow all sorts of liberal and radical speeches

---

[14] Who, after all, particularly deserves to be quoted in a chapter titled "War and Peace."

in Reichstags, as well as workmen's associations and socialist demonstrations, and they even pretend themselves to sympathize with those things, knowing that they are of great use to them in diverting people's attention from the great and only means of emancipation. But governments never openly tolerate refusals of military service, or refusals of war taxes, which are the same thing, because they know that such refusals expose the fraud of governments and strike at the root of their power.[15]

Liberals sometimes face a dilemma. Most of them do not share Tolstoy's vision of personal responsibility transcending government misbehavior. Far more than conservatives, however, liberals are likely to condemn war, seeing it as an evil and an abomination, or at minimum, an error and something that reasonable people, behaving rationally, should be able to avoid. The dilemma is that sometimes war appears unavoidable, or even desirable: to overcome injustice, achieve freedom, or defend societies with liberal democratic values from the menace of totalitarianism (of either the extreme right or left). Sadly, when it comes to resolving this dilemma, liberals have been no better than anyone else.

Case in point: Iraq's invasion of Kuwait. This event, a possible watershed in the post–Cold War world, was not marked by a comparable divide between liberals and conservatives. Indeed, representatives of each have been found on either side of this difficult issue. Such liberal members of Congress as Stephen Solarz and Les Aspin were hawkish, for example, while conservatives, including columnist Patrick Buchanan, as well as Senator Sam Nunn, were dovish. By and large, however, liberals took a moderate and responsible stand, willing to go to war if need be, but only as a last resort. They generally supported the initial deployment of United States forces to prevent further aggression by the minions of Saddam Hussein, and then urged that we stand by the stringent economic sanctions imposed by the United Nations. In this, they were consistent as well as principled, since liberals have long argued for multilateralism over unilateralism, and for the usefulness and, if possible, even the primacy of the United Nations.

---

[15]Leo Tolstoy, *Writings on Civil Disobedience and Nonviolence* (Philadelphia: New Society Publishers, 1987).

They are generally far more leery than conservatives of initiating war, and certainly more reluctant to do so as self-appointed world policemen rather than as part of a genuine
international enforcement effort. When the Senate finally voted
to give George Bush the go-ahead for war, the resulting tally
was 52–47, with only two Republicans opposed.

By contrast, conservatives have not only been more receptive to a kind of flag-waving jingoism, they have also been
inconsistent almost to the point of intellectual dishonesty, with
the same folks who not long ago wanted "the UN out of the
US and the US out of the UN" suddenly singing the praises
of the United Nations and averring the need to abide by UN
resolutions. (Or at least, for Iraq to do so.) And it was the
liberals, overwhelmingly, who insisted that if the United States
was to go to war, it was for Congress—and not the President,
acting unilaterally—to decide.

THERE IS a widespread notion that liberals are unwilling
to employ military power. For better or worse, this is false.
From this author's perspective, the world might be a better
place if liberals had actually been a bit more circumspect about
throwing their weight around, internationally. Theodore Roosevelt, Woodrow Wilson, Franklin Delano Roosevelt, Harry
Truman, John F. Kennedy, Lyndon Johnson: All these liberal
presidents used force against other countries, sometimes justifiably, sometimes not. Like it or not, the truth is that liberals
have not been wimps. (The image of liberals as antimilitary
doves derives in part from liberal opposition to the Vietnam
War in its later stages, but this should not overshadow the
fact that it was JFK and Lyndon Johnson—two notable liberals—who got us most deeply involved in that sorry endeavor
in the first place.)

And so, we come to liberalism's most regrettable chapter, a
blight on an otherwise estimable politics: I refer here to Cold
War liberalism. Cold War liberalism has been, in part, an effort to give the lie to Heywood Broun's criticism that a liberal
is someone who leaves the room whenever a fight begins. It
is also a result of liberal anxiety, a felt need to prove their
bona fides, to demonstrate that even though they fancy themselves left of center, they are most assuredly not communist,

procommunist, communist sympathizers, or well-intentioned but naïve communist dupes.

The Cold War liberal combined[16] traditional liberal domestic policies with a hard-line, promilitarist, and devoutly anticommunist foreign policy. Senator Henry Jackson of Washington state was probably the quintessential Cold War liberal. Others included Harry Truman, Hubert Humphrey, and—especially in his early political career—John Kennedy.[17] Jimmy Carter, never very liberal, became more of a Cold Warrior as his administration went on. Even today, many politicians (no matter how progressive) often prove to be Cold War liberals when it comes to closing a military base or terminating a military contract within their state or district.

The specter of being soft on communism has haunted liberals since the Second World War; JFK and LBJ were perhaps most hard-hit. And so, liberals indulged in a prolonged bout of macho interventionism, while conservatives were isolationist, even opposing NATO, for example, during the late 1940s and early 1950s. Dwight Eisenhower's secretary of state, the arch Cold Warrior John Foster Dulles, saw the world in traditionally conservative, good guy versus bad guy terms, while Eisenhower himself tried to keep military spending within bounds. As a result, John Kennedy inherited a military prepared to fight a nuclear war, but little else. He built up a conventional, interventionary capability, supposedly to provide other, nonnuclear options for the use of force. Kennedy then wound up running numerous covert operations (only Ronald Reagan has come close) and beginning the long slide into the swamps and jungles of Vietnam.

According to sociologist Alan Wolfe:

> Kennedy and his advisors were convinced that the public was far to the right of themselves, and therefore they were wary of doing too much. But at the same time, Democrats claim that

---

[16]I use the past tense in the expectation, and hope, that the Cold War will indeed prove to be over, and with it, Cold War liberalism as well.

[17]Following the Cuban Missile Crisis, Kennedy became much less enthusiastic about prosecuting a moral crusade against the U.S.S.R., and by the time of his assassination in 1963, he had launched a notable series of conciliatory gestures toward the Soviets, overtures that were reciprocated and which—for a time—substantially lowered East-West tensions.

the Republicans are the "do nothing" party, and in order to distinguish themselves from stand-patism, they have to do something once in power. Torn between the need to do something and the fear of doing anything, Kennedy was left with the traditional course of waging full scale battles against universally recognized enemies. Primary among these was the Soviet Union. From the moment of his Inaugural—when he called for increases in air power, the building of nuclear missiles, and the development of the Polaris submarine—to the end of his presidency, Kennedy sought to expand the military budget. And his advisors searched the world to find a place where the new military might could be demonstrated. For Kennedy, the answer to this domestic political dilemma was to be aggressive around the world, and thus to rekindle the fear of the Soviet threat.[18]

The Vietnam War represented the zenith (or, should we say, the nadir?) of liberal interventionist forays, after which the interventionist bee has become firmly ensconced within the bonnets of conservatives, who agitated for United States involvement in Central America, Afghanistan, Cambodia, Angola, and God knows where else, while liberals seem finally to have learned a bit of overdue humility. Conservatives, by contrast, have nurtured a schizoidal view of the power of the United States to influence events: They eagerly assert America's ability to manage events in foreign cities, such as Managua, Kabul, or Saigon—even if their preferred outcomes run counter to the wishes of the local population—while arguing passionately that the federal government could not possibly effect meaningful changes right here at home, in the ghettos of New York, Detroit, or Los Angeles, where the goal of social improvement is widely shared.

Never was this more apparent than in 1991, when the United States liberated Kuwait City while at the same time losing Washington, D.C. Conservatives in the Bush administration see no contradiction between pursuing a "new world order" abroad while tolerating—even encouraging—the same old "national disorder" at home. And, in fact, there is little real contradiction, since the conservatives' goal is basically the same

---

[18] Alan Wolfe, *The Rise and Fall of the "Soviet Threat"* (Washington: Institute for Policy Studies, 1979).

in both cases: to support the status quo on behalf of the privileged well-to-do.

The danger for liberals has long been that affirmative government at home had a tendency to spill over to affirmative government abroad, an excess of the problem-solving "can-do" attitude: for example, Teddy Roosevelt's Big Stick, Woodrow Wilson and World War I (after campaigning in 1916 on a pledge to keep the United States out of the European war), FDR and World War II, LBJ and Vietnam. Activism, with all its self-confidence and do-it-yourself, fix-it enthusiasm, has a penchant for walking on water . . . sometimes right across the Atlantic or Pacific Oceans.

In its origins, Cold War liberalism was also energized by the Keynesian recognition that federal spending was good for the economy. Coming at a time when most American businessmen and other conservatives feared that government activity would result in unacceptably higher budgets and higher taxes, President Truman's economic advisers hit upon military spending as a way of stimulating the economy in a manner that would be acceptable to the political right wing. In addition, vigorous anticommunism would also help cement the liberal-Democratic consensus in the West and South (where much of the money was spent), and to some degree insulate activist domestic programs from conservative criticism.

Then came Vietnam. Lyndon Johnson escalated that war partly to demonstrate his own anticommunist credentials as a good Cold War liberal, and thereby, he hoped, to protect his Great Society programs from attacks by the right. But ironically, the Vietnam War split his own liberal supporters. As one observer puts it:

To the New Left and left-liberal thinking of the time, the entire spectacle [of LBJ's political difficulties at home and in Vietnam] laid bare the bankruptcy of establishment liberalism, representative primarily of the well-to-do, manipulative of the underclass but superficial in its concern for them, and prone to disastrous military adventures abroad.[19]

---

[19] Alonzo L. Hamby, *Liberalism and Its Challenges* (New York: Oxford University Press, 1985).

The Vietnam War was a tragedy of many dimensions, for the Americans and Vietnamese who fought it, the innocent civilians who suffered and died, the moral values of the American superpower that prosecuted the war, the economies of both the United States and (even more so) Vietnam, which were so deformed by the awful experience. It was also a tragedy for United States liberalism, not only because it was Cold War liberals who got us so enmeshed in the first place, but also because liberal critics of the war—who saw it as predatory, imperialistic, and immoral—came across as anti-American and un-American to many others in mid-America. Many liberal opponents of the Vietnam War, in their anger and frustration, became more and more countercultural, leading to a mutual alienation: them from mainstream America, and vice versa.

Liberals cannot escape their responsibility for Vietnam, and from the obloquy that Cold War liberalism richly deserves. But once the Cold War was underway, there can be no doubt that conservatives feasted on it, while liberals barely munched. Consistent with their tendency toward absolute moralism, conservatives came to see the Cold War as melodrama: simplified, larger than life, a cosmic battle between righteousness and evil. Liberals, as is their wont, saw it as a kind of tragedy, made all the more tragic by the fact that it could have been handled differently. Specifically, a different outcome could have occurred if both sides had been blessed with better leadership, clearer communication, etc. (The conservative response has typically been that the tragedy, if any, lies in United States weakness, in FDR's failure to "stand firm" at Yalta, to resist the infiltration that supposedly made American policy-makers the spineless tools of international communism, or perhaps our failure to have bombed the hell out of the Soviets before they developed nuclear weapons.)

As Arthur M. Schlesinger, Jr., sees it, the origins of the Cold War reflected many of the problems that earlier liberal theorists had identified as the "security dilemma." Thus, it "was the product not of a decision but of a dilemma." He goes on:

> Each side felt compelled to adopt policies which the other could not but regard as a threat to the principles of peace. Each

then felt compelled to undertake defensive measures. Thus the Russians saw no choice but to consolidate their security in Eastern Europe. The Americans, regarding Eastern Europe as the first step toward Western Europe, responded by asserting their interest in the zone the Russians deemed vital to their security. The Russians concluded that the West was resuming its old course of capitalist encirclement; that it was purposefully laying the foundation for anti-Soviet regimes in the area defined by the blood of centuries as crucial to Russian survival. Each side believed with passion that future international stability depended on the success of its own conception of world order. Each side, in pursuing its own clearly indicated and deeply cherished principles, was only confirming the fear of the other that it was bent on aggression.[20]

Schlesinger contends America set on this path by folly and unfortunate circumstance:

For the next fifteen years the Cold War raged unabated, passing out of historical ambiguity into the realm of good versus evil and breeding on both sides simplifications, stereotypes and self-serving absolutes, often couched in interchangeable phrases. Under the pressure even America, for a deplorable decade, forsook its pragmatic and pluralist traditions, posed as God's appointed messenger to ignorant and sinful man and followed the Soviet example in looking to a world remade in its own image. In retrospect, if it is impossible to see the Cold War as a case of American aggression and Russian response, it is also hard to see it as a pure case of Russian aggression and American response.[21]

Again, the liberal interpretation of the Cold War turns out to be fundamentally middle-of-the-road, convinced that there is enough blame to go around. And the funny thing is, it is probably correct.

Liberals—not the Cold War variety—have been accused of being naïve vis-à-vis the Soviet Union. But as George Kennan has pointed out, there can be a naïveté of distrust no less than a naïveté of trust. There is very little evidence that liberals have erred on the latter side, and substantial reason to think

---

[20] Arthur M. Schlesinger, Jr., "Origins of the Cold War," *Foreign Affairs*, October, 1967.
[21] Ibid.

that they (and conservatives even more so) have erred on the former.

Up until recently, in any event, worldwide communism has made many Americans nervous, liberals most especially, since, as we have seen, they have regularly felt the need to cover their flanks lest they be accused of being "soft on communism." By contrast, the specter of being seen as "soft on fascism" has only rarely dampened the ideological fervor of American conservatives. No one seriously worries that Alfredo Stroessner (formerly) of Paraguay, or the ghosts of Ferdinand Marcos, Papa Doc Duvalier, Anastasio Somoza, or Fulgencio Batista—not to mention Hitler, Mussolini, or Tojo— have been sponsoring the machinations of today's conservatives. There is genuine irony here, since the "friendly fascism" of Ronald Reagan and Ollie North threatened the integrity of the United States far more than did the mildly leftist sympathies of Henry Wallace, George McGovern, Eugene McCarthy, or Michael Dukakis.

But if we really want to ferret out the fundamental, underlying cause of Cold War liberalism, it is to be found not in excesses of naïveté, in fear of communism, or even fear of being mistakenly thought to be a quasicommunist, but rather in the absence of a genuine, credible left in the United States. Because of this vacuum, liberalism spent a lot of time guarding the ramparts, anxious not to be perceived as procommunist, and vulnerable to being egged on by the conservatives, whose advice they have often implemented, despite the fact that it has nearly always been bad.

ALL OF US—liberals no less than conservatives—would do well to refrain from excessive smugness and self-congratulation about the victory of the democratic West over the rapidly disintegrating communist East. To be sure, the West provides more freedom and consumer goods. That's like saying that summer is warmer than winter, or New York is bigger than Dubuque. The danger in such self-congratulation is that it blinds us to our own shortcomings. The democratic West is better than the communist East, but it is still not nearly as good as it should be. (Here, of course, we are encountering another of liberalism's distinctive traits: optimism combined with a fussy, almost grumpy kind of divine discontent.)

Whatever the lessons and whatever the need to maintain their uniquely hopeful-critical perspective on modern society, the collapse of communism and end of the Cold War offers American liberals a double opportunity. First, it deprives conservatives of what has been in large part their raison d'être: anticommunism. Of course, conservatives may well continue running against the Reds, and muttering darkly about the international communist menace, but fewer and fewer people will take them seriously. So much the better. For decades, Democrats ran against the Depression (the "Hoover Depression"), and then ran into trouble when the memory of it grew thin. Now, conservatives will have to make do without their beloved bogeymen, glaring at us from the Kremlin walls. Conservatives, far more than liberals, have defined themselves negatively: opposition to the welfare state, to democracy, to innovation, to communism. With communism disappearing as an enemy, conservatives have begun to suffer an identity crisis of large proportions.

Despite the virulence of Cold War liberalism, conservatives have consistently been able to present themselves as the party of national military strength, and electorally it has worked. Even during the divisive and ill-conceived Vietnam War, a hawkish conservative was elected twice, and at the heart of the revitalized Cold War and the nuclear scare it engendered, another hawk (Ronald Reagan) was reelected in 1984. Absent the Cold War, conservatives will be losing one of their most effective campaign issues. It remains to be seen, on the other hand, whether conservatives will be able to replace communism with a parade of Third World despots such as Manuel Noriega and Saddam Hussein.

Second, the collapse of communism may finally liberate liberals from their fear of being tarred as "soft on communism." Maybe at last, liberals will be able to chart a course in international affairs based on humane and enlightened liberal principles, without having to talk and act like the international bullies that the anticommunist paranoids have typically demanded . . . and in which liberals, all too often, have acquiesced.

Both liberals and conservatives sometimes say that one half the world lives in misery. To conservatives, this means communism. To liberals, they mean those who are hungry, without adequate housing, a remunerative job, medical care, clean water and education . . . and political freedoms as well, but not exclusively. Conservatives turn a blind eye to socioeconomic misery; so long as such misery takes place within a free-market system, they—at least—are not offended. The real affront to conservatism is not human misery per se, but an improper ideology (hence, the spurious distinction between authoritarian and totalitarian regimes). Liberals, by contrast, are far more pragmatic. Liberals can live with communism, so long as it is respectful of fundamental human rights; and, contrary to the assertions of conservatives such as Jeane Kirkpatrick, communism has shown itself able—even eager—to undergo reform, and even, perhaps, to disappear.

A Puritan has been defined as someone haunted by the awful thought that somewhere, someone might be happy. A conservative is someone haunted by the notion that somewhere, some people might be living in a noncapitalist system and enjoying it.

Compared with conservatives, liberals are far better suited to going beyond the Cold War, for several reasons. They are more comfortable with pluralism and diversity, less mired in the rigidities of ideological purity. Also, conservatives are wedded to the old East-West confrontation, which was congenial to their penchant for melodramatic good guys versus bad guys, us-versus-them, simplifications. Furthermore, conservatives, almost by definition, are partial to the way things have been rather than how they can be; hence, they have a terrible time just recognizing change, not to mention welcoming it, even if it hits them over the head.

In addition, a smooth transition to a nonmilitary economy requires "economic conversion," whereby military industries switch over to producing civilian goods. Conversion is hardly the disaster that conservatives make it out to be; rather, it is an immense and very welcome opportunity, long overdue. But it requires affirmative planning and implementation at the level of government, something for which liberals are suited, and conservatives are not. (It is interesting that conservatives long ago became perfectly comfortable—indeed, downright exuberant—about government-inspired military spending, but when it comes to a government-led conversion in favor of human needs, they are notably stingy and withholding.) And finally, liberals are far more likely to recognize peace as an opportunity rather than a threat, to applaud it and move on to our pressing economic and environmental problems, both at home and throughout the world.

Chapter 10 Into the 1990s: Advice from the Cheshire Cat

LYNDON JOHNSON liked to tell about the no-nonsense politician who boldly declared, "Let's seize the bull by the tail and look the situation square in the face." So far, we have been trying to seize liberalism by the tail; now let's look the situation in the face.

Although the L *word* has been unpopular lately, L ideas and L programs—the real stuff of liberalism—are held in much higher esteem. And this is good, because liberalism is precisely what we need for the 1990s and beyond.

The world has been turning itself inside out and upside down. All but the most obtuse and resistant have come to realize that the "Soviet threat" is essentially self-destructing, leaving environmental and social problems the major threats to our security. Crushing poverty, inadequate and unavailable medical care, drugs and violence, Third World debt, depletion of the ozone layer, the greenhouse effect, destruction of forests (rainforest ruination, temperate zone logging, the effects of acid rain), erosion and loss of soil to salinization and desertification, the population explosion—these are the problems of the 1990s and the twenty-first century (assuming, of course,

201

that we get nuclear weapons under control). As Thomas Paine put it two hundred years ago, we have it in our power to make the world anew . . . not only in America but perhaps elsewhere too. This tendency to look at things afresh, with energy, enthusiasm, and optimism, is an impulse that is not so much revolutionary as it is liberal, one that has illuminated and given hope to some of our darkest times, as with FDR and the New Dealers during the Great Depression in the 1930s, or Eugene McCarthy and the anti-Vietnam War movement of the 1960s. It was liberals, then, who pressed an agenda of responsibility, responsibility for one another and for the world. And it is liberals, now, who continue doing so. Which is just as well, because good planets are hard to find.

But how have the Bush Administration and other conservatives responded to today's challenges and opportunities? Hardly at all. Instead of leading the charge, seizing the opportunities and rising to the challenges, the current federal government resolutely does as little as possible. George Bush, for example, has used his veto power more frequently than any president in recent memory. Conservatism in the 1990s seizes nothing; it refuses to look anything in the face . . . except for public opinion polls. And as to solutions, forget it.

This should not be surprising. Conservatism is made up of about equal parts complacency and cruelty: complacency toward planetary threats (the environment, nuclear weapons) and cruelty toward those less well-off than themselves.[1] Moreover, unlike liberals, conservatives have a terrible time even acknowledging that the world has changed, that the communist "threat," for example—like the Wicked Witch of Oz—is melting away. What, then, are they left with? "No new taxes." Hardly a rallying cry with which to mobilize a nation and inspire it to new heights of greatness, although it pretty much exhausts the conservatives' agenda, which continues to be limited to indifference, inaction, and reaction. (As well as overreaction, as in the Persian Gulf.)

---

[1] Such cruelty is typically not of the overtly sadistic or even nasty sort. Rather, it resides in denial and in a philosophy of "self-reliance," buttressed by the myth of rugged individualism, which adds up to the self-serving satisfaction that if people are doing poorly, it is their own fault.

As to George Bush's now infamous "no new taxes" pledge, Senator Lloyd Bentsen presciently called it "pure Bushlips," even before the renowned presidential flip-flop.[2] Certainly, it ill behooves liberals to complain about a presidential willingness to entertain taxes. The point is that liberals have long recognized the need for taxes, so long as they are fairly applied, thoughtfully spent, and honestly acknowledged. Under conservatives, none of these criteria have been met. Thus, conservatives vigorously oppose a progressive tax code, which levies a higher rate upon wealthier citizens. So much for "fairly applied." They insist on throwing money at the military—notably in "Big Ticket" strategic weapons systems, where typically it is not needed, is woefully wasted, and actually reduces our security—rather than spending it on domestic problems, which desperately need it. So much for "thoughtfully spent." And all the while, they pose as champions of the embattled taxpayer, whereas in fact they defend only the worried rich. So much for "honestly acknowledged." Bush's reversal on taxes wasn't despicable in itself; something else was despicable, however: the cynical, self-serving lie in which he initially claimed he would oppose taxes (knowing full well that they would be needed), a claim that succeeded in its only purpose, namely to fool enough people to get him elected in 1988.

The regrettable truth is that taxes are necessary in order to run a country. And they are especially needed if that country is to have any hope of greatness, or even OK-ness. There is an old-fashioned notion, one that once upon a time, long ago, might even have been considered characteristic of conservatives: You get what you pay for. But these days, conservative opposition to taxes, when it isn't simple demagoguery, is typically based on just what modern-day conservatives claim to abhor: the idea of getting something for nothing, getting the benefits of living in a wealthy, happy, secure modern nation-state, without paying for it.

Liberal ideals and liberal programs are the wave of America's future (at least in the short- to medium-term, until, God

---

[2] Which should probably be called a flip-flop-flip, since Mr. Bush now claims—once again—that he will oppose new taxes. But maybe, like Milli Vanilli, he was only lip-synching the first time.

help us, the cycle shifts back again). Thus, a 1990 poll of nearly
three hundred thousand college freshmen conducted by
U.C.L.A.'s Higher Education Research Institute and the
American Council on Education, found that—as predicted in
our discussion of liberal-conservative cycles—the times are indeed a-changin' . . . once again. Thirty-seven percent of the
freshmen interviewed in 1990 had "participated in an organized demonstration" the previous year, more than twice the
percentage found in that heyday of activism, the late 1960s.
Sixty-five percent supported abortion rights, 68 percent felt that
the government was not doing enough to promote disarmament, 86 percent thought that the government should do more
to control pollution, and whereas in 1969 and 1970, 34 percent
felt that "influencing social values" was "a very important goal"
for their own lives, 41 percent responded this way twenty years
later. With their honesty in identifying problems and their optimistic, forward-looking, activist approach to solving them,
liberals are well-positioned to ride the coming crest of idealism
and public good that seems likely to develop in the 1990s, as
in the 1930s and 1960s.

At the same time, it is simply inconceivable that conservatives will rise to the occasion, that they will call upon the
American people to sacrifice for the benefit of others, or even
for their own long-term interest. Sacrifice wasn't part of the
Reagan vocabulary, and George Bush is, if anything, even less
idealistic, less willing to make waves, and not at all inclined
to rise above petty, shortsighted interests. But the American
people are not unfamiliar with idealism and vision, and their
long love affair with change, progress, and self-sacrifice is
overdue to be rekindled. Perhaps the inspiring successes of
Eastern Europe, and the courageous progress being made even
in that citadel of conservative reaction, South Africa, will also
help inspire Americans in their next, forthcoming rendezvous
with liberalism.

CASTING ABOUT for a program to carry them into the 1990s,
conservatives began floating something called their "new paradigm." (Brother, can you para-digm?) It involves a retread of
the old inaction, dressed up with such new phrases as "local
empowerment." The new paradigm will essentially give the
needy of America a smile and a wave, along with the same

dispirited—and dispiriting—message: Don't expect anything from the rest of us. Also likely to emerge, a version of racist pandering, masquerading as opposition to "quotas." Those who gave us such intellectually meaty, high-toned campaign issues as Willie Horton and the Pledge of Allegiance are going to strike again.

But is there a liberal program for the 1990s? Of course not. There are many. "It's easy to stop smoking," wrote Mark Twain, "I've done it hundreds of times." It's also easy to identify a liberal program; there are hundreds of them. Partly because of their tolerance—maybe even craving—for diversity, liberals have a tendency to jump on their hobbyhorses (usually the Democratic donkey) and gallop "madly off in all directions." And, to their credit, most of these directions in which today's liberals would take us are worthwhile. Unlike the poor horse of Stephen Leacock's epigram, most of the programs supported by liberals are not mutually exclusive.

No one on the American political scene is more attuned to genuine family values and their integration into public life than Governor Mario Cuomo. Senator Albert Gore would have us pay attention and resources to the global environment and the pending ecological crisis in which we are all simmering (especially in the summers, as the greenhouse becomes more effective). Jesse Jackson is a tireless voice for the oppressed and dispossessed, and for redirecting government resources to social needs. Representative Richard Gephardt has had the effrontery and courage to call for affirmative world leadership on the part of the United States, for a recognition that the Cold War is over and that our interests lie in helping the U.S.S.R. reform itself, economically and along democratic lines. Senator Daniel P. Moynihan has shown that liberals can even favor tax cuts; moreover, he proposes making these cuts where they belong—in the bite the IRS takes out of the poor and middle class—through reductions in the social security rate. The existing social security levy, as most liberals acknowledge, is unacceptably regressive, exacting the same percentage from all paychecks up to fifty-one thousand dollars annual income. It also has been generating a huge surplus that the Bush administration has sneakily been using to disguise the true size of the federal deficit.

Representative Dan Rostenkowski has suggested a comprehensive, detailed plan for eliminating the federal deficit within five years. Senator Edward Kennedy has equally specific plans for extending health care coverage to needy Americans. Nuclear freeze activist and military specialist Randall Forsberg has been analyzing and presenting detailed strategies for "nonprovocative defense," a strategic and force posture that would restrict the military to nonoffensive operations. Such a policy shift, to be carefully initiated over a decade or so, has been receiving favorable attention in Europe as well as the Soviet Union. It is precisely the kind of "new thinking" that we desperately need, and that comes naturally to liberals, unencumbered as they are with the conservative baggage of permanent American-Soviet ideological enmity. Restricting the military to real defense would immensely increase our military security, while also saving literally hundreds of billions of dollars, desperately needed for achieving *real* security. Representative Ted Weiss has introduced legislation for comprehensive economic conversion from a military to a civilian economy. Investment banker and financial analyst Felix Rohatyn has specific plans for investing in the United States infrastructure, and for revitalizing American industrial productivity, while Senator Bill Bradley has proposals for refinancing Third World debt. And this is only a partial list.

Other worthy ideas pop up all the time, such as a Police Corps, whereby college students receive a waiver of their student loans if they spend a specific period as inner-city police after graduation. The liberal agenda will also include an ongoing commitment to civil rights, freedom of reproductive choice, equal pay for equal work, environmental cleanup and protection, workplace safety, educational reform, an end to the national scandal of homelessness, a national health plan that includes nursing care as well as catastrophic insurance for the tens of millions of people who currently have no health coverage whatever, and much more. Just as there is no shortage of problems, liberals have no shortage of solutions. And this means real solutions, not just window dressing, the Potemkin villages of feel-good political theater which, under conservative "leadership," have passed for national policy.

To some extent, liberal policies will have to be carefully packaged, since, as sociologist Seymour Lipset has said,

Americans tend to remain "ideological conservatives" while being "operational liberals." In a *New York Times*-CBS poll, for example, when Americans were asked, "Do you approve of most Government-sponsored welfare programs?," 58 percent answered "No." But as it turns out, they do in fact favor welfare *programs*; what they don't like is the word *welfare*, just as many Americans simultaneously reject the label *liberal*, while embracing liberalism. Thus, in that same *New York Times*-CBS poll, when respondents were asked whether they supported "helping poor people buy food for their families at cheaper prices" (the liberal program achieved by food stamps), 81 percent agreed; when asked if they approved of the government "providing financial assistance for children raised in low-income homes where one parent is missing" (the liberal program known as Aid to Families with Dependent Children), another 81 percent agreed; and 82 percent approved of government programs that "pay for health care for poor people" (another liberal program, known as Medicaid).

Liberals have given us programs—many of them welfare programs—that Americans admire and continue to need, even though they would rather call them something else. What, in the meanwhile, have conservatives given us? A sense of drift and escapism, a nonnourishing diet of political bread and circuses. A staggering national debt, decaying inner cities, a dilapidated national infrastructure and a countryside overflowing with toxic dumpsites: a thousand points of blight. After a decade of conservative governance, the poorest 20 percent of Americans currently earn a paltry 3.8 percent of the nation's income, the lowest since the 1950s. At the same time, the wealthiest 20 percent bring home a whopping 46.3 percent (the highest ever). More than thirty years ago, liberal stalwart J. Kenneth Galbraith explained that whereas liberalism aims at "buttressing weak bargaining positions," conservatives strive for "the protection of positions of original power."[3] True to form, those who crow loudest that conservatives have brought economic prosperity are almost exclusively those who occupy "positions of original power." For the rest, it has been mourn-

---

[3] John Kenneth Galbraith, *American Capitalism* (Boston: Houghton Mifflin, 1956).

ing in America. In a democracy, however, bargaining positions are not weak when they are widely shared.

Satisfaction with America as it now exists is a mile wide and an inch deep . . . pretty much like the support for George Bush and 1980s conservatism generally. Not that people don't love this country. Indeed, that is just the point. They love the United States so much that they are becoming increasingly restive and frustrated with its failure to live up to its potential, impatient to—as JFK promised thirty years ago—"get this country moving again." And only liberals are likely to do this, or even to try.

Despite such reasons for optimism, the success of liberals in recapturing the Democratic Party[4] is by no means assured. Following the 1988 elections, a bevy of self-appointed experts emerged, many of them from the "blame liberalism first" school. Thus, southern conservatives such as Sam Nunn and Charles Robb would like to see the Democratic Party become less liberal, which is to say, more like the Republicans. And some northern Democrats have joined the bandwagon, calling upon liberals essentially to back off from their principles. Meg Greenfield, editorial page editor of *The Washington Post*, suggested that liberals must resolve three major issues. In particular, they should begin by:

> . . . recognizing the difference between effectively using governmental intervention to do good things, and indulging that instinct mindlessly to the point of heavy-handed coercion. [Second, is] . . . stopping short of harshly and unjustly penalizing one group of Americans by way of trying to help another that is in trouble. [And finally, promoting] . . . a rational foreign defense policy that acknowledges the existence of American interests abroad and the legitimacy of the assertion of American power to defend them.[5]

In *My Fair Lady*, Professor Henry Higgins asks in exasperation, "Why can't a woman be more like a man?" Ms. Greenfield asks why liberals can't be more like conservatives.

---

[4]In theory at least, liberals can exist within the Republican Party as well, as witnessed by such holdouts as Oregon's Senator Mark Hatfield and Rhode Island's John Chafee. In general, such liberal Republicans have become an endangered species, although several liberal-moderate Republican governors were elected in 1990.

[5]Meg Greenfield, *The Washington Post*, October 25, 1988.

There is, after all, nothing new in the politics of imitation. If Hollywood can give us "Police Academy XXVI" and "House on Elm Street, Part 47," not to mention Ronald Reagan, why shouldn't politics give us comparable retreads? During the 1950s, conservative Republicans following the leadership of Robert Taft derided the liberal—and mostly eastern—wing of their own party as "Me-Too Republicans." People such as Ms. Greenfield and those making up the center-right Democratic Leadership Council would like to see a resurgence of "Me-Too Democrats." (Not "Me-Too Liberals"; Heavens no, they wouldn't even use the dreaded L word.)

The liberal's answer can be borrowed from Harry Truman: Give the voters a choice between a genuine conservative and a pretend conservative, and they'll choose the conservative every time. But let's make Truman's point more explicit: Give them a choice between a genuine (or pretend) conservative and a genuine liberal, one not afraid to espouse and explain liberal values, ideas, and programs, and they'll choose the liberal. If not every time, at least often enough.

H ERE IS a radical suggestion: Liberals don't need new ideas nearly as much as they need faith and confidence in their old ones. And they certainly don't need to repackage conservative notions. The future of liberalism is essentially old wine in new bottles, so long as the wine is of good vintage. One of the few good things about conservatism—perhaps its only good thing—is its penchant for preserving what is worthwhile about the past. (A notable difference with liberalism is that to conservatives, such phenomena as inequity and authoritarianism are among the past's more desirable components.) Old remedies are not by definition outdated; so long as old problems keep repeating themselves, old remedies keep working.

In any event, the honest, beneficent kind of conserving conservatism is what liberals need; not a craven retreat to the right, but a staunch support of what has always been worthwhile about liberalism's heritage: pursuit of the common good, social conscience, optimism, democracy, a vigorous humanism. The P word (progressive) is far more popular—at least in opinion polls—than liberal, populist, or conservative. Call it anything, although I confess a fondness for just plain old liberalism. But whatever it is called, for all of our sakes, make sure it isn't ersatz conservatism. Not many Americans will quiver with excitement at a motto such as, "Just like the Republicans, only less so."

The liberal message has not failed America, or its political followers; rather, many of our politicians have failed liberalism, by compromising liberal principles, or moving away (or claiming to move away) from traditional liberal values, trying to be oh so neo. The value of affirmative government, of commitment to civil liberties and social equity, environmental protection, democracy, optimism, a positive orientation toward the future, confidence in rationality with respect to the solution of human problems, a hardheaded willingness to promote and plan for peace: These hallowed liberal traditions are every bit as valid for the 1990s as they always were. Liberals don't need neo so much as *brio*. What they do need—especially among their presidential candidates—are better leaders, more appealing and charismatic personalities than George McGovern, Walter Mondale, or Michael Dukakis. They also need to avoid becoming the me-too party, a pale imitation of the neo-Neanderthal conservatives.

During the 1988 campaign, George Bush claimed that the liberal vision was of "big government, higher taxes, a weaker national defense." And liberals in fact favor responsive, affirmative government, equitable taxes (higher for those who can easily afford it, lower for those who cannot), and real national security, not the illusion of military power actually leading to profound insecurity. As Princeton University's Paul Starr puts it, the trick is not moving to the right, or even to the center, but getting to the core, to the fundamental interests shared by all Americans. And this is precisely where liberalism's greatest strength can be found: Liberal ideals are America's ideals, liberal goals are the goals of most Americans.

Actually, conservative politicians often admire liberals, but only after they are dead. While in office, Ronald Reagan referred far more often to Franklin Roosevelt, Harry Truman, and John Kennedy than to Herbert Hoover, Warren Harding, or even his supposed favorite, Calvin Coolidge. This is not surprising, since liberal presidents remain especially beloved by the American people. Compare Barry Goldwater on Harry Truman: "The greatest president of the last one hundred years," with "Mr. Conservative's" view of Richard Nixon: "The biggest liar I ever met in my life." It is not simply that for these conservatives, the only good liberal is a dead one, but that conservatives have come to recognize that liberal programs are generally successful and popular, and they want to associate themselves with their positive aspects. Liberals need to be at least as self-congratulatory.

They also need to be firm and assertive, unblushing about defining themselves before the likes of media advisor Roger Ailes—with help from racist innuendo, Boston harbor, an M-1 tank, and the Pledge of Allegiance (an unlikely combination that only conservative duplicity could have drawn together)—do it for them. Their greatest need is not to change their philosophy but to clarify and enunciate it, not to cling forlornly to an outdated worldview but to show how that view is not, in fact, outdated at all.

Nearly everyone, it seems, has a prescription for liberals. Become tougher on crime, on the wealthy, on business, on communism, on the poor, on the environment, or easier on our wallets, on business, on the poor, on separation of Church and State, on the military, on the environment. Can liberals keep the faith by tinkering with the system? Or should they aim less high? Or higher, becoming more radical? There has been no shortage of good, specific advice, of which perhaps the best has been offered by the Three Roberts: Robert Reich,[6] Robert McElvaine,[7] and Robert Kuttner.[8] Let Reagan be Reagan, chanted many conservatives, a suggestion whose wisdom never fully revealed itself. My advice: Let liberals be liberal.

This is not to recommend that liberals just talk more and better, that is, mere gliberalism. Rather, they must combine rhetoric with a clear understanding of reality—but in fact, this has long been a special strength of the liberal outlook. Perhaps because of their long-standing fondness for the right to dissent, liberals have become associated with relatively unpopular issues, with which many Americans disagree, like flag-

---

[6] Robert Reich, *Tales of a New America* (New York: Random House, 1987).
[7] Robert McElvaine, *The End of the Conservative Era* (New York: Arbor House, 1987).
[8] Robert Kuttner, *The Life of the Party* (New York: Viking, 1987).

burning, pornography, tolerance of social deviance, and prison reform. They have been rather too quiet on those other important issues on which the overwhelming majority of Americans are strongly on their side: environmental protection, a more equitable tax burden, social investment in education, health care, public transportation, and job training, to mention just a few.

No harm would be done, as well, by clarifying that it isn't illiberal to insist on an honest day's work for an honest day's pay, or that all students—black as well as white, Hispanic as well as English-speaking—be held to reasonable academic standards, that the social contract includes not only self-expression but also self-discipline, or that criminals should be punished as well as rehabilitated. And then there is the matter of "traditional values." For conservatives, this means patriotism, social stability, and family life as eternal verities. At the same time, for some liberals traditional values have come to mean intolerance, provincialism, selfishness, meanness of spirit . . . and liberalism's condescending attitude toward those espousing such values has itself reflected a kind of social intolerance that liberals deplore in their conservative opponents.

Such an attitude, by liberals, is a surprising example of social insensitivity, by people who traditionally pride themselves on being aware of social issues and attuned to socially mediated disaffection. Worrying about crime is not necessarily racist, and being genuinely fond of the United States does not necessarily reveal narrow-minded jingoism. In short, values do matter, and liberals need to be reminded of this, while also emphasizing that their policies as well as their philosophy are profoundly value-oriented. (It also bears repeating that ironically, while conservatives have gained ground somewhat among advocates of "family values," conservative policies in fact are significantly *anti*family, since they restrict nutrition, child-care and employment programs, health-care and education efforts, and so forth. Moreover, as we have seen, the fundamental American values of fair play and defense of civil liberties are among the basic strengths of liberalism.)

WHEN A corporation or an individual elects to spend resources, hoping that this expenditure will grow and eventually result in a larger payoff, we say that an "investment" has taken place. Prudent and farsighted investing is generally seen as a good thing. Accordingly, most financial analysts, even conservative ones, would like Americans to invest more, not less. That is how enterprises grow: when people choose to invest capital in them, resulting in new ideas, new capacities, a more modern industrial plant, etc. On the other hand, when the government elects to do the same, this is often derided as government "spending," and is almost by definition considered wasteful, shameful, and something to be reduced.

For absolutely no good reason, "investment" has been considered the sole province of private individuals and corporations. Governments, by contrast, are supposed to count only income and outgo. It is high time to reformulate the notion of spending, and to see it as *investment*, something laudable and worthwhile, so long as it is done intelligently and with foresight. When the government spends on education, drug-abuse prevention, prison reform, low-income housing, workplace safety, health care, museums, scientific research, parks and wildlife refuges, wilderness areas, clear water and air, prenatal care, day-care centers, energy and resource conservation, adult education, job training, and so forth, it is *investing* in America and in our future. Not that all these things should be done willy-nilly. And certainly, there must be regard to suitable priorities, available revenues, and attention to whether each kind of expenditure brings appropriate returns. The point, however, is that government spending is not simply a case of throwing money away; it is—or rather, it should be and it can be—money well spent . . . like investing in Apple computers in the mid-1970s, or Teenage Mutant Ninja Turtles in 1988.[9]

The idea of government spending as investment is an important one, especially for liberals. Robert B. Reich[10] recounts the well-known fisherman's fable: Give someone a fish, and you feed him for a day, but teach him to fish, and he will feed

---

[9] Actually, wise social spending would be a far better investment than Ninja Turtles, because in addition to making money (like the Turtles), in the long run it also contributes to bettering the country, something for which Ninja Turtles, or an improved kind of underarm deodorant, for example, are likely to have a slimmer claim.

[10] Robert B. Reich, op. cit.

himself for life. Reich then adds an important twist: Eventually, the fisherman will also help us. Once he has enough for himself, or grows tired of being exclusively piscivorous, our fisherman will trade his surplus fish to the butcher, baker, or candlestick maker, making his catch available to them, just as he purchases goods and services from these worthy merchants. Accordingly, society is better off when someone knows how to fish (assuming that he doesn't abuse the opportunity, and catch too many, thereby endangering the fishery).

Investments, by society in society, are the very stuff of liberal politics. They are also crucially important for us all. Conservatives, by contrast, would rather have each of us make *private* investments—assuming we have the money, of course—instead of public ones. The result is that those who have, get more, and those who don't, don't. It is worth noting in this regard that whereas the rich can, in most cases, take care of themselves, the nonrich are more generally dependent on the economic and social health of society as a whole. Not only are they in greater need of being invested in, they also rely to a greater extent on society functioning well in the future. Contrary to what most people think, for example, social security payments are not accumulated for each taxpayer in a personal fund, specially earmarked to be paid out to every individual wage earner later on, like an annuity. Rather, when today's lower- and middle-income earners retire, they will rely upon the next generation—those now young—to earn their social security payments, based on what that next generation is paying into the system. Hence, except for those who are independently wealthy, we cannot succeed economically unless we invest in the education, health, environment, and freedom of others . . . in short, in ourselves. Human capital is "where it's at."

And yet, children are the poorest age group in the United States. The Bipartisan Commission on Children reported in 1990 that malnutrition affects nearly five hundred thousand kids in this, the wealthiest country on earth. One hundred thousand children are homeless and one in five lives below the poverty line. So what? Aside from the simple ethical outrage, as commission chairman Senator Jay Rockefeller put it, "The health and vitality of our economy and our democracy are increasingly in danger," because of our failure to invest adequately in the young.

The Fisherman's Fable notwithstanding, we don't need to operate fishing schools, but we do need vocational schools, as well as day-care centers, nutrition, housing, and education programs: not simply because there are needy people who require assistance, but because such schools (and other, comparable social programs) represent an opportunity for society to invest in itself, for its (that is, our) own benefit. Our country and our planet are filled with investment opportunities of this sort, crying out for programs that are softhearted and hardheaded: in a word, liberal.

Our cities are broke, we are told. They can't afford to provide public transportation, pick up the garbage, educate their children, provide decent health care, and housing. And yet, are they really so destitute? Vast sums of money pour into our cities—particularly into the financial districts, selected upper-crust high-rent communities—every day. The *public sector* is broke. In a sense, therefore, the people are broke, while individual persons, and corporations, are raking it in. Part of this is a result of an intentional conservative strategy: Starve the local communities by depriving them of federal revenues. Then, make speeches (à la George Bush on the environment, transportation, education, etc.) that sound like the government is concerned and caring, ready to be an active player . . . but with the fine print saying that it's up to the communities to provide the resources, that is, to make the necessary investment.

As we have seen, disillusionment with "big-spending liberals" has occurred in part because the nonrich (primarily the middle class) have been squeezed to support programs that benefit the very poor and the very rich; those paying the most derived the least tangible benefits from their sacrifices. Corporations and conservatives have sought—largely successfully—to shift the burden of tax payments to those who work, while also (and here is the real trick) convincing them that their money has gone to provide luxury Cadillacs for lazy welfare chiselers and an army of arrogant, muddleheaded bureaucrats who revel in suffocating stacks of paperwork and a penchant for minding other people's business.

But the problems of our society are real, requiring that we move beyond hypocrisy and easy words, and actually *do something* about them. In short, they require liberals, with enlightened policies of social investment.

Even those who do not directly require to be "invested in" very definitely require that such investment take place, "in" the society of which they are inseparably a part. The term "independently wealthy" is an oxymoron: Even they are not really independent. They are not entirely insulated against war or social upheaval, environmental collapse, or even the vagaries of the stock market. There are also moral and ethical connections that have a legitimate claim on the attention and resources of the rich. None of us, in short, is an island.

So long as liberal programs are seen as isolated from each other, however, they are vulnerable to the right-wing ideology of selfishness, which seeks tirelessly to divide and conquer by isolating various "special-interest groups" that profit at the public expense. The "public" must therefore be seen as having a deep and overriding "interest," which is very "special" and fundamentally indistinguishable from private interest as conservatives would narrowly define it.

Our mutual boundaries are long, complex, and intertwining. Just as we neither exult nor suffer alone, our very survival depends on others. For example, we have long been hostage to the prudence and restraint of those people in the Kremlin who have their fingers on the nuclear button. But we are also hostage to events elsewhere in the world, to the decadent oil emirs of the Persian Gulf, to the industrialists who spew acid rain that kills our forests and lakes, to the destroyers of the world's rainforests, to carbon dioxide emissions which threaten to change the earth's climate, to worldwide population growth, with its far-reaching impact on just about every aspect of quality of life. Between now and the year 2025, for example, given current rates of growth, the population of Mexico will increase from 88 to 150 million, Brazil from 150 to 246 million, Nigeria from 118 to 301 million, Bangladesh from 114 to 235 million, and India from 853 to 1,445 million. Moreover, population growth within the "developed world," although slower, actually levies an even greater toll on planetary resources, since countries such as the United States use far more energy and other resources, and produce far more pollution, per capita, than the increasingly overcrowded Third World.

It has widely been suggested (and may even be true) that the 1990s will be the environmental decade, a make-it or break-it time for the world ecosystem, and a crucial challenge to our politics. There can be no doubt that the politics of environmental protection and renewal are liberal. The conservative right is enamored of laissez-faire, which literally means "leave to do," a concept that might be taken to imply environmental protection: leave natural ecosystems to "do their own thing." But alas, laissez-faire really means leaving the despoilers, polluters, and rapists of the environment free to do *their* own thing. Sadly, the radical left has been no better: Worshipping production goals with a fervor almost indistinguishable from the laissez-faire capitalist kowtowing to profits, communists in Eastern Europe and the Soviet Union have heedlessly plundered their natural environment and piled up increasingly lethal levels of pollution and ecological abuse.

Enter, liberalism, the middle way, and perhaps the only way we can have production and freedom, combined with some degree of environmental harmony. It is but a short step from liberalism's social commitment to moderating the worst economic excesses of capitalism to an ecological commitment to moderating capitalism's most serious environmental excesses as well.

Senator Albert Gore has proposed that the United States engage in a Strategic Environmental Initiative, funded at least as well as the ill-conceived Strategic Defense Initiative of which conservatives have been so fond. Star Wars, in short, can be replaced by Earth Peace. Conservatives can be counted on to salivate on cue when it comes to funding national projects of vast scope, so long as they are military. Not surprisingly, however, it will take liberals to propose and enact national— and international—projects of vast scope, which are designed to save lives, heal the planet, and point us toward a sustainable future.

In one of his most liberal moments, President Jimmy Carter had sought to initiate a far-reaching energy policy for the United States, notably a comprehensive mix of conservation and re-

newable energy sources. Carter was absolutely correct in calling for the "moral equivalent of war," a crusade that Ronald
Reagan utterly squelched during the 1980s. In its place, we
got the immoral equivalent of sloth and greed: The auto industry was permitted to relax gasoline mileage standards; tax
incentives for home energy conservation were abolished; and
federal supports for wind, solar, and other creative energy solutions were slashed. (By contrast, nuclear power was smiled
upon.) And when Iraq invaded Kuwait in 1990, more than
five hundred thousand United States citizens were mobilized
to defend—not democracy, not principle, not a "New World
Order"—but oil, the same old oil that we could have been
saving, several times over, had we only chosen war's moral
equivalent over its bloody reality.

Any way you slice it, the environment is liberal territory.
Despite the common root verbally linking "conservative" and
"conservation," conservatives are—and have long been—hand
in glove with the destroyers of our natural realm, the profi-
teers who would benefit from the rape of the land, the water,
and the air, for whom other living things have no intrinsic
role except as obstacles to "development." And increasingly,
people are realizing that concern for the environment is not
limited to an effete, elite class. After all, the great majority of
toxic waste sites, for example, are located in areas that are
predominantly low income, often black, Latino, or Native
American. Environmental politics are the politics of economic,
social, and racial justice, as well as common decency and ele-
mental planetary hygiene. As an editorial in *The Nation* put it:

> In New Jersey, tackling a chemical polluter should mean orga-
> nizing with workers, arguing for reparations and retraining. In
> Montana preserving wilderness should mean fighting for Indi-
> ans' treaty rights and religious freedom. In Hawaii saving the
> tropical rain forest and its unique species from a mad geother-
> mal project should mean uniting with opponents of hyperde-
> velopment and supporting indigenous sovereignty claims.[11]

The list goes on: Defending ground water means taking on
the agrochemical companies with their passion for long-last-

---

[11] "After Earth Day," *The Nation*, April 30, 1990.

ing fertilizers, insecticides, and herbicides. Reversing deforestation means standing up to the rapacious timber interests. Preserving open space and natural habitats means bringing pressure to bear on land-development interests. Limiting water and air pollution means modifying the way big business does business. All these actions, and many more, must be taken in the name of society, in support of a greater good, and despite the vigorous opposition of entrenched financial and social interests. It is a job for liberals. Anyone who thinks otherwise would believe that George Bush, or Ronald Reagan for that matter, is an "environmentalist." (And probably also believes in the tooth fairy.)

As ecologist (and liberal-progressive) Barry Commoner[12] has pointed out, there is much that an activist federal government can do, not only to preserve critical ecosystems, defend wildlife, carry out a future-oriented population policy, establish and enforce prohibitions against pollution and energy wastage, but also to stimulate—directly—the development of Earth-friendly technologies.

During the late 1950s, the United States government decided it needed small, powerful, highly accurate computers to provide guidance mechanisms for long-range missiles. The federal government proceeded to underwrite research and development toward that end, and as a result, efficient, inexpensive microchips have become a part of the modern commercial landscape. There is no reason why the federal government could not similarly turn its supportive eye toward technologies substantially more benign than endowing nuclear weapons with pinpoint accuracy . . . and giving us pocket calculators as a distant spin-off. The government could encourage—even demand—the development of efficient, inexpensive photovoltaic cells, which would provide cheap, altogether safe energy. Similarly, the United States currently purchases literally billions of dollars' worth of motor vehicles each year: If the feds insisted on buying only highly fuel-efficient models, you can bet that Detroit would figure out how to produce them, just as the creative, proenvironment use of farm-subsidy and child-nutrition programs could do wonders for organic farming, or

---

[12] Barry Commoner, *Making Peace with the Earth* (New York: Pantheon, 1990).

procurement policies could provide the equivalent of venture capital for recycled paper, glass, and metals, and so forth. Enlightened, proenvironment policies of this sort can only be driven by the liberal recognition that the good of society and of the entire biosphere—and not private greed—is the real "bottom line."

Eager to make their own, individual contribution to protecting the environment, many Americans have been rushing to learn "what you can do" to help save Mother Earth. This is fine, as far as it goes. But the truth is, it doesn't go very far. You can ride your bicycle, compost your garbage, recycle your newspapers, and even boycott selected manufacturers, but the basic problems of environmental destruction will go on, largely unaffected. All these "hints from Heloise"–type solutions simply aren't enough, laudable as they may be. Problems as large as the environment require not only individual solutions, but also a response that is comparably large, at the level of society. Former British Prime Minister Margaret Thatcher revealed the standard conservative attitude toward such responses when she commented to a women's magazine: "There are individual men and women, and there are families [but] there is no such thing as society."[13] Mrs. Thatcher is wrong, of course, but her view reveals why conservatives cannot be trusted to be environmentalists: They are too much taken with the individual, and insufficiently attuned to the role of society in causing problems and, potentially, in solving them.

It will take liberals to shake off the misguided complacency that—except when it comes to the "Red menace"—conservatives find so hospitable. With communism failing left and right, it may seem that the United States is sitting pretty, in the best of all possible worlds. But, the fact is that there is only one world, and we are irrevocably enmeshed in it. Its problems— environment, poverty, social injustice—are ours. (Only a liberal, of course, would write this, or believe it.) Conservative "leadership" has given us a unique dependency on foreign capital, a scarcity of long-term investment, inadequate and outmoded industrial facilities, threats to our privacy, our health,

---

[13] Quoted in Christopher Hitchens, "Minority Report," *The Nation*, April 30, 1990.

our environment, and our education level, as well as nearly 20 percent of our children living in poverty. We are less than 6 percent of the world's people, yet we consume more than 30 percent of the planet's resources and 50 percent of its hard drugs. In short, we could desperately use some *perestroika*— social as well as environmental—of our own, and make no mistake, only liberals will undertake it.

PERHAPS THE major theme of this book has been that liberalism has much to recommend it, and that liberals should be proud. It also presumes that liberal ideas are so worthwhile that they need primarily to be articulated rather than reformulated, that liberals are more in need of an explication of their creed than a new, detailed guidebook for the future. Thus, liberal themes present themselves in virtually every aspect of modern life. Although the details will vary depending upon the problem to be addressed, the liberal approach is best seen as just that—an approach—rather than a precise blueprint for every eventuality. Armed with liberal precepts, activists, politicians, voters, and citizens should be well equipped to deal creatively, effectively, and humanely with whatever the future presents.

As we have seen, there are numerous threads that unite to form the liberal approach to society and politics: optimism, faith in democracy, an orientation toward the future, a belief in the fundamental decency and connectedness of people and in their responsibility to work together for the common good, a respect for capitalism combined with a recognition that its worst excesses must be ameliorated, a profound belief in the virtues of moderation and reason as well as a deep devotion to civil liberties and freedom.

Let us close, therefore, by suggesting a suitable unifying theme for liberal activists of the 1990s and beyond: human rights. Human rights can narrowly be defined as political and civil freedoms: the right to vote, to express oneself without fear of reprisal, freedom of association, freedom to petition one's government for redress of grievances, freedom from cruel and unusual punishment, the right to a fair trial, and so forth. These crucial rights trace their ancestry directly to liberal thinkers and activists, especially in the Western World.

More recently, however, theorists and activists in the Third World have expanded the notion of human rights to include a new range of concerns: social and economic rights. These would include the rights to a decent education, to medical care, to housing, to food, to a job. In the words of Leopold Senghor, former president of Senegal, "Human rights begin with breakfast." And human rights can and should be extended yet further, to include the right to a safe and sustainable natural environment, as well as the right to live in a world that is not threatened with nuclear annihilation.

But why should human rights—defined both broadly and deeply—be so appropriate as a project for liberalism? Basically, because liberals are humanistically inclined, life-affirming, oriented positively toward people and their problems, and away from rigid, hierarchical, authoritarian, and militarist approaches. This is why if we know someone's stance on civil rights and nuclear weapons, for example, we can, with a high degree of confidence, predict his or her attitudes toward environmental preservation, or toward a national health-care policy. On the surface, it isn't immediately obvious that this should be so, and indeed, there are exceptions: Some antinuclear Catholics, for example, take an antiabortion stance, whereas most liberals are likely to oppose nuclear weapons but favor the availability of abortion. In most cases, however, we can identify clusters of political and social concern, which tend to be found together. The unifying principle is a humane orientation, toward people, life, and decency, if need be at the cost of higher taxes, restricted room for selfish maneuver, etc.

And this is where human rights comes in. It provides an aegis of sorts, a wide umbrella under which liberal, thinking individuals might be able to rally, enlist additional adherents, and work toward a livable world of which we can be proud. All of us. Human rights not only belongs on the liberal agenda, in many ways it is an embodiment of that agenda, waiting only to be recognized as such.

WHAT IS it that we really want, from society, from government, from ourselves? Maybe we can learn from Alice, who, lost in Wonderland, asked the Cheshire Cat:

"Would you tell me, please, which way I ought to go from here?"

"That depends a good deal on where you want to get to," said the Cat.

"I don't much care where—" said Alice.

"Then it doesn't matter which way you go," said the Cat.

"—so long as I get *somewhere*," Alice added as an explanation.

"Oh, you're sure to do that," said the Cat, "if you only walk long enough."[14]

But perhaps we can learn more yet from the Cat. If we stick with the conservatives, we shall get nowhere, and probably even slip backward (as the United States has begun doing). If we follow the liberals, on the other hand, and walk long enough, then surely we shall get somewhere. But exactly where, and how quickly, is up to us.

---

[14] Lewis Carroll, *Alice in Wonderland* (London: Dent, 1971), p. 55.

Index